The sexual dynamics of history

8

This collection represents the views of the individual authors and not of the London Feminist History Group as a whole.

The London Feminist History Group

The sexual dynamics of history

Men's power, women's resistance

Pluto  Press

First published in 1983 by
Pluto Press Limited
The Works, 105a Torriano Avenue
London NW5 2RX and
Pluto Press Australia Limited
PO Box 199, Leichhardt,
New South Wales 2040, Australia

Cover design by Marsha Austin

Photoset by Alan Sutton Publishing Limited

Printed in Great Britain by Photobooks (Bristol) Limited
Bound by W.H. Ware and Sons Limited, Clavedon, Avon

British Library Cataloguing in Publication Data
The Sexual dynamics of history.
  1. Feminist—History
  I. London Feminist History Group
  305.4′2′09   HQ1154

ISBN 0-86104-711-7

Contents

Part four: Sexuality

Preface: Writing our own history

The prospect of doing our own research can be daunting, particularly for those without experience of academic work. But anyone who has listened with interest to an older woman describing her earlier experience has already begun to do history – in the sense of trying to imagine and re-create the past.

Interviews – or 'oral history' – can provide information not often covered by traditional histories about people's everyday lives. It often works best to just let people talk – you can fill in any gaps by asking questions later. You can tape the conversations, or take notes and reconstruct them later. The Department of Sociology at Essex University has a national collection of oral history tapes, and there are some local collections, for example that made by *History Workshop* in London. A good written example of the use to which oral history can be put is *Dutiful Daughters* by Jean McCrindle and Sheila Rowbotham (Harmondsworth: Penguin 1979).

For some subjects – like the experience of twentieth-century immigrant women in Britain – oral history provides a unique opportunity for women whose experiences are often silenced or ignored to speak for themselves. Recently, young women at Vauxhall Manor School in South London produced a play – *Motherland* – about the lives of their mothers and grandmothers, who had been immigrants from the Caribbean in the 1940s and 1950s (see *Spare Rib* 123, October 1982).

You might choose to interview women in a particular area for a local history project, or women who have been involved in particular campaigns. Just as our knowledge of the suffragists still provides inspiration to the Women's Liberation Movement today, finding out about women's early struggles over abortion, contraception, equal pay and peace can provide inspiration for present-day campaigns. There is a history of women involved in the Women's International League for Peace and Freedom (Gertrude Bussey and Margaret Tims, *Pioneers for Peace: Women's International League for Peace and Freedom, 1915–65*, published by the League in 1980) but many other women must have been involved in more local campaigns. Some local organizations have lists of former members, or an advert in a local newspaper or organization's newsletter often attracts great interest.

At some stage, and of course for projects outside living memory, you are going to want to consult written sources. It's best to check through bibliographies first, to give yourself some idea of work that's already been done, and for leads to where the sources are. Local libraries should have books on women's history (if not, ask them to buy some!) to give you ideas. They will also have collections of local newspapers – Anna Clark's piece in this book shows what an invaluable source they can be.

Other generally available sources include novels, biographies and autobiographies of women's lives. Women's magazines provide insights into the expectations held about women in a particular era: Cynthia White's *Women's Magazines: 1693–1968* (London: Michael Joseph 1970) provides a comprehensive introduction.

There are also specialist libraries. The Women's Research and Resources Centre in London has a collection of women's history books, as well as journals printing recent research. *Feminist Review* and *Signs* often carry articles on women's history, as does *History Workshop Journal*. The Fawcett Library in London has archives of the women's movement, as well as printed books. There is a feminist archive in Bath, and a group has been set up in Manchester to create a national lesbian archive. The Museum of Labour History in London has a large photographic collection, including photographs of women workers.

Unprinted sources (censuses, church records, letters, maps, minute-books, etc.) are held by local record offices. You can find out where they are from your local council. It is a good idea to write and tell them what you're interested in looking at first, and they will let you know what's available, and get it ready for you when you visit. There is also a National Register of Archives, listed by family name, in London.

Births and marriages for England and Wales after 1847 are registered at St Catherine's House in London, and deaths at Alexandra House across the road. Registers there can be consulted free of charge, but copies of certificates cost £4.60 each, plus postage and a search fee if you ask for them by post. Wills are often more informative, and can be read for a charge of 25p each at Somerset House in London. The system in Scotland is different, where official record-keeping started much later.

Court records are also a rich source of information about women's lives (see Nazife Bashar's paper in this book). Quarter Session records are held by local record offices, and records from the higher courts are held at the Public Record Office in Chancery Lane (though many have now been moved to the PRO at Kew).

Printed Parliamentary Papers – copies of which can be found in most university libraries, and the British Library – contain reports of enquiries by Select Committees into such varied topics as divorce, marriage and emigration. These sometimes contain verbatim evidence given by women. Also Commissioners' Reports made after inspecting factories, public institutions etc. give insights into women's everyday lives, for example the lives of women mine-workers or the lives of women asylum-keepers (as Charlotte Mackenzie's paper shows). Just looking in the indexes under 'women', 'girls', 'marriage', etc., will produce leads.

Obviously this guide is not comprehensive. A good preliminary bibliography of work which has been done on women in the nineteenth century (and sources) has been put togother by S. Barbara Kanner in two volumes edited by Martha Vicinus – *Suffer and be Still* (Illinois University Publications 1972) and *A Widening Sphere* (Indiana University Press 1977). The 1982 *Spare Rib* Diary contains introductory bibliographies for immigrant women's history. Dee Beddoe has written a book on local history for women, *Discovering Women's History* (Pandora Press 1983).

Research doesn't have to be written up in an academic way. It could just as easily lead to an article in the local paper, exhibition at your local library, play, slide-show or historical walk – like those described in the *Spare Rib* diary for 1982.

Useful Addresses

Alexandra House
Kingsway
London WC2

Bath Feminist Archive
c/o 8 St Saviours Terrace
Larkhall
Bath

Fawcett Library
City of London Polytechnic
Calcutta Precinct
Oldcastle Street
London E1

London History Workshop
New Mary Ward Centre
42 Queens Square
London WC1

Lesbian Archive
c/o Lesbian Link
62 Bloom Street
Manchester

Museum of Labour History
Limehouse Town Hall
Commercial Road
London E14

National Register of Archives
Quality House
Quality Court
London WC2

Public Record Office
Chancery Lane
London WC2

St Catherine's House
Kingsway
London WC2

Somerset House
Strand
London WC2

Women's Research and
   Resources Centre
Hungerford House
Victoria Embankment
London WC2

Introduction

Resistance, men's power, the dynamics of history: these are strong words which have emerged out of months of discussion in our collective. A group of diverse feminists, we reflect the wide-ranging concerns of the Women's Liberation Movement, and are involved in campaigns such as women in trade unions, abortion, and women against violence against women. Our link with contemporary political struggles gives our work as historians a special edge, because our analysis is constantly being reworked and developed. Recent discussions on racism within the Women's Liberation Movement have made us aware of assumptions we may have been making in our work. We do not assume our analysis will be comprehensive enough to deal with the experience of women who are not part of the dominant white Christian tradition.

We have chosen the title, 'The Sexual Dynamics of History: Men's Power, Women's Resistance', because we see history as a dynamic process of struggle and change. Male domination is not a fixed monolithic system, but it changes in form and intensity in response to social and economic transformations such as capitalism or the rise of Protestantism – it also changes in response to women's resistance. Men's power over women, and the form of women's resistance will differ, depending on whether the women concerned are women of colour or white women, and according to their access to social and economic power.

To carry out our feminist aims, we want this book to be of use to all women interested in feminism and our past, not just academics. We want to look outward, away from the universities. All of us occupy a marginal – if any – place within academia. Some are students, some work full-time at other jobs, and some teach part-time in adult education. We describe ourselves as feminist historians rather than students of women's history.

Women's history has come to mean history about women and usually done by women. It began with the necessary task of resurrecting women's hidden experience by focusing on great women in history. We needed the inspiration of discovering Miss Beale and Miss Buss, pioneers in girls' education; the suffragist Pankhursts; scientists such as Marie Curie; political economists such as Harriet Martineau. This tendency, however, has rightly been criticized as elitist. In response, another type of women's history has arisen: revealing ordinary women's lives as part of history. From this we learned about the changing role of women in the household, and women's work in the fields, factories, and workshops of industrializing England. Women have not just been *hidden* from history, they have been deliberately oppressed. Recognition of this oppression is one of the central tenets of feminism.

Another popular tendency in feminist history has concentrated upon the victimization of women. Horrific depictions of the witchburnings of early modern Europe, or gynaecological horrors such as clitorectomies, have rightly fuelled feminist indignation. But these works do not give an adequate explanation of how or why women were oppressed, or illuminate the changing nature of men's power. We need more than a history of women which is tacked on to the existing history of men, but by looking solely at women, we run the risk of ignoring the dynamics of relations between the sexes.

Yet another tendency has taken a more historically and theoretically sophisticated route in order to explain women's oppression – marxist, and some marxist feminist history. Work in this area has been tremendously helpful in showing the oppressive effects of class and imperialism on working-class women's lives. The marxist approach has proved that women's oppression benefits capitalism in many ways, through the contribution of domestic labour to the reproduction of the labour force, and through the exploitation of women in wage labour. But even when men's power is acknowledged as a factor, the main cause of women's oppression is nonetheless always seen as capitalism.

Our commitment to feminist history challenges the exclusive concentration on class which has dominated much British social history. We are no longer willing to contort our theory and our facts into a rigid terminology which ensures that any discussion of women's status attributes our oppression to capitalism. It is time to add the missing dynamic in history – men's power, and women's resistance.

We approach our work from different political persepectives within feminism. Some of us consider the pivotal social conflict to be that between women and men, whilst others view patriarchy as a force equal to, and intertwined with capitalism. Whatever our differences we are all trying to provide feminist answers to feminist questions.

We think it is centrally important to address the problem of how women's oppression benefits men, and how the dynamics of men's power have changed. After the 'second wave' of women's liberation in the 1960s had attacked male dominance, we wanted to concentrate our attention on women rather than men, whether in consciousness-raising groups or feminist research. Furious at the way in which we had always put men's needs first and suppressed our own, we worked from our own experience to understand women's oppression. We banished concern for men from our minds in order to find out what we really wanted and felt. Women's experience *is* the basis of the feminist movement. Our own experience is for each of us our own feminist history. But now we need to understand how our oppression works, how men's power operates. If we only look at women's lives, the reasons for our oppression can appear mysterious and obscure. Women's oppression has not withered away after being exposed as unjust, because it in fact benefits all men in some ways as individuals and as a group.

We still need more subtle arguments to explain the ways in which men's power over women has been instituted and maintained. Every man is born into a world in which language, the family, gender roles, class structure, education, religion, and the state give him advantages over women of the same class. To take two examples: a patriarchal language in the early nineteenth century prevented women from articulating their experiences of rape. This was because language had been constructed around a male point of view; it was not necessarily a deliberate strategy evolved to confuse women. Another of the deep structures that serve male domination is heterosexuality. Through this women's domestic and reproductive labour can be exploited by men on the basis of a sexual relationship. By the periods on which we focus in this collection (1600s–1930s) highly complex structures already existed through which male domination was organized. In our papers some of us wish to emphasize the persistence of these deep structures of male power.

Others of us have focused on the way they are maintained by men's specific strategies. We see the oppression of women as being organized in the interests of individual men as well as men as a group. We do not suggest that changes in the form and structure of women's oppression are considered consciously in the form of a conspiracy. Rather, individual men adjust their relationships with women in order to maximize the benefits that accrue to them. Together, powerful groups of men (the medical profession, the church, the state) may introduce ideas or policies which are aimed at furthering their interests at the expense of women. The actions of individual men, in concert with the aims of representative groups of men, form men's strategies as a whole.

The oppression of women is often conscious and deliberate. Men impose restrictions on women, however, in the context of the existing assumptions about the biologically based 'natural-ness' of men's power. For example, the introduction of a marriage bar effectively controlled women's access to employment in important areas of well-paid work such as the civil service and teaching in the inter-war years. Similarly, but less overtly, the new emphasis on marital equality in the 1930s can be interpreted as a deliberate strategy on the part of sex reformers to reproduce male domination and female subordination in sex, and to attack the early-twentieth-century suffragists who had criticized male sexuality and found strength in celibacy. Such strategies are pursued in the context of men's need to retain their privileges in politics, the workplace, and the family.

The structures and strategies of men's power for the oppression of women are elaborate and various, precisely because women are not easily kept down. If the sexual order were 'natural', men would not need to exert overt legal, physical or ideological power to convince women that they are silly, weak and feminine.

We can safely assume that at least some women have always been active, strong and enterprising. Women have been 'actors' as well as 'victims' in history – taking action against men's power as well as suffering under it. Some women have acted individually, while others have joined with their sisters in order to fight better. Women's actions fall along a continuum of survival, resistance and challenge.

Survival

Throughout history, women's immense energies have mostly gone into keeping alive. They had to work for low pay, or scrounge, or grow food to provide for themselves and their families. A continuing tradition of bread riots can be seen as a part of the struggle to survive. They were a relatively acceptable way women could demand food for themselves and their children. Women got married to survive economically. They kept back from prosecuting for rape because an unsuccessful prosecution could bring disgrace and despair. A pregnant servant would abort herself in order to keep her job. Most importantly, women helped each other to survive, exchanging knowledge, favours, and emotional comfort through neighbourhood or group networks.

Resistance

History also shows that women found ways to resist the suffocating confines of the traditional female role, but which did not consciously challenge the sexual order, and indeed, could fit into the framework of the existing sexual order. On the individual level, they might become hysterical, and avoid domestic responsibilities. They could remain single but make their living by writing about the joys of married domesticity. They could try to prosecute for rape and risk disgrace. They could refuse to allow their husbands to sleep with them, in order to have fewer children. They could dress as men and live as men, enjoying male privileges.

Women could form a 'female world of love and ritual'* in which their strongest emotional and supportive relationships were with other women. (One of the strongest forms of resistance is lesbianism, which repudiates men's sexual control.) On a collective level, women could use their energy for political action, claiming their right as feminine moral arbiters, in the temperance movement or philanthropic organizations.

Challenge

Finally, women could and did and do challenge the sexual order, breaking through men's power to challenge male dominance and female subordination and rigid gender roles. Women's resistance becomes a challenge when it is politically conscious. It involves identifying your condition as a woman as similar to that of other women, seeing that condition as a consequence of male domination, and with this understanding acting either individually or with other women to change it.

Women's resistance has not been without effect. Not only did it lay the groundwork for the feminist challenge, it required adjustments in men's power to contain women's resistance – hence the sexual dynamics of history. But the challenge involved recognizing and confronting male structures and strategies and forcing them to change. Women in the nineteenth century acted together to open up higher education and the professions to women. The suffragists demanded the vote as a right in itself and as a tool for further change. Past and present feminists demand that men should change their sexual practices, for

---

* See Carol Smith-Rosenburg, *The Female World of Love and Ritual* in N. Cott and E. Pleck, eds, *A Heritage of Our Own*, N.Y.: Simon & Shuster, 1979.

example in campaigns to ensure an acceptable age of consent for girls.

Our work falls into four areas: sexual violence; domesticity; women and public life; the state and sexuality – and in each we will look at forms of men's power and women's resistance. At the beginning of each section we outline these themes and the way the articles relate to them.

We hope the past as well as present existence of feminist challenge will be a constant presence throughout the book. When you read about rape, think about Reclaim the Night marches; when you read about education remember the now well-established women's studies courses in adult education; when you read about women's work recall the efforts of Women in Manual Trades and the feminist struggle in the trade unions; when you read about sex reform, think about the feminist critique of male sexualtiy.

The challenge of feminist politics, finally, has enabled us to write this book.

Part one

Sexual violence

Introduction

Sexual violence against women has been a crucial issue for the women's movement. Contemporary feminist theory, especially Susan Brownmiller's *Against Our Will* (New York: Bantam 1981) has revealed how male sexual violence plays a critical role in keeping women in their place. The fear of rape hinders us from moving about freely; we're told we need a man to protect us from the threat of male violence. If we're attacked, we know we can rarely derive redress from the legal system, despite the help of Rape Crisis Centres. To conduct an effective campaign around the issue of rape we need to understand the history of rape law and women's experience of rape in the past. How has it varied? What has been the effect of changing definitions of women's role, especially her sexuality? In order to disprove the notion that rape is an inevitable and excusable result of 'natural' aggressive male sexuality, we need to demonstrate that the incidence and character of rape vary in different historical circumstances. How have changing social and economic conditions, as well as changing sexual dynamics, shaped sexual violence?

The two papers in this section address these issues, contributing to the development of the history of sexual violence as a new area of feminist research. Nazife Bashar traces the history of laws on rape and looks at the discrepancies between legal theory and practice as revealed in court records of the sixteenth and seventeenth centuries. The reasons why theory and practice varied so widely can be related to the changing definition of rape in early modern society after the decline of feudalism. But neither law nor the courts protected women against rape, though Nazife Bashar points out that women did try to manipulate masculine definitions in their own favour. Anna Clark, focusing on the early nineteenth century, uses a controversial rape-murder case to reveal class-based attitudes toward female sexual behaviour. These attitudes concealed the realities of rape and prevented women from protesting against male aggression.

Today, we are still struggling against such ploys as blaming the victim and excusing rape as an expression of 'natural' male sexual aggression. Feminists provide support to rape victims in crisis centres and battle to change the laws on sexual violence. Now, women are seizing control over definitions of rape. We regard all forms of male sexual violence as crimes against women's right to physical and sexual self-determination.

1. Rape or seduction? A controversy over sexual violence in the nineteenth century*

Anna K. Clark

Early one morning in May 1817, the lacerated and bruised body of servant Mary Ashford was pulled from a pond in the fields of Erdington, a rural district near Birmingham. She had been raped and drowned. Only two hours earlier, a neighbour had seen her sitting on a stile with Abraham Thornton, a bricklayer whom she had met at a public house dance the previous evening. Thornton was later acquitted of rape and murder, sparking off a national controversy.

Today, feminists use such controversies to protest against the way sexual violence keeps women in fear. Such protests were muted in the Thornton controversy, for not only were the assumptions of the debate patriarchal, but the debate itself kept women in fear.

The debate over Mary Ashford's death reveals the changing function of sexual violence in the dynamics of men's power and women's resistance. On one level, it focused on men's concerns – conflicts between men or between conceptions of manhood. Some saw Mary Ashford's death as a crime of class domination rather than of sex. Others asserted Thornton's innocence because they believed violence was an acceptable means of 'seduction'. Their opponents repudiated this 'libertine' masculinity and promulgated a chivalrous manhood in its place. On another level, the controversy was also addressed to women; many polemicists used Mary Ashford's fate to warn women to

* I would like to thank Leonore Davidoff for the stimulation of her own work, and her helpful supervision of this research project. My gratitude also goes to Raphael Samuel, Barbara Brookes, Alison Oram, Sheila Jeffreys, Frances Jarman, Judith Zeitlin and Immy Humes for valuable comments on various drafts of this article.

behave according to restrictive middle-class standards of feminine behaviour. Finally, Mary Ashford's death epitomises the ways sexual violence kept all women in fear – through threats, through direct violence, and through the silencing of women's resistance.

The Thornton controversy was particularly significant in exposing tensions over standards of sexual behaviour because it occurred at a time of social and political turbulence. Political agitation, agricultural depression, and unemployment followed the French Revolution and the Napoleonic Wars. Labouring people were beginning to gain consciousness of themselves as a working class. The situation intensified when middle-class Evangelicals launched a moral offensive against working people, with a two-pronged attempt to reform what was seen as their lax morality, and to deter them from emulating the French Revolution. A middle-class identity was also forming at this time, in part through the doctrine of 'separate spheres'. This ideology encouraged women to leave productive labour and retreat to the shelter of the home, while men were supposed to protect them and venture forth into the competitive public world.

Because almost every woman's economic position was so vulnerable, chastity was her most valuable possession. The importance placed on chastity stemmed from patriarchy, a word which I am using in its particular sense to mean a type of male domination characterized by the rule of fathers (or father figures) over wives and children. Chastity did not necessarily imply physical virginity. It meant that if a woman was unmarried, she was under the control of her father, who could use her labour power and exchange her in marriage. A chaste wife was faithful and obedient. The loss of a woman's chastity was believed to damage her father or husband's honour and financial interests. In fact, two often-used actions in English law enshrined women's status as property in the early nineteenth century. A father could sue his daughter's seducer for the loss of her services in an action for seduction, but the daughter could not use this method to gain redress for herself. Similarly, a husband could claim damages from his wife's lover.

During the early nineteenth century, the importance of a daughter's chastity varied by class and this became a significant issue in the Mary Ashford case. In areas where women could support themselves with high wages, bartering chastity for the support of marriage was less necessary, so the illegitimacy rates were high. Such regions were few, but in the labouring classes an acceptance of prebridal pregnancy and common-law marriages was common. In times of economic hardship, however, men found it difficult to live up to their promises, and women found it more difficult to support themselves. If a daughter's lover abandoned her, her loss of chastity could have serious consequences for her father. It added a baby to feed to the household and deprived the daughter of her ability to contribute to family survival. In the middle class, when female labour lost its respectability and economic value, a woman's chastity became a crucial ornament to her husband's and father's respectability, and ensured that the property would be passed on to the rightful heirs.

Mary Ashford and Abraham Thornton unwittingly became part of the turbulence of this era when they stepped out of a crowded pub into the fields of Erdington. As testimony from this and other trials shows, Mary Ashford was following local plebeian custom by 'walking out' with a young man she did not know very well. A neighbour, John Hompidge, had seen the couple on a stile at three o'clock in the morning because he had been courting his sweetheart in the parlour while her farmer father slept upstairs.[2] In an action for seduction near Birmingham in 1824, Mary Turner admitted she had walked in the fields in the evening with various young men, and met her seducer at a public house dance. She spent the night with him in a pub when he bought their wedding ring, and no one in her family or at the pub questioned their behaviour.

Few voices in the debate, however, admitted that an ordinary man had violently raped and murdered a woman he was courting, and that Mary Ashford had been behaving respectably according to local custom. In part, this was due to the fact that Mary Ashford's behaviour was not only judged by her rural peers, but by middle-class lawyers and clergymen. While a

Birmingham melodrama and many ballads attest to the furore her fate aroused in the locality, her story also reached the genteel pages of the *Gentleman's Magazine*.[4]

It was not only class differences in standards of chastity that determined Mary Ashford's status as innocent heroine or a woman who deserved her fate. Some plebeian and middle-class sources revealed similar opinions about acceptable masculine and feminine behaviour. An examination of the three main positions in the Thornton controversy – the 'libertine' view which excused violence in seduction, the chivalrous view which urged women to submit to male protection, and the view of Mary Ashford as a working-class heroine – will show how both patriarchy and class shaped the interpretation and function of sexual violence in the early nineteenth century.

Those who took the 'libertine' position (so-called by its opponents) saw no basic contradiction in saying women 'consented' to violence. Their argument has two implications: first, that violence was merely one (although not a universal) technique of seduction; and second, that a woman's reputation as chaste or unchaste defined others' perceptions of her consent.

The first idea could be found on all class levels. A jury consisting of farmers, artisans, and a tradesman found Thornton innocent of rape and murder even though he admitted he had had intercourse with Mary Ashford. They followed Judge Holroyd's hint that Thornton had merely used 'great importunity' to gain her consent, and thus would not have murdered her in order to silence an accusation of rape.[5]

What 'great importunity' could mean was revealed in the evidence of the surgeon who examined Mary Ashford's body. He stated of her wounds, 'The lacerations might have been produced if the sexual intercourse had taken place by consent.' He asserted this in the face of testimony by witnesses who examined the field where her body was found. They had seen footsteps, matching the shoes of Thornton and the victim, which showed a man chasing a woman across a field and her efforts to escape. They saw the imprint of her body on the grass, with quantities of blood where her crotch had been, prints of a man's knees and toes beneath the prints of her legs, and on her body, bruises caused by a man's hands pressing into her arms.[6] This surgeon merely followed the principles expounded in all contemporary texts on medical jurisprudence. In such works, men wrote 'contusions on various parts of the extremities and body . . . are compatible with final consent on the part of the female', or 'it is to be recollected that many women will not consent without some force'. They also asserted that it was impossible for one man to violate a conscious, healthy woman.[7]

Evidence from trials reveals that defendants, attorneys, and judges alike consistently confused surrender to violence with consent. In the case of a London publican prosecuted for raping his barmaid, his solicitor brought forward a young man 'who would admit that it was he who violated the young woman, and that she had been a consenting party'. An engineer charged with the attempted rape of a 14-year-old pauper girl pleaded that he had been intoxicated and 'had no recollection of having used any violence or persuasion toward the girl'. *The Independent Whig* stated, 'Violence, in a manner, is acknowledged by Thornton himself to have been committed by him, only, he added, that it was with her consent'. In the trial of William Hall for the murder of Betty Winshull, landlady of a Warrington pub, the judge asked the jury to consider 'if though violence was used, it was with her consent'.[8]

Popular songs reveal the assumption that a woman's lack of consent was not important in the face of a man's determination. Copies of these songs were sold and sung in the streets. They sprang from traditional folk melodies, but in the early nineteenth century commercial printers distributed them nationally, so that they may be seen as the equivalent of today's pop music. In many songs a roving swain comes upon a pretty girl and steals her virginity while she faints. He leaves her pregnant and penniless and goes on to more adventures. Other songs illustrated the coarse cliche that when women say no they mean yes, or imply that it doesn't matter if she says no, she'll like it anyway. In 'By the Light of the Moon,' the hero sings,

How this fair maid blushed and grumbled
    Let me alone, I pray forbear;

Pray be easy, do not tease me,
  Touch me again and I'll pull your hair;
How this fair maid blushed and grumbled;
  You have spoiled my gown and new galloon.
  But well pleased my Sally by the light of the moon.[9]

Seducers and their critics shared the idea that violence was merely one means of seduction. Those who disapproved of seduction also disapproved of violence, but they were concerned with immorality, or damage to family integrity, rather than rape. One moralist wrote, 'Are not all the arts and flattery imaginable, the most infernal stratagems, and perhaps, direct violence, had recourse to, in order to make these devoted victims stoop to their desires?'[10] In 17 per cent of the actions for seduction I have examined, the daughter claimed her seducer had used violence against her. In one case involving an artisan's daughter the prosecuting attorney described her 'fall' as follows:

> He locked the door and endeavoured to commit violence on her person. She resisted and screamed for help, when he, after much trouble, promised to marry her if she consented to grant his desires. She yielded to his violence and entreaties and promises to marry her, and her virtue, character, and her happiness were gone forever.[11]

As this quote reveals, violence became significant only when it led to the father's loss of a daughter's chastity. In almost all actions for seductions reported in newspapers, fathers (or other relatives) were awarded heavy damages – usually running from ten to over one hundred pounds. The seduced daughter, even if raped, did not elicit sympathy, for the action served only to indemnify her father's loss. If a daughter prosecuted for rape on her own behalf, she had very little chance of gaining justice. Between 1815 and 1819, only 22 per cent of men tried for rape were convicted.[12]

In fact, it was a woman's own behaviour which determined whether violence committed against her would be regarded as a peccadillo to be fined or ignored, or as a capital crime. Edward

Holroyds, a defender of Thornton, expressed the tendency to blame the victim as well as a willingness to accept violence as 'seduction' when he tried to explain away the injuries evident on Mary Ashford's corpse. He contended,

> There were no appearances but what have been from connection obtained by consent after considerable earnestness, exertion, and importunity . . . the deceased, after some efforts to get away, and struggle, and resistance at first, yielded, a yielding obtained most probably reluctantly, and by artifice, promise, and oaths, and urgent importunity, to which her own extreme imprudence in remaining alone with a man, especially one so shortly known to her, all night in the fields, she was unfortunately exposed.[13]

By describing the victim's behaviour as culpable, he excused Thornton's violence as an acceptable technique of seduction. It was always women's responsibility to defend themselves against men's allegedly uncontrollable passions. A victim's failure stained her, rather than her attacker, with dishonour. Another advocate of Thornton argued that Mary Ashford committed suicide in shame after yielding to Thornton (although witnesses saw only Thornton's footprints and a trail of blood on the edge of the pond).[14] This claim loses even more credibility when we consider the apparently easy acceptance of premarital sex in the locality. As these defences of Thornton reveal, class as well as patriarchy shaped standards of chastity.

Her chastity, not her refusal or acceptance of a certain act, determined a woman's consent. Legal authorities did declare 'It is no mitigation of [rape] that the woman at last yielded to the violence, if such her consent was forced by death or duress', or if she were a 'common strumpet' yet judges and juries often excused rape on the grounds of a woman's bad character.[15] Defence attorneys could introduce evidence alleging that a woman was unchaste. Chastity, in fact, meant that she behaved as the exclusive sexual property of one man rather than common property to all men. If a woman had a 'bad character', her consent could be assumed – or became irrelevant – to any violence, even gang rape. In such cases, even clear evidence that the defendants had committed a rape would not often deter juries from acquittal.

In the case of Anne Keystone, a weaver in Gloucestershire who was brutally gang-raped in front of 100 people on a village common, the jury refused to convict after learning she had been drinking gin in a pub.[16] Mr Justice Stephens epitomised this notion of consent in 1868, when he 'submitted that the true rule must be, that where a man is led from the conduct of the woman to believe he is not committing a crime known to the law, the act of connection cannot under any circumstances amount to a rape'.[17] English law did not repudiate this precedent until 1975, after the notorious case of Morgan in which three men were acquitted of rape on the grounds that the victim's husband had told them she liked rough treatment.

Even those who opposed sexual violence, such as Mary Ashford's defenders, exploited such crimes as warnings to women to conform to restrictive feminine standards of behaviour. Instead of excusing violence as seduction, they attacked Thornton as a 'libertine' who endangered chivalry. The Rev. Luke Booker pronounced, 'The female sex is authorised to look up to man as its Protector, rather than its Destroyer,' but he also made clear that women must deserve such aid.[18]

Booker used Mary Ashford's fate to warn young women to submit to chivalrous protection instead of acting freely and independently. She was blamed for putting herself in a situation where she would be vulnerable to such a licentious man, even though she was behaving according to local custom. Booker stressed her 'imprudence' in going to a dance 'unattended by a discreet Male Relative, or a prudent Matron-Friend'.[19] (She had, in fact, accompanied her intimate friend Hannah Cox.) Booker even went to the length of distributing the inscription on her grave as a broadsheet,

As a warning to female virtue, and a humble monument to female chastity, this Stone marks the grave of Mary Ashford, who, in the 20th year of her age, having incautiously repaired to a scene of amusement, without proper protection, was brutally violated and murdered on 27th May, 1817.[20]

One writer satirically noted of Booker, 'Really, if the doctor goes on in this manner, his cookmaid will not be able to cross the street with a pie to the baker's without a chaperon.'[21] Booker's stress on chaperonage, admittedly laughable in circumstances when young women earned their own livings, stemmed from an increasingly prevalent middle-class morality. Since a woman's sexuality was regarded as the property of her male relatives, she was not considered capable of regulating her own actions, but had to be guarded until she could be handed over to her husband.

Booker was not eccentric in conjuring the threat of crime to control women's behaviour. Judges often used their position to pronounce warnings to women. In 1824 a judge at Chester Assizes found a man guilty of raping Jemima Cooper, even though her character was not 'respectable'. As he sentenced the man to death, he told him, 'The treatment this girl has received from you, will be a warning to others, not to enter into that familiarity with, and form an acquaintance with persons so unknown to them as it appears you were to her.'[22]

Versions of this theme surfaced as well in the more popular genre of ballads. Although the Birmingham ballad 'Mary Ashford's Tragedy' attacked Thornton, it ended with the requisite moralistic note,

Now all you virgins that bloom as I bloom'd,
  Keep at home in your proper employ;
    Ne're in dancing delight,
    Nor in the fields roam,
    With a stranger from home,
Lest you meet a fate as wretched as I.[23]

Such songs and Booker's warnings clearly show that rape could be used as a means of controlling women's behaviour.

Yet this use of chivalry did require a demonstration that some men would protect women from some other, dangerous, men. The proponents of chivalry attacked Thornton because he undermined the premises of this protection racket. They portrayed him as a wild, inhuman, diabolical creature, in much the same way the Yorkshire Ripper was described as insane. 'Mary

Ashford was savagely seized like a Sabine, and inhumanly immolated by her rapacious defiler!' proclaimed Booker. Thus differentiating him from ordinary men, they blocked any suspicion that his actions merely stemmed from an exaggeration of normal masculine behaviour. The execration heaped on Thornton served to define the limits of acceptable sexual aggression. Following Evangelical tenets, Booker also used Thornton's example to warn young men to live up to the principles of chivalrous manhood by controlling their passions. As a melodrama about the case admonished,

> In viewing well this act of dark despair
> Or crimes like his – Oh giddy youth beware
> May virtue, sense, and honour hold control
> Ere furious passions stain the spotless soul.[24]

Despite the focus on Mary Ashford's 'imprudence' according to middle-class standards, her reputation as an innocent heroine persisted. The third position in the debate celebrated Mary Ashford as the innocent victim of an evil man. The ballads called for revenge on Thornton:

> May the thorn that could wound a bosom so fair,
> Yet wither, be sapless, of nature despair;
> And blasted the soil be where'er it is found
> Till it droops on the pit where poor Mary was drowned.
>
> Or should it in spite of all nature remain,
> And seek social comfort, may it seek it in vain;
> Let barren rocks receive it, deserted let it dry,
> So killed without pity, unpitied let it die.[25]

Although Thornton, as a bricklayer, did not exactly fit the nineteenth-century stereotype of the aristocratic libertine preying on village maidens, two melodramas (and apparently popular opinion) interpreted the murder as a case of class exploitation. (Statistically, a woman was much more vulnerable to a man of her own class, but this fact was rarely publicly acknowledged.)[26] They claimed Thornton was acquitted because his rich father bribed the jury. After the trial, a reporter noted,

Among the lower classes of people about the neighbourhood,
there is a sense of horror against Thornton, that amounts
almost to ferocity; and this is accompanied by a most
indecorous and general outcry against all the means which
led to his dismissal.[27]

In the play *The Murdered Maid*, 'Maria' cries to 'Thornville' as
he chases her, 'Begone, and learn that the humble and lowborn
Maria abhors the wretch, though a diadem sparkled on his
brows, who would shock her ears with such base proposals, and
try to lure her from the paths of rectitude and honour.'[28] A
Birmingham play, *The Mysterious Murder*, described Thornton's father as an independent gentleman and places the whole
play in the context of hard times for the poor.

Even when they did not highlight class differences, Mary
Ashford's defenders tended to present her male relatives as the
true victims of the rape and murder, consistent with the
principle that loss of a woman's chastity damaged her father's
honour. The legal entanglements following Thornton's acquittal exacerbated this tendency. Mary Ashford's young brother
resurrected an obscure precedent in order to appeal against the
verdict of innocence. In response, Thornton challenged him to
a 'wager of battle' (to prove his innocence through single-
handed combat). A weak boy, the brother did not take up the
challenge, and Thornton went free.

Mary Ashford could only become a heroine because she died
defending her virtue. *The Mysterious Murder* ends with a
tableau in which 'Maria Ashfield' ascends to heaven to the
accompaniment of choruses praising her purity.[29] This melodrama belonged to a long tradition, featuring the classical heroine
Lucretia, and Clarissa in Richardson's eighteenth-century
novel, in which women die after losing their chastity. In an 1825
edition of *The Terrific Register* (a magazine of gothic romance
and horror) the victim of a 'brutal violation' tells an aged
woman before drowning herself,

That after she had thus lost her honour, which was the only
thing for which she wished to live, she couldn't think of
enduring life – that never anyone should point her out and

say, There is the girl who has become a wanton, and dishonoured her family – that no friend of hers should be reproached with the tale that she consented to her ravisher's will, but that she would give manifest proof, that although her body had been violated by force, her mind was unstained.[30]

In *The Murdered Maid* (the more genteel melodrama) it is clear that what defines a woman as pure is her physical virginity. 'Thornville' remembers Maria crying before he violates her, 'Oh reflect, if once a female falls from virtue, abandoned by all, she exceeds man in the extent of wickedness.'[31] According to this morality, only death saved Mary Ashford from becoming a degraded female. If a woman's resistance to rape failed, she lost her place in the patriarchal system. As Chitty, a writer on medical jurisprudence, noted,

Universally, in England, an unmarried woman who has had sexual intercourse, even by such force that she was unable to resist with effect, is in a degree disgraced, or rather no longer retains her virgin purity in the estimation of society, and there is a natural delicate, though perhaps indescribable feeling that deters most men who know that a female has been completely violated, from taking her in marriage.[32]

One voice did honour Mary Ashford as an innocent heroine in her own right, without insinuations that she had behaved imprudently. The *Ladies Monthly Museum* featured her as one of a series of celebrated ladies, usually queens or famous writers. It described her according to the romantic conventions of the time:

She promised, at a very early age, to rise superior to her station by the graces of her mind and person . . . so lovely a girl could not have been without admirers, but it was proved, that although she had a great share of vivacity, it was so tempered by discretion, that scandal itself could not cast an aspersion on her fair fame . . . she was of a retired and domestic turn.[33]

This account could be interpreted as an instance of women's reluctance to accept patriarchal definitions of sexual violence.

Such a celebration of Mary Ashford from a female point of view was the exception rather than the rule. It was very difficult for women to protest against sexual violence, or even to prosecute. 'Respectability' prohibited women from speaking out on any sexual matter, let alone sexual violence committed against them. As a Lambeth magistrate noted with reference to indecent assaults on the streets, 'the more decent or respectable females were, the more reluctant they were in coming forward to give public details of such gross outrages.'[34]

If the constraints of propriety did not hold a woman back, more brutal methods could be brought into play. Although rape-murders were not common, Thornton's technique of throwing his victim into a pit or pond seemed to be a pattern in such cases. Men could use many other means, however, to ensure that the living victim of sexual violence could never obtain redress. Mary Ashford would probably never have succeeded in prosecuting Thornton if she had survived.

Both assailants and police often blocked a woman's complaint. Assailants could bribe or harass their victims in order to keep them from prosecuting. For example, Henry Collier was accused of raping, robbing, and attempting to murder Amelia Marshall, the young wife of a hawker, to whom he had given a ride to Sheffield. At the Warwick Assizes where he stood trial, she did not appear to prosecute, and 'it was supposed that the absence of the witness had been procured by means of a sum of money furnished by the prisoner's friends.' The runaway daughter of a Hereford farmer, Rosetta Addis, was indecently assaulted by several lodgers. The next day they dragged her from the Brentford lodging house, tied her up, and threw her in a cart to be taken to the madhouse at the urgings of the landlady. One assailant was committed to prison for two months in default of a five pound fine.[35] Middle- and upper-class assailants, of course, could escape imprisonment by paying a fine in all but the most severe cases.

Assailants sometimes ordered constables to arrest their victims on charges of theft if they protested.[36] A woman could even be arrested for indecent exposure if a man pulled her clothes about.[37] Even more astonishing, some victims themselves were imprisoned after pressing charges, if they were too poor, or did not have a husband to post bond to ensure that they would prosecute. Mary Rich, a 14-year-old workingman's daughter who accused a lawyer of raping her, was imprisoned for a month in solitary confinement and fed on bread and water while the lawyer went free on bail.[38] If a woman's prosecution for rape failed, the man she accused could prosecute her for perjury.[39] If she were found guilty, the humiliation and imprisonment resulting from a trial could effectively deter other women from seeking justice.

Despite these difficulties, many women did prosecute, and some resisted sexual assault. A witness in an 1834 case testified that when publican Edward Thomas of Grosvenor Mews molested a Mrs Kenwick, 'he got so roughly handled by that lady, as to be obliged to keep to his bed for several weeks'. 'Respectable married women' often 'collared' the drunken young men who grabbed them on the street, and indignantly hit them with their reticules or umbrellas. After a 60-year-old man raped a 12-year-old girl, her mother and several other women 'dragged him through a pond', but when he was brought to trial, he was acquitted.[40]

Women's resistance to violence in the early nineteenth century was limited to such individual incidents. Although sexual violence was widely publicized, patriarchal assumptions shaped any organized protests against sexual victimization. For instance, the Associate Institute for Improving and Enforcing the Laws for the Protection of Women claimed it had 26 'Female Auxiliaries' to protect girls all over the country. But male leaders controlled this organization's campaigns against the entrapment of young girls into brothels and their violation there, focusing on the necessity of repentance for fallen women, and on the prosecution of madams rather than brothel customers.[41] Any women who spoke out on sexual matters from a feminist point of view, such as Mary Wollstonecraft and the Owenite socialist-feminists, were reviled as the nadir of female impropriety. By the late nineteenth century, however, women began to campaign against sexual violence and aid its victims.[42]

Today, judges still exploit rape cases as opportunities to blame victims for their fates, warning women not to hitchhike and excusing male sexual aggression. Sexual violence still restricts our freedom by keeping us in fear. But feminsts are fighting back. We campaign to ensure that victims of sexual violence can prosecute successfully. We refuse to accept patriarchal definitions of women's consent and proper female behaviour. Instead of being defined as chaste or unchaste, we try to define ourselves as desiring or refusing when we wish, for 'However we're dressed and wherever we go, yes means yes and no means no!'

2. Rape in England between 1550 and 1700

Nazife Bashar

Despite the emergence in recent decades of crime history, social history and women's history, the historical study of rape has not been extensive. Historians of crime and society in early modern England, (the period between 1550 and 1800) have readily given their attention to other crimes affecting women such as infanticide and witchcraft, but not to rape. When, in his article 'The Nature and Incidence of Crime in England 1550–1625: A Preliminary Survey', James Cockburn[1] is forced to consider rape – having found about fifty cases of it in the Calendar of Assize Records that he had compiled – he shuns the subject, dismissing the identification of a pattern of sexual offences as virtually impossible. One could agree that 'rape was probably reported', and his sample was small! But even so a pattern of few prosecutions, young victims and a low conviction rate could be seen to emerge from his cases. It seems that rape is too risky, too contemporary, too political a subject, to be dealt with comfortably by the present-day male historian.

Similarly, Geoffrey Quaife[2] does devote a few pages to rape in *Wanton Wenches and Wayward Wives*, his book on peasant attitudes to sex in seventeenth-century Somerset. His main source is ecclesiastical records, which do not deal with rape *per se*. He finds, however, that 'one in ten of the girls consented to sexual intercourse through fear of violence' and another one in ten consented when drunk. Occasionally emotional blackmail was used to gain consent from a 'girl'. Yet Quaife does not analyse his material, being content to give a rather prurient account of the molestation of a 12-year-old by her schoolmaster. He does not ask why so many of the rapes tried at Quarter Sessions involved children. He fails to speculate that the historical record may not be a reliable mirror of reality, that adult women were raped but their cases usually did not come to court. He proceeds after a few descriptions of the sexual assault of young girls ('It was not only little girls that had to fear sexual harassment') to some lengthy quotes on homosexual aggressors. He fails to comment on the high incidence of sexual assault by Somerset men or on their seemingly widespread sexual attraction towards children.

The middle ages, with its abundance of rape law, have been investigated from a legal aspect by John Post[3] and E.W.Ives[4] in a number of articles in academic books and journals. But after 1500 few laws on rape were passed and the interest of legal historians declines.

A reading of the works of legal authorities and of the texts of laws and statutes relating to rape gives one impression of rape law in England between 1550 and 1700. A study of the records of the main law courts that dealt with rape gives quite a different impression. Feminist historians cannot rely on the assurances of legal authorities and the existing laws and statutes for an accurate portrayal of the treatment of rape in sixteenth- and seventeenth-century England. Much more revealing court records are accessible in the Public Record Office in London and in numerous county record offices.

Records of the Assize court for the home counties (Essex, Kent, Hertfordshire, Surrey and Sussex) between 1558 and 1700 are held in the Public Records Office. Records of the north-eastern counties, which include Yorkshire, Westmoreland, Cumberland, Northumberland and Durham, for the period 1646 to 1700, are also held in the PRO. James Cockburn has published the extant records of the home counties Assizes for the years 1558 to 1625, making these records particularly accessible to the historian.[5] In my research on rape, I also used printed and manuscript records of the lower court of Quarter Sessions for the five home counties and for the county of Yorkshire.

Legal authorities, laws and statutes

From Anglo-Saxon times until the sixteenth century rape

featured prominently in English statute law. This prominence was due to the law's concern with the protection of male property, rather than to its concern with the welfare of women. The language of medieval rape statutes defined rape and abduction interchangeably. Both involve the *theft* of a woman. Writing in the nineteenth century, Pollock and Maitland [6] concurred:

> The crime which we call rape had in very old days been hardly severed from that which we call abduction; if it had wronged the woman, it had wronged her kinsmen also, and they would have felt themselves seriously wronged even if she had given her consent, and had, as we should say, eloped.

The 1275 Statute of Westminster placed rape and abduction side by side: 'the king prohibiteth that none do ravish, nor take away by Force' and provided the same punishment for them both. Section 34 of a further Statute of 1285 dealt with three issues together: 'Punishment of Rape: of a married Woman eloping with an Adulterer; for carrying off a Nun'. The economy of words, in using 'punishment' only once, and their conjuction together seems to emphasize their classification as one. For 'rape', the woman's non-consent was made less relevant, thereby facilitating legal action by her family even if the woman had *willingly* gone off with a suitor who was not welcomed by her family. For elopement, the husband was to recover his goods taken by the eloping wife, and she was to lose claim to dower from her husband. A nun was 'owned' by the church but her property value was less than that of an heiress, so a man who carried a nun from her convent, even with her consent, was liable to the comparatively light sentence of imprisonment and a fine. All three issues revolved around property, its theft and its recovery. Section 35 was entitled 'Ravishment of Ward' but was actually about wards of children 'taken and carried away' before they were suitably and profitably married according to their guardians' desires. Rape as we know it may not have been involved.

A statute of 1382 reinforced the principle that rape law was about the protection of male property and that the woman's consent was irrelevant. Women who 'consented' after 'rape' were to lose all claim to their husband's property. Henry VII's Act of 1487 indicated that wealthy women were sometimes the victims of abduction:

> Women, as well Maidens, as Widows and Wives having Substances, some in Goods moveable and some in lands and Tenements, and some being Heirs apparent unto their ancestors, for the lucre of such Substances been oftentimes taken by Misdoers.

The statutes of 1285, 1382 and 1487 were all directed at the protection of the property of the wealthy. Family land and wealth was increased by carefully placed marriage alliances. A liaison that went against family interests and wishes was anathema. In order to put an end to the relationship (indeed to put an end to the suitor, for after 1285 the penalty for rape was death) the girl's family charged him with rape. John Post[7] argues that the 1285 Act was 'aimed at consenting sexual relationships . . . the material and familial aspects of a consenting illicit relationship', and that many 'rape' cases brought in the thirteenth, fourteenth and fifteenth centuries concerned relationships between men and women not approved by their families due to the unhappy consequences for ancestral fortunes:

> The emphasis of the law of rape was thus drawn away from the actual or potential plight of the victim of a sexual assault, and placed upon the unacceptability of an accomplished elopement, or an abduction, or an abduction to which the victim became reconciled.

The 1382 and 1487 Acts were both passed to aid individual families. Sir Thomas West had extensive lands in a number of counties including Hampshire, Wiltshire and Devon. According to West, his daughter Eleanor was abducted and 'ravished' by an upstart – a landless younger son who later married Eleanor West.[8] Margery Ruyton, daughter of a leading Warwickshire gentleman, was abducted and married by Robert Bellingham, a member of the same social class, but a man whom her father disliked.[9] In both these cases, as in many other medieval 'rape' cases, the property dispute was settled amicably, the families were reconciled to their sons-in-law and the cases were dropped before the death sentence could be considered.

Whether the woman had actually been raped, was irrelevant. Medieval rape laws were meant for the wealthy, for the protection of their property, rather than to protect a woman's rights and sexual self-determination.

By the beginning of the sixteenth century, the law of rape was prominent and severe. A further act of 1576 took away the benefit of clergy from offenders in rape and burglary. 'Clergy' meant that the convict who could read a verse from a prayer book was branded on the hand rather than put to death. Death was left as the only penalty for the convicted rapist. Rape was classed with crimes such as theft and murder, in the 1576 Act. Michael Dalton,[10] a seventeenth-century lawyer, citing Sir Francis Bacon, proclaimed: 'if a Woman kill him that assaileth her to ravish her: This is justifiable by the Woman, without any pardon.' Rape, even attempted rape, was serious enough to justify killing, and officially classed with other serious crimes in which the killing of a thief or a murderer was also justifiable.

Consequently, eminent legal writers through the centuries: Glanvill, Bracton and Britton in the middle ages, Edward Coke, William Lambarde, Fitzherbert and Dalton in the sixteenth and seventeenth centuries, William Blackstone in the eighteenth century and Pollock and Maitland in the nineteenth century, discussed the statutes and legal provisions for rape, and included chapters on rape in their tomes on English law. They described at length the severe penalties for rape, and were punctilious in detailing the various forms of castration and mutilation supposedly used in pre-Norman England as punishment for rape. They assumed that rape, because cleared as a serious crime, would be actually punished as a matter of course. Sir Anthony Fitzherbert[11] deemed rape to be more important than any property crime: 'The most greate offence nexte unto murdre semyth to be Rape.' In 1586 the distinguished Justice of the Peace, William Lambarde[12] stressed rape's seriousness and the need to punish it severely: 'let us not be afraid to cut off treasons, murders, witchcrafts, rapes and other felonies that be the highest and top boughs as it were of this tree of transgression.'

Nicholas Brady in his *The Lawes Resolution of Women's Rights* or *The Lawes Provision for Woeman,* written in 1632, devoted a large chapter to rape, ostensibly as an important aspect of women's rights. Brady proclaimed his book 'a publique Advantage and peculiar Service to that Sexe generally beloved and by the Author had in venerable estimation'. It is interesting however, that in advising women on the law's provision for them on rape, Brady drew almost solely on legal authorities and on laws and statutes concerning rape.[13] He did not think to consider the unsatisfactory *usual* treatment of rape cases that came before the Assizes and Quarter Sessions in the late sixteenth and seventeenth centuries.

Thus, from the point of view of the legal authorities and statutory law, rape was regarded very seriously. There were quite a large number of statutes on rape. Rape was classified as an important crime and incurred severe penalties which were becoming even more severe by the end of the sixteenth century. There was a prevailing belief that rape should and would be punished.

Reinforcing this last point was a play, *The Rape, or the Innocent Impostors,* a tragedy written and performed at the end of 1692. It portrayed a king as being completely prepared to punish with death his own son who was accused of rape:

> Be witness for me Gods how much I loathe
> A villainy like that ! How much my heart
> Deplores with Tears of Blood the Virtuous Princess!

Court records

Yet, when I studied the law's *practical* application at the Assize courts and at Quarter Sessions, a completely different picture of rape and punishment for rape emerged.

The Assize records contain only a very small number of rape prosecutions. In Sussex during the forty-five-year reign of Elizabeth I over 1,000 cases of larceny were prosecuted, about 150 burglaries, about 100 homicides and only 14 rapes. In

Hertfordshire over the thirty-year period 1573–1603 there were almost 200 cases of larceny, 50 burglaries, 50 homicides and 4 rapes prosecuted. Rape usually constituted less than 1 per cent of all indictments.

There are a number of ways of interpreting this material. One can accept the evidence at face value and conclude that, in the sixteenth and seventeenth centuries rape was a rare occurrence. The severity of the penalties deterred men from rape. In stressing the severity of rape penalties, legal authorities tended to explain the increasing harshness of the law in terms of the increasing incidence of rape and the state's desire to put an end to it. Alternatively, one can look behind the facts and suggest that, for a variety of reasons, theft and murder were more likely to be reported than rape. Theft involved a material loss of property, and murder a missing person or dead body. Even so, it is unlikely that over nearly one hundred and fifty years, 1558–1700, in Sussex for example, only 48 women were raped, or in Hertforshire, only 21.

The number of rapes appearing in the court records was remarkably small. Either rapes were not reported, or, though reported, some cases did not get to court. The problem is highlighted by Pollock and Maitland's [14] observation of rape law prior to Edward I: 'Concerning these matters we find little "case law". Appeals of rape were often brought in the thirteenth century, but they were often quashed, abandoned or compromised.' Pollock and Maitland imply there were no more rapes than actually came to trial, which leads on to the second point produced by the court records about rape.

Most of the small number of men charged with rape were acquitted, 'not guilty', reprieved, not captured and described as 'at large', or released without trial. [15] A finding of 'ignoramus' meant that the case was rejected before trial due to lack of evidence. Clearly, 'evidence' for a rape case was as difficult to find then as it is now, because the proportion of rape cases rejected 'ignoramus' in the seventeenth century was usually more than twice as high as for cases involving other crimes.

Of the 274 rape cases for the five home counties between 1558 and 1700 which did come to court, 45 men were found guilty, and 215 were not; 14 verdicts are unknown. Of the 45, 31 were hanged, 6 pleaded clergy and were branded and released, 6 were reprieved and 2 sentences were not given on the document. Of the 215, 141 were acquitted outright, 6 were released or 'delivered by proclamation'; 15 remained at large and 53 cases were rejected 'ignoramus'.

A change occurs over the period. Between 1558 and 1559, 59 men brought to trial for rape were found 'not guilty', and 25 were found guilty of whom 2 were reprieved, a conviction rate of more than one in four. For the period 1600–49, 50 were found not guilty and 14 guilty of whom two were reprieved, a conviction rate of one in five. For 1650–1700, 32 were found not guilty and 6 guilty of whom 2 were reprieved, a conviction rate of about one in eight. Not only was the total number of rape cases coming to court decreasing markedly, the proportion of men being convicted of rape was decreasing as well. (These figures do not include the men who remained at large and the cases rejected 'ignoramus' before trial.)

The effect may have been cumulative. Women would have become more reluctant to charge a man with rape when the probability of his conviction was decreasing. Further, prosecution at assizes required an outlay of time and money in travelling to and attending at the court. The emotional cost of a rape prosecution has always been very high for the victim. In 1632 Nicholas Brady[16] cited medieval authorities on the procedure a woman should follow when she had been raped:

> She ought to go straight way and with Hue and Cry complaine to the good men of the next towne, shewing her wrong, her garments torne and any effusion of blood, and then she ought to go to the chiefe constable, to the Coroner and to the Viscount and at the next County to enter her appeale and have it enrolled in the Coroners roll: and Justices before whome she was again to reintreat her Appeale.

Such open and repeated display of what was described at the time as a 'loathsome leprosie' would have been extremely difficult for a woman then, as it is now. The ravished princess in the 1692 play, *The Rape or the Innocent Imposters,* cries,

Let me for ever hide my Face in Darkness:
I am not fit for light; a stain like mine
Should seek for Everlasting Night to cover it.

In the end death by suicide was the only release from her shame, as it was for Lucrece in Shakespeare's poem.

Because of all these deterrents, it is possible that only the strongest cases came to court. But even, what seems to us the strongest possible case, was not guaranteed a verdict of guilty. In 1683 Sibila May, 'a woman of about eighty years old' was raped. The accused was also charged with robbing her of a ring from her person and with robbing her house. A pamphlet of the time detailed the judgement: 'Upon the latter two Indictments, the proof being plain, he was found guilty, but upon the former acquitted, the party ravished not being able to say he was the man, by reason as she alledged, he Blindfolded her'[17] It did not appear to have satisfied the criteria for a 'strong case' at the early modern courts. The judgement also indicates the relative ease of conviction for theft as opposed to rape.

Another factor limiting the number of rape prosecutions was the widely held legal dictum that conception proved consent: 'Rape is the forcible ravishment of a woman, but if she conceive it is not rape, for she cannot conceive unless she consent.'[18] Many rapes, especially where the woman was raped repeatedly during the time of an employment contract that she could not leave, would not have been prosecuted because the woman had fallen pregnant. Evidence of these is found in bastardy depositions. The woman concerned was interrogated at Quarter Sessions as to how and by whom she had become pregnant, in order to get the man to maintain her child. Sussex Quarter Sessions records show that often sexual intercourse was had 'more by force than persuasion'. Considering the limited available forms of contraception, the dangerous forms of abortion, the death penalty for infanticide, the imprisonment, whipping, ostracism, job loss involved in bastardy, as well as the sundry other adjuncts of heterosexual intercourse, this is not surprising.

Francis Haddon, master of Lydia Prince, 'did sweare by the

Lord Jesus hee would teare her in peices if shee did not let him lye with her'. Elinor Symonds said that she was pregnant because Ralph Brown overtook her on the road, 'Carryed her forcibly into John Pinkes barne and had Carnal knowledge of her body against her Consent 2 or 3 times and threatened to kill her this Examinant if she made the least noise'. Esekiell Filder stopped his servant's mouth with a sheet and when she resisted threatened to kill her if she told anyone.[19]

Some rapes come to light even more by chance than those found in the bastardy depositions. In the course of a dispute over a gold ring at Kent Quarter Sessions, it was revealed that Mr John Turner, vicar, 'would have got out of ye bed, But he would not let her But caught hold of her'. It was not pregnancy stopping Mary Bean from prosecuting, but rather the other deterrents of time, money, emotional trauma, humiliation and the small chance of the rapist's conviction.[20]

Simultaneously with the decrease in prosecutions and convictions, there was an increase in the age of rape victims prosecuting. Over the whole period 1558–1700 there was a preponderance of cases in which the victim was under eighteen years. But by the end of the period proportionately more adult women appeared at court as rape victims compared with the beginning of the period when more girls appeared. During 1558–99, 48 cases involve girls under eighteen, of whom 22 are under ten; 16 cases involve adult women of nineteen years and over. The years 1600–49 saw the numbers becoming somewhat more even and the proportion of victims under ten decreasing: 48 cases involved girls under eighteen, of whom 17 were under ten; 24 cases involved adult women. By the period 1650–1700 the balance had tipped: 19 cases involved girls under eighteen, of whom 5 were under ten; 31 cases involved adult women.

However, this did not mean that the conviction rate in cases involving adult women increased proportionately. Of the 15 victims of men hanged for rape in the home counties between 1558 and 1599, 5 were under eighteen years, 2 were spinsters, one unmarried and one a widow, though the man in the latter case was also charged with burglary. Details of 6 of the victims were not given. For 1600–49 all 9 of the victims of men hanged for rape, were under eighteen. Between 1650 and 1700, of the 4 men hanged for rape, 2 had raped girls under eighteen, one had raped a spinster of twenty-three years, but it may be significant that she was declared on the indictment to have been a virgin at the time. The age of the other woman was not given on the indictment.

While the rate of prosecutions and convictions, small though it always was, decreased even further and the ages of victims at court changed, the relative ease of conviction of men accused of raping girls under eighteen was a stable factor through the years 1550–1700. It seems that rape cases rested on the issue of virginity. Men who raped children, who were assumed to be virgins, and women designated on the indictments 'virgins', were more likely to be tried and convicted. Of the 53 cases rejected 'ignoramus' before trial two-thirds involved adult women. Rape of an adult woman was generally considered by the Assizes to be a case not suitable for trial. The courts were far more willing to prosecute for rape where virginity was involved, but not for the same reasons current today – sexual morality, 'virtue' and its logical consequence, likelihood of consent.

In the seventeenth century the accused's defence was more apt to rest on a denial that sexual relations took place, rather than on a claim that the woman consented. Surprisingly little is made of the victim's past sexual history. When mentioned in evidence, it relates to her past sexual relations with the accused, not with her general standard of 'virtue'. Lambarde[21] held that a man could not rape his own mistress, but he could be prosecuted for raping the mistress of another. Indeed, the man's sexual history is more at issue. In 1649 Christopher Shackleton was charged with the rape of Martha Redman. A neighbour testified that 18 years earlier his wife, by this time dead, had told him that Shackleton had attempted to rape her.[22] Past sexual history of the accused was allowed as evidence, even though it was long since past and a second-hand account. Included in the evidence against another man accused of rape was the information: 'the said Shaw is suspected by his neighbours to be a man of lewd behaviour'.

The emphasis on the man's character and actions rather than on the woman's character and consent suggests that, as a hangover from medieval times, the woman's volition was still fairly irrelevant. Severe restrictions on children giving evidence further negates the possibility that cases involving virgins were prosecuted because their evidence of non-consent would be more convincing.

Moreover, although more rapes involving *adult* women appeared at court in the seventeenth century, they probably represented only a fraction of rapes actually committed on such women. An adult woman had little chance of having her attacker indicted or convicted of rape at Assizes. In the second half of the seventeenth century, men were indicted at Assizes for the lesser crime of attempted rape. Most of these victims were adult women. Of the 22 men charged with attempted rape in the home counties, 4 were found guilty and fined, fines ranging from £100 to £10 to 20s. – all substantial amounts – 3 were found not guilty, 7 verdicts were not given. Eight were rejected 'ignoramus', a very high proportion indicating that even attempted rape was a difficult charge to lay. Moreover, the convictions were passed on the few cases of girls under eighteen.

In the seventeenth century many adult women prosecuted for rape and attempted rape at the lower court of Quarter Sessions, where the penalty was a smaller fine. In 1667 in Surrey, John Lee was fined 5s. for the attempted rape of Anne Killick.[23] But the verdict in most of these cases is not given, and probably the usual action was binding the accused over to good behaviour.

Some cases show rather extreme efforts to avoid prosecuting for 'rape'. In 1693 John Chesham was indicted in Sussex for assaulting Anne Willet and keeping her from her husband against her will for six hours.[24] In a Lancashire case of 1603 Ellen, wife of Richard Johnes, charged John Heywoode with assault. She claimed that he assaulted her and 'forced her into adultery'.[25] They avoided the charge of sexual assault, clearly a very hard one to lay. Instead, they focused on the husband's rights and religious aspects of adultery.

Some indictments simply involve assault of a woman by a

man, but other evidence by chance available reveals that the man actually attempted to rape the woman. These were all methods women used to try to have their attackers punished. A rape charge at Assizes was patently ineffective. Yet these lesser charges turned out to be almost as ineffective.

Thus, reluctance to impose the death penalty was not the factor preventing indictment and conviction of rapists. On the contrary, the removal of clergy in 1576 which left death as the only penalty for rape was followed briefly by an increase, not a decrease, in convictions – small as these figures always were. (Only well into the seventeenth century did the decrease in prosecutions and convictions occur and it was not related to the legislative change of 1576.) It was not a question of all-male judges and juries being loath to convict and send to their deaths members of their own sex. Male judges and juries were loath to punish in any way other males for any sexual offence against females.

In Kent, 1558–99, 150 persons were tried for burglary of whom 80 per cent were convicted: 88 were hanged and 34 granted clergy. By contrast, 26 were tried for rape: 4 were hanged and 2 granted clergy. Male judges and juries were quite prepared to send to their deaths members of their own sex for crimes other than rape.

Contradictions

The harsh impression of rape law given by legal authorities, laws and statutes (and even the play I have mentioned) was contradicted by the evidence from the law courts themselves. Very few rape cases were prosecuted in the period 1558–1700. Of those that were, only a small proportion ended in conviction. There was an overall preponderance of child victims in the cases that came to court, and a tendency to convict men accused of raping children and to acquit when the victim was an adult woman. Changes occurred over this period too. From 1558 to 1700, the number of rape cases at court declined, as did the number of convictions. By the end of the seventeenth century the victims who prosecuted rape cases were predominantly women, but the tendency to convict where the victim was a child did not change through the period.

I will suggest a possible explanation for the contradiction or gap between what the law claimed to do, and what it actually did regarding the prosecution of rape. Of course, today in the late twentieth century there is still a gap between the law's occasional declarations on the heinousness of rape and its treatment of rape in the courts. The situation in the sixteenth and seventeenth centuries could stem from the same hypocrisy. But I would suggest there is another factor at work.

Rape law in the medieval period was constructed around the protection of male property in the form of their movable goods, their wives and daughters, their bequeathed inheritances, their future heirs. Rape was seen as a crime against property. Those same medieval laws applied for the period 1558–1700. However, it seems that in the late sixteenth century, the legal view of rape changed. Rape came to be seen as a crime against the person, not as a crime against property. Statutes of 1555 and 1597 treated abduction separately from rape, and had the indirect effect of establishing rape and abduction as separate offences.

Moreover, at the sixteenth-century Assizes where information of the social status or occupation of the victim or accused is given, there is not the pattern of class and wealth that emerges for rape cases in earlier centuries. Men accused are no longer mainly 'gentlemen' but yeomen, husbandmen, laboureres or tradesmen, representing a fair range of the lower classes. Victims are servants in great number; daughters and wives of ordinary men. There is no mention of property, inheritance, abduction or illicit marriages.

Depositions from the northeast describe the sexual assault of ordinary women. In 1646 a young woman was on her way to Leeds where she was to work as a servant. She met John Cawvert on the highway, drank ale with him at an inn, and according to his deposition, 'he offered her if she would carry kettles of water she should stay at his house until she could be better provided'. She charged him with rape.[26] In 1647 Jane Bingley was in a close milking her mistress's cows, when Francis

Barber approached her. 'After some few words he forceibly and violently threw her downe on the ground there and did hould both her hands in one of his hands and lay upon her body and had Carnal knowledge of her body against her will . . . when she Cryed out for help he sware . . . he would kill her.'[27]

Because ordinary women of little or no property in any form appeared as victims in rape cases at Assizes and Quarter Sessions in the late sixteenth and seventeenth centuries, rape was not treated very seriously by these courts; there were few cases and even fewer convictions. The only convictions that were imposed were on men accused of raping young girls. Perhaps the contemporary connection between virginity and property explains this phenomenon. When Thomas Rockingham, an alehousekeeper, petitioned the king in the mid-sixteenth century about the rape of his daughter Elizabeth, he complained she 'haith lost hir maryag that she might have had and hir good name in that Contie.' Rape of a virgin, a young woman, was regarded as the theft of her virginity, the property of her father to be used in procuring an advantageous marriage. Only the rapes that had in them some element of property, in the form of virginity, ended in the conviction of the accused.

In the medieval period, rape law disadvantaged women because it focused on the protection of male property, not the sexual invasion of the raped woman. In the sixteenth and seventeenth centuries, rape law in its practical operation in the courts focused on the sexual assault of the women, but convictions were nonetheless rare. Whether regarded as a crime against property or a crime against the person, rape was a crime by men against women, and the law as an intrinsic and powerful part of patriarchy operated for men against women.

Certainly some very strong patterns emerge from Assize and Quarter Sessions records about rape, patterns that contradict the impression of rape given by other sources. The assurances of contemporary statutes and legal men cannot be trusted.

Part two

Fitted for her place

Introduction

The three papers here are primarily concerned with the idea and practice of domestic ideology. They are case studies in an area which attracted early attention from women historians looking at the restrictions which bound them so firmly to a particular place of work – the home.

Using mainly primary sources (local archives, biographies, diaries, letters, state and business records) feminist historians such as Patricia Branca, Leonore Davidoff, and Catherine Hall[1] started to reconstruct the conditions of domesticity. This was separate but complementary to work being done on women's paid occupations and professions (such as domestic service, education, nursing, medical and manual trades), and the collection of women's experiences through oral history recording. Interest in the historical analysis of domesticity has been strengthened by political demands within the movement – particularly the 'wages for housework' campaign – which focused attention on the economic function of housework, and its sociological structure. In practical terms, it was found that the sexual division of labour to a great extent revolved around the issue of domesticity. The proposed reforms needed, amongst other things, more information, and in the wake of early enthusiasm called for the intensive study of 'what housework is, and has been'.[2]

It is of particular interest that each paper in this section presents an original view of domesticity *outside* the home, e.g. in science, education and emigration. Ginnie Smith looks at domestic advice for women contained in a body of work by one man, Thomas Tryon, exploring the medical and moral bases of his prescription for women's home lives. Charlotte Macdonald has scoured London and New Zealand for records of all types relating to the lives of a single body of colonial women immigrants. Gill Blunden has gone to administrative records for a reconstruction of the legislation, curriculum, and politics surrounding domestic training in three local areas.

They have attempted to set their work in a wider context, drawing on feminist research as well as historical work in other areas. Ginnie Smith highlights the early importance of science and scientific concepts in rationalizing the Puritan mythology of femininity and domesticity. Charlotte Macdonald has taken the myth into the reality of mid-nineteenth century colonial exploitation, where women were crucial to the physical survival of pioneering communities. In late Victorian Britain the myth was being fitted out and expanded with all the paraphernalia of state education, the reality being that domestic service was the key to preserving the material gains of middle-class prosperity. Gill Blunden notes that working-class women saw no need to subscribe to this doctrine. All three contributors examine the variety of ways in which domesticity served male interests and how social expectations compelled women of different classes into conforming to the oppression of domesticity.

3. Thomas Tryon's regimen for women: sectarian health in the seventeenth century

Ginnie Smith

One of the strengths of women's history has been the necessary discovery and use of new sources. We know of women's physical and legal subordination from 'value-free' sources such as mortality rates, wage indices, commercial and legal records, etc. Just as frequently, however, we are faced with what seems an impenetrable barrier of social and cultural attitudes stacked against women – the ideology of gender divisions, patriarchy, as written out by men. These are the 'value-laden' social sources – fiction, prose, most social reading matter – which categorize women in the public mind. So total has this consensus been made to appear, especially from the nineteenth century onwards, that we can even have great difficulty as seeing it as 'history' at all. But all objects, even the printed word, lie in some concrete historical situation, and language itself has been called 'structural'.[1] By deconstructing and reconstructing the meaning of words, symbols, images, patterns of logic by investigating philosophies and those who wrote them, the theory of patriarchy can be traced to its social and economic base.

When we talk about the language of patriarchy, we are talking about a theology, a belief system grounded in the religious observances and doctrine associated with a male God. What we call 'domesticity' is a way of life based on this original gender division – the sexual division of labour. For women it meant in effect domestic seclusion and their withdrawal from the public trades and professions. So powerful was this social phenomenon in the nineteenth century that it has attracted a mass of historical rumour and generalization, with male historians being primarily interested in its function rather than its cause.[2] The more detailed work being done by women historians is beginning to correct this imbalance; and what evidence there is suggests that religion, not economics, has to be seen as the key.

In order to look at what she calls 'domestic ideology', with its constant nineteenth-century image of the 'angel in the house', Catherine Hall has found a rich source in the letters and activities of the Evangelical 'Clapham Sect'.[3] These were the influential families who bridged Old Dissent and orthodox Anglicanism, and they successfully publicized a new model morality. They wrote and preached, but above all lived, the ideal of the family life. Their powerful influence in social and political matters came directly from their religious faith and they regarded the home as the centre of their spiritual inspiration. Catherine Hall concludes that they helped to establish the crucial 'middle ground' of Victorian liberalism by putting religious interest above both class and gender – these were sunk into the doctrine of personal salvation harmonizing with the common good. Refined domesticity, however, meant a sufficient male income – doubled at least – to support the woman who had become the consumer rather than the producer of goods and services. Hence the economic riddle – which came first, function or belief? Catherine Hall suggests that while domestic ideology was indeed 'partly a response to the development of productive forces', it primarily consisted of beliefs which had their own internal logical history. It was these, rather than a desire to stimulate the Industrial Revolution, that created the 'angel in the home', and ordained the separation of the spheres.

As Catherine Hall notes, Evangelism and the idealization of family life were not new to the nineteenth century. We cannot realize the depth and influence of domestic ideology unless we trace its origins to an earlier Protestant or Puritan world view. Its reforming strength lay in the ideals of sanctity and anti-materialism which were first heard in the aftermath of a far more radical period of religious revolution. The seventeenth century in Britain was a ferment of religious ideology that between 1640 and 1660 quite literally 'turned the world upside down'.[4] The Protestant belief in individual revelation shattered the fixed idea of hierarchy and energized every area of social life. Amongst other things, it attempted to revolutionize the sexual relationship by replacing property marriage by the spiritual bond of love, celebrated in its most radical form outside marriage.[5] An unknown number of Puritan women were active revolutionaries, asserting their individual rights at the same time as forwarding the political and religious cause.

After the Restoration, however, the political tide turned against all radical activity. Led by the example of the Quakers, many sectaries forswore the world and turned inwards towards 'quietism' and the communities of fellow-souls, living together in strict religious observances, i.e. the sects 'became sectarian'.[6] Two things happened as a result. First, the public withdrawal reduced their numbers steadily thoughout the eighteenth century. Old Dissent (Quakers, General Baptists, Presbyterians and Unitarians) disappeared even more rapidy from public view after 1750, when their religious influence was challenged from below by the new 'enthusiasm' of the Methodists, then by the sects of New Dissent, and later by Evangelism within the Anglican Church. Second, their exclusivity made them wealthy. By the nineteenth century, Old Dissent had become 'more and more disproportionately represented in the upper middle classes, and among the wealthier merchants and manufacturers of industrial England'.[7] The political troubles of Dissent following the failure of the Glorious Revolution had created a new urban middle class that rivalled the landed wealth of the Anglican squirearchy. The same religious cohesion that made them a financial force (no Quaker was allowed to go into debt – therefore they could get endless credit, and many of them went into banking, e.g. Barclays, Lloyds), also ensured the survival of a strong moral code which deliberately bound together the sect, the family, and individual. The protective, inward customs of the old dissenting sects provided some of the most extreme examples of the philosophy and practice of moral domesticity (one of which was the puritanical household of John Wesley's Presbyterian mother). Here the distinctions between New and Old Dissenters breaks down, for in practice they were all sectarian in the same sense of shared and codified values.

Even more importantly, however, with regard to the long-term influence of Puritan beliefs, were those who refused to join anything – the sectaries who vanished after 1660, the groups of the population who provided the surge of revivalism between 1750 and 1850. Their public beliefs were either hidden or transferred publicly to orthodox Anglicanism; we can only guess at their private beliefs, which are historically far less exposed even than those of the sects. We can assume that they helped make up a large reservoir of religious belief after 1660, stretching across class boudaries, that became apolitical on principle, and directed its energies instead towards economic survival and the perfection of domestic life.

We know that between the late sixteenth century and the early nineteenth century the life of the formal religious groups was one of emigration and financial consolidation. For those that stayed 'at home' we know as yet little in detail about their impact on social affairs. We know that groups were centred in particular parts of the country, and that they formed social circles which relied heavily on inter-marriage and kinship ties.[8] The practical reason for this protective network was that they could be self-sufficient, since as non-conformists they were officially barred from a range of supportive state and local activities. Some clue to their history may be found not only in records of their activities, but in books which hint of their beliefs and goals. Dissent had long claimed the right to publish, with the aim not only of essential self-enlightenment, but of breaking the monopolistic grip of Latin on the professions and sciences. They believed in education, and they were not shy of authorship – in fact, they were probably also disproportionately represented in the growing book trade. Intellectually, they were represented at all levels and in all areas, but especially in those areas which directly involved religion and belief. One of the areas which they considered to be closest to their interests, and which reveals a great deal about them, was medicine.

Within the range of medical publications there was a type of work in which dissenting views are strongly stated. These were the medical advice books, containing recommendations and advice on health for the lay reader. They were a separate genre from the medical textbooks or specialized treatises addressed to the profession. In market terms they had something in common with etiquette books and domestic manuals, with which they were often but not always associated. Their history runs from the widely circulated hand-written texts of the medieval period, to the mass publication of books on 'domestic medicine' from the end of the eighteenth century. The advice they contained formed the core of what came to be called 'preventive medicine'; from the beginning they were concerned with the prevention of disease or ill-health, rather than the cure of a disease in progress, or the mending of shattered limbs. Built into the function of these works were the practicalities of self-care, where specialist aid was non-existent, insufficient, or simply disliked. Their recommendations were based on the Greek preventive health code known as 'regimen of the non-naturals'. Regimen was a precise 'ordering' of the six non-naturals of air, food and drink, sleep and watch, motion and rest, evacuation and repletion, and passions of the mind.

A strongly political view of health and medicine emerged, however, from the religious revolution. Dislike or suspicion of the medical profession became an increasingly important feature of medical advice books in the seventeenth century, when doctors, and their theories, came to represent the caste-ridden old order. The religious view emphasized the idea of self-help and responsibility for self as a personal and spiritual duty; and through publication, the populist 'empirics' could attack orthodoxy and publicize new and distinctive alternatives. This took the form not only of slating the medical profession, but of propounding radical, utopian visions of health.[9]

It was at this time that Greek ideas were inspiring all areas of science, through natural philosophy; the problems and possibilities of Nature dominated eighteenth century thought. Nature also had a particular meaning for believers. Those dissenters who looked to science to support their beliefs recognized them in the naturism of the early Greek science of hygiene. They were among the main promoters of the simple natural therapy of Hippocrates, which reduced 'artificial' medical interventions (drugs, surgery) to a minimum.

The main contribution of the religious view to preventive medicine was that health ensured the perpetual state of well-being neccessary to ensure salvation. This 'total' and continuous health philosophy was well known to the ancient Greek sects and priest–physicians. Between the seventeenth and the nineteenth centuries the preventive ideal became slowly more scientific, and less spiritual, less a question of faith. However, the religious beliefs involved in health care were so comprehensive that to many, academic 'proof', though desirable, was not really required. Amongst the many dissenting medical advice books the works of Thomas Tryon stand out.

I came across Thomas Tryon (1634–1703) during a study of medical advice books in circulation between 1770 and 1850. His books were immediately obvious because of their sheer quantity. In content they were even more intriguing, because at first sight they appeared to be entirely miscellaneous but amongst them all were constant references to women. The twenty separate titles[10] gave advice on every area of life, from metaphysical philosophy to housecleaning. But it soon became clear that his main preoccupation was the particular type of ascetic health that was attuned to the spiritual existence, and that the extensive advice to women was not simply coincidental. The fundamentalist and mystic interpretation of health that Tryon presented, I subsequently found recurring in dissenting or 'alternative' medical writers up to the nineteenth century and beyond. What is interesting to us in this purist version of sectarian health was the way in which women were being defined as sect members, and their activities programmed to fit the needs of the sect.

The 1680s and 1690s were still a lively intellectual period for the sects, at a time when they were reorganizing themselves and seeking new certainties. What Tryon said, and what was being absorbed by his wide audience of readers in the late seventeenth century, is best described by looking at the content of some of the works in detail.

Tryon clearly was a popular writer of some influence. In a comment writen in 1805 he was described, a century after his death, as 'one of the most extraordinary self-taught geniuses, and original writer that ever existed in this country, particularly on the subject of health and Temperence, to which all his writings allude.' A contemporary writer in 1692 listed his sect as one of 45 different orders of religious opinion existing at that time – 'Tryonists are such as forbid eating of Flesh, Fish, or anything that is killed, as contrary to Scripture.'[11] A lapsed Anabaptist who moved from the West Country to settle on the outskirts of London, he was certainly known and respected amongst the Quakers, who published his work on their presses. His self-taught, broad, empirical philosophy would have appealed to a range of seventeenth-century sectaries; and there is evidence that he was particularly popular in America. Benjamin Franklin read Tryon in his youth, and Franklin was later celebrated for his radical views on health care (mild vegetarianism, and bathing). A volume of memoirs brought out after Tryon's death, in 1705, treated him as an exemplary prophet figure – 'patriarchal, primitively good'. Tryon himself hoped that his work as a sect leader would be continued by a 'Society of Clean and Innocent Livers'. But his real influence would have come, not from any band of obedient followers but from the twenty-odd works, several of which were republished in his lifetime, and which were available split up into cheaply produced tracts or bound in book form. Many Puritan writers felt the urge to write at length, but Tryon must have dominated the advice-book market during the 20 years he was writing. It started after his call from God in 1682 to 'recommend to the world temperence, cleanness, and innocency of living'.[12]

'Temperence' and 'cleanness' were two key words for Tryon. He was an ascetic, and the strength of his faith came through rigorous self-denial – or as he called it, 'temperance'. Asceticism was an ancient tradition which had been practised amongst others by the Greek sect of the Orphics, the Roman Stoics, the medieval monastics, and which had been revived in Tryon's time by the radically anti-materialist Anabaptists. Like other Puritan fundamentalists, Tryon looked to Scripture, and admired the life and spiritual values of the wandering Hebraic sect or tribe. To him and to others the simple, hard, ascetic life was Innocency before the Fall; the Fall was encapsulated by the filth and corruption of the modern world.

Tryon, who wrote approvingly of 'labour hard, cloathing thin, open Air, cold houses, small fires, hard beds',[13] had no doubt that this type of innocency could be perfected only by a pure 'cleanness' of the actual internal and external body – 'for by thoroughly cleansing the outward court of terrestrial nature, it opens the windows of the inward senses of the soul.'[14] For spiritual or psychic purity, Tryon's advice was to quite literally cleanse the body of all gross matter, i.e. of fat, and filth. This was done by vegetable diet, and simple drinks which cleansed inwardly; plenty of cool fresh air, bathing, and exercise in rural surroundings; and simple clean clothes, rooms, and bedding. The effect he found was that he was 'more nimble, brisk, eesie [sic] and lightsome'.[15]

Tryon had spent 20 years on the study of astronomy, chemistry, philosophy, and 'physic'. It enabled him to build in a persuasive 'scientific' structure to support his personal experience of revelation. His own intellectual turning point, when he rejected fashionable radical Paracelsian chemistry in favour of the Greek God of Nature, was actually described by him as a dream. Dreams were important to Tryon – he specialized in interpreting them. The Greek philosophy of medicine with its ideas of physical and metaphysical harmony leading to unity, were obviously congenial. Through the system of regimen or regulation of the six non-naturals in accordance with the four natural elements (earth, air, fire, and water – translated as hot, cold, moist, and dry) the Greeks harmonized body and soul with the natural environment. Temperance was to them the balance of opposites, the 'mean' between extremes, and the reconciling of all elements. Tryon approved of the order, regularity and self-discipline. He likened temperate regimen to the pruning or training of a tree – it would 'suffer no superfluous branches to grow but would cut them off in the bud; and inform man, in all the particulars of his life, which is right and the contrary.'[16]

Asceticism pushed the connection with the natural world much further through symbolism. A pristine state of Nature as he knew it was to Tryon symbolic of Heaven – a cool countryside, pure and unsullied by human destruction. If Heaven was cool, Hell was hot. The Tryonite vision of the world was guided by this ancient distinction between temperatures, a moral polarity which had also been emphasized by the Greeks. They had described heat as the centre of the passions ('vital heat') and of life itself ('animal heat'). To sublimate the gross and terrestrial animal passions the body heat must be cooled, moderated, and kept in check. The moral qualities of hot and cold, and their physical link with the (sinful) passions are one of the most familiar themes in medical advice books, particularly those at the turn of the eighteenth century. Through a complicated process it left the legacy of hygiene as we know it, but the symbolic ramifications of the idea went far wider than that. In Tryon (and others) the distinction produced a didactic version of regimen which cited quite precisely all the paraphernalia of a higher standard of living as belonging to the 'soft' life, or 'hot' regimen – such as an increased and richer diet in food and drink, especially 'hot meats', better clothing, more comfortable housing, the congregation of people in towns, the reduction of physical labour, and the new imported luxuries of hot tea, coffee, and tobacco. It was a truism amongst Puritans that these produced unnatural heat, and the poisonous dirty vapours of diseases. The vegetarianism that Tryon was famous for was not ly lived the part, and undertook to describe the spirituality of the new 'cool' regimen. By the mid-eighteenth century, cool regimen was being widely used by doctors for treating infectious disease. The vegetarianism that Tryon was famous for was not as he stated it so much to do with the sinful taking of life, but it was because vegetables were overwhelmingly cool, clean, and natural. If romanticism is the attribution of all that is good, then Tryon was supremely romantic about Nature, and her works.

It is easy to argue that he was as romantic about women. Yet his widely publicized views on the godly way of life contained many explicit condemnations of the conduct and status of women. Taken together, they represented a strong critique (again, one shared by other male authors) of the misuse of female authority in household and family affairs. The answer was that women, like Nature, had been corrupted. The impure woman was unnatural, the pure woman was 'natural'. Women, like men, were natural objects to be slotted into Tryon's patterned and logical spiritual schema, though women were naturally more 'inanimate' than men. Once women had been identified with Nature, the symbolism was endless. The reason for women's supreme naturalness was according to Tryon, quite simple – women looked after the bodily needs of the spirit. The customary special responsibilities of women in family health, birth, education, dress, and houswifery were all to be included in the 'authorized' regimen. Tryon's miscellany consisted of detailed advice on all these subjects. Thus in his second work, *Health's Grand Preservative, or the Woman's Best Doctor* (1682), Tryon outlined the theme of cold regimen as 'highly fit to be pursued and observed by all that love their Health, and particularly necessary to the Female Sex'.[17] Women had control of the 'natural' areas:

> The whole preservation of Men's Health and Strength does chiefly reside in the Wisdom and Temperance of Women . . . Also Women have the entire management of all things that concern our health, during the whole time of our lives.[18]

He clearly recognized women's power in their customary roles, and expressed some resentment against what he saw as the matriarchy of the household:

> Whatever women do or say touching the Preparation of Food, and other ordering of their families for Health, most men believe, not making the least scruple or question thereof. As well they may: For the chiefest doctors of our times do bow before them, and are altogether as subject to the Rules and Directions of women as other Men.

He upbraided men, 'There is not one man in a hundred that understands or takes any notice whether his Food be well prepared or not; and if his Bed stinks, he is used to it, and so counts it all well.'[19] This could not be said of Tryon, who prided himself on his cooking, brewing, and bed-making. Again, he drew out the moral distinction between hot and cold. Women were the dispensers of a destructive 'hot' regimen which wasted the bodies of men, children, and themselves in pregnancy. The life-style of the leisured, housebound, consuming woman was an obvious target, 'warm clothes, hot Houses, an idle soft life, and the like effeminacies'. Thus corrupt, women were weak, soft, idle and (unfortunately) warm.

Tryon cited as scientific evidence the evils of heat in fevers and child-care, in a call for cold regimen:

> A great part of the Children that die, especially in Towns and Cities, is occasioned either by the Intemperance of their Mothers, during the time they go with child, or afterwards by their unnatural and badly prepared food . . . also by their keeping them too warm, and too close from the Air, and lapping them up in several Double Clothes and Swathes, so tight that a Man may write on them, and putting them into warm beds . . . Besides, the Window-curtains are drawn, and also the Curtains about the bed; by which means the Air become hot and sulpherous, that it causes great Disorders to attend both Mothers and children. This ill kind of management does also cause such a Tenderness . . . that on every small occasion they are liable and apt to get colds, and divers distempers.[20]

This is an early reference to the swaddling issue, which medical historians have long seen as a turning point in hygienic child-care.[21] Tryon was, however, not concerned with professional rights and privileges – he wanted the reform of the woman herself, by herself, guided by the truth of male Reason.

Science to Tryon was a useful aid, but his Voice of Wisdom came directly from a mystic God whose rites and observances were to him paramount. Clearly women were not being accused of simple neglect. Tryon's concept of proper health overlay a fear which he expressed frequently, both obliquely and openly – that of women's propensity to passion, or love, leading to intemperate sexual release and spiritual defilement. Hot regimen was not confined to externals; it included the psychology of the passions. Tryon had a constant objection to maternal affection and warmth, specifically the

> Common and frequent kissing of children by Mothers,
> Nurses, and all . . . by which use and continual custom as it
> were forced thereto; which sort of Carriage and behaviour
> hath Originally sprung from Mothers and Nurses Foolish Hot
> Fantastick Passions of Love.[22]

Children should not be hugged, but coolly rested on the knee.
Another godless habit was the drinking of Cherry Brandy which
heated and inflamed the passions and filled women with 'Fury
and Madness, and many other indecencies which are no less
pernicious than shameful in a woman'. She was then the scarlet
woman, or the harlot. Only women had proper 'shame' from
heated sexual activity, for according to religion, men were free
of this burden. Underlying Tryon's theory of the double
standard was the old ghost of chastity. The act of birth and
everything associated with it was the physical cause of the
patriarchal view of women's weakness and dependency; added
to this was a spiritual impurity which male cultists ascribed to
'pollution'.

In many respects, Tryon's conception of the cleansing of the
body of gross humours emerges as a seventeenth-century
version, in full religious mystical language, of what has been
described as 'cult hygiene', and which has been broken down
from ethnographical evidence by Mary Douglas.[23] In this 'pollution theory', regular or ritual bodily purification and dirt
avoidance can ensure divine favour as the symbolic expression
of deference and commitment, a continual and repeated
affirmation of the permeability of spiritual boundaries – the
idea that bodily impurites contaminate or pollute the spirit. The
ritual of bodily boundaries (i.e. salival, nasal, genital, men-
strual, vaginal, or anal bodily excretions) involves cleansing,
eating, and food preparation; and has a particular application in
the sexual entry of women. Women, who were more fun-
damentally interdependent in their body were therefore more
'unclean'. In many societies these emerge as a set of 'purity
rules', often associated with a cult, such as the hygiene observances of Judaism, or the purity rules of Greek Orphism. Other
anthropologists and historians note that women were and are

frequently connected in various societies with an inauspicious sexual polarity, i.e. male/female, right/left, light/darkness, good/evil.[24]

These traditions were maintained in Greek science and society, which was firmly patriarchal, through such theorists as Pythagoras and Aristotle.[25] The religious sexual polarity was redefined by them primarily through physiological description. Women were not so much a mystery or a danger (as suggested by many of the matriarchies scattered about the Greek hinterland), merely a weaker animal. In the medieval period, religious supernaturalism was re-established, and with it some of the polluting fear of women, who were believed to be sexually irrepressible. The permanent sexual separation and inferior moral position of women was confirmed both by hierarchical theological doctrine, and the uncritical absorption of Greek physiological theory.

Tryon wrestled with these ideas in a long passage where he attempted to persuade men – 'though many men do believe the contrary' – of women's 'natural chastity'. His Rules of Cleanness frequently included the sexual reference. The mind could either have 'clean inclinations' or become 'a cage of unclean thoughts'; the body should be 'clean, chaste and healthy', a 'well-prepared Temple to receive the sweet influence of God's spirit and company of good angels'.[26] Guiding his readers scrupulously through the complex intellectual arguments, Tryon described the moral and medical constitution, and the regimen, of pure natural womanhood:

> Their spirits and Balsamick body, whence their true life shines, is more volatile and tender than Men's, and their natural heat is not so strong, for this cause Women cannot bear or endure any extremes, either in Meats, Drinks, or Exercises, without manifest danger to their Healths, they being naturally more sanguine than men, and their Central Heat weaker, therefore all kinds of inequality make a deeper impression on them, and they are sooner moved to all kinds of Passion; for Women in their Radix are compounded more of the sweet friendly Sanguine Nature, their dignification

being chiefly the element of water, but the Root of Men's Nature is from the stong might of Fire. And for the same cause Women are more chaste than men, and of colder natures, though many men do believe the contrary, but they are greatly mistaken in this particular, having no true understanding of Nature; they have judged thus hardly of women because many of them are so easily drawn into inconveniences by the pretended friendship of Men, but I do affirm, that their being so easily overcome, is not from their unchaste desires, but chiefly from their Friendly, Courteous, effeminate Natures, being of yielding temper, which is essentially at the root of their Lives, and when a Man has once awakened in them the 'Love-string', which is quickly done, he may command them as he pleases; now finding that they comply, they imagine that of them which they find in themselves. Not but that some Women are as unchaste as men, but then such, through the power of their depraved free wills and wanton imaginations, have forced Nature out of her simple innocent ways, compelling her often to do that which she perfectly loathes. The Wise Ancients understanding this Nature and Constitution of Women and considering that the whole welfare of mankind depended chiefly on their Temperance and descreet Conduct, did therefore direct them to a higher degree of Temperance, and thought it requisite, and so absolutely necessary, that both the Drinks alotted to Women in most countries, was, and is to this day, 'pure water', and their Food as innocent and natural; they eat Flesh sparingly, living much on raw and boiled herbs, Fruits, and Grains, which is a most sublime diet.[27]

The passage is worth quoting in full since it sums up Tryon's various preoccupations, and gives a view of words and language in context. The problems he had making the abstract constructs of science and religion fit apparent reality are reflected in the buoyant but anxiously hectoring assertions.

It did, however, take the form of a lengthy defence of women. These were Tryon's idealized, romantic woman who 'like a good angel', lived on a 'sublime diet', suppressing the inchastity which she 'perfectly loathes'. The sexless physical purity of the monk or nun was not ordained for the Protestant priesthood of believers living in tribal and sectarian groupings. The Puritan woman was not to be physically locked away from the world; but from the mystic view her neccessary purity could only be ensured by the regular practice of asceticism. Innate chastity can be seen as an attempt to resolve pollution fears; theologically it was of great importance in redefining and spiritualizing women's role within the sect. Those who had 'judged thus hardly of women' could be reassured that women were naturally godly companions, fit keepers of the Temple, and 'clean' Vessels for the Seed.

We do not know whether Tryon's Society, or its followers, ever existed except on paper. But there is evidence that he attracted support not only from male sectaries, but from women themselves. The clue lies in the appeal to the intellect. In his early works he apparently addressed himself to the families of independent labourers and craftsmen from the cities and the countryside, similar to those of his own experience. Religious or 'sober' women from the diligent and dissenting lower middle class were themselves intelligent and literate, and they might well have been receptive to Tryon's religious authority, as well as to the practicalities of his attacks on sloppy and inefficient household management. Tryon's contempt for women's customary illiteracy was, however, barely concealed. By the end of his life he had abandoned the task of persuasion and simply issued in his sectarian Laws a list of 'Rules and Orders proper for women to observe'. The earthy style gave way to prophet-like commandments, strong paternalism, and a form of religious romanticism that traded on the intellectual life of religious fantasy. Beauty entered as a positive female virtue, and a further constraint on their activities.

There were apparently middle-class women intellectuals to whom the leisured aesthetic appeal of such things as Beauty was a liberation. Such women as the radical playwright and poet Aphra Benn seem to have regarded Tryon as an inspiration rather than a threat. There are traces of Aphra Benn's link with Tryonism in a poem handwritten onto the flyleaf of an edition of his *Way to Health*, and inscribed 'Mrs Ann Behn'. In the midst of her struggles as a professional writer, and regardless of the implications for female doctoring, and feminine authority in the home, 'Mrs Ann Behn' saw at least part of herself as a philosophical, enlightened, Tryonite woman. In a lyrical hymn of praise to Tryon and his vision of Beauty before the Fall she wrote of

that blest Golden Age when Man was Young . . .
When Nature did her wonderous dictates give
When every sense to innocent Delight
Th'agreeing elements unforc'd invited
When Earth was gay and Heaven was kind and bright
And nothing horrid did perplex the sight;
The unpruned roses and jasmine grew,
Nature each day drest the world anew
And sweets without Man's aid each moment grew;
Till Wild Debauchery did Men's minds invade
And Vice and Luxury became a Trade.[28]

In the glory of primitive Nature Aphra Benn's poem highlighted not only Beauty but sexual innocence. To her Tryon was the 'learned Bard' and 'saving angel' who held out the hope of a sexless cerebral purity existing beyond the decadence and crude sexual divisions of the contemporary world. By surpassing their sexuality, women could gain

A new Earth and a new Heaven; new senses and a new understanding. Those are the blessed fruits of adhering to the Voice of Wisdom, in self-denial and separation; for they are the only inlets to all true knowledge, whether it be of God, of Nature, or our Selves.[29]

Nevertheless, the physical constrictions of self-denial and separation which Tryon proposed were very real, and so demanding that they excluded the majority of women simply on grounds of subsistence. In her ideal form the Tryonite woman could only exist through the support of others. The precise Orders which he issued posthumously to his Society are revealing. They show a Puritan woman of almost Asiatic caste –

separated, beautified, and saved from contaminating work. As a high-caste woman, she spent her leisured time on religious study, children's education, and supervision of the household. Her practical economic contribution was limited to needlework, though she should be 'busy' in all other domestic affairs so that they should be well conducted. It is hard to imagine the intinerant Puritan woman of the revolutionary period being bound by this fastidiousness. It is less hard to see it as advice which fitted the life of women closed within sectarian groups driven under after the Restoration. Physical retreat, physical moderation, self-help, and education combined virtue with necessity. In its most extreme form it was inevitably moderated by a period of prolonged economic expansion. But while the purist religious meanings of the Orders gradually became obscured, the principle of physical segregation survived. These are some of the base-line instructions which Tryon issued in 1705:

> You shall not read any books, but such as tend to the praise of your Creator, and the building you up, and confirming you in Temperence, Cleanness, Innocency, and Vertue; and the Improvement of Innocent Arts and Sciences. 16. You shall keep one Fashion in your garments or Apparel, which shall be grave, decent, easie, and convenient for Travel, Labour, Work, and Business, either for within or without Doors. You shall use no superfluous Trimmings, nor Fantastick Ornaments . . . Let all your words and Discourse be clear, free, and mellow, spoken from the Throat or Breast, as Musick-masters teach . . . 17. All Women above the age of seven years, shall be veiled when they go abroad. This will not only mightily preserve the Female Beauties Power, but advance the Natural Esteem, and render them more valuable. 18. No Girl, Maid, nor Woman, shall carry Burthens, do any Field Labour, sell nor cry anything about the Streets, nor do any dirty work. All Robustick Labour shall be done by Men: the Fair Sex are naturally unfit for dirty mugling [sic] Imployments. Besides, the Preservation of Mankind, principally depends on the good education, and discreet conduct of

> Women; whose Noble characters of Beauty, Innocency, and
> tender affection are sullied; and as it were obliterated in
> many of them, by their being employed about unclean things,
> and hard and dirty slavish labour. And therefore Women
> should be allotted all clean, easie, Imployments, as the
> making of all Sorts of Garments, Dresses, Beds, and the like;
> All things that are performed with the needle, for Men,
> Women, or Children.[30]

This lengthy statement is partner to Tryon's earlier view of the
natural and scientifically 'healthy' woman. It is entirely non-
medical in intent and language, but the two clearly relate to
each other. It's social description sums up in accurate detail the
image of nineteenth-century Victorian womanhood, particularly those enshrined in fiction. This, as Catherine Hall has shown,
derived its strength largely from Evangelical example; they
were the womenfolk of the 'new rich' emerging from old
Dissent.

Much of the detail of Evangelical sectarianism is more fully
illustrated by reference to their fundamentalist past. Wilber-
force's statement on women, that 'We would make them as it
were the medium of our intercourse with the heavenly world,
the faithful repositories of the religious principle, for the benefit
both of the present and the rising generation,'[31] makes the
seventeenth-century framework leap from the page; it is just
one of many points of similarity.

Tryon, of course, was only one part of this strongly patriarchal Dissenting tradition, but he illuminates it. Because of his
intellectual range, his accessible and powerful prose style, and
the spectacular amount of information he put out on all
subjects, he must be considered to have been an enduring
influence in sectarian ideology. Not least, he was capable of
attracting and inspiring women as an educationalist. We should
also note that the Greek physiology that he used was not
scientifically fully undermined until the late nineteenth century,
so that, in this sense, his works were 'valid' for at least two
centuries. However rough and ready he might have appeared to
the refinement of the Evangelicals, our understanding of their

world is enhanced by the fine detail of Tryon's medical and moral description of women in their 'protected space'. It was a powerful individual contribution to a mythology and ethic of female domesticity.

4. Ellen Silk and her sisters: female emigration to the New World

Charlotte J. Macdonald

Ellen Silk[1] Harriet Brasell, Eliza Lambert, Maria Payne, Abigail Atkinson, Mary Murphy – these are just six of the more than 4,000 young single women who landed at the port of Lyttelton, in the province of Canterbury, New Zealand between 1853 and 1871. They all went out on government sponsored passages offered to 'eligible SINGLE FEMALES above Twelve and not exceeding Thirty-Five Years of Age; who must be sober, industrious and of good moral character and *free*, from any *bodily* or *mental* defect.'[2] In the same period, on similar schemes, at least another 8,000 young women landed elsewhere in New Zealand and tens of thousands disembarked at ports throughout Australia and Canada.

This exodus of young women was part of the massive emigrant stream to the New World destinations from England, Wales, Scotland and especially Ireland throughout the last century. Emigration as a major aspect of nineteenth-century Europe has been studied by social, political, economic and labour historians as well as demographers. For historians of North America and the British colonies immigration is of overwhelming importance. Only rarely, however, have women been the focus of attention or given more than passing mention. This paper is intended to examine some aspects of the dynamics of female emigration, with particular reference and illustrations drawn from the experience of women who went to New Zealand in the 1850s and 1860s as assisted migrants. The study of female emigration merits consideration, not only because of its neglect, but also because patterns of migration are distinctive for women and men. In the complementary and integrally related aspects of internal migration and emigration the numbers of women and men occur in inverse proportion. Far more men emigrated than women, whereas a larger number of women moved once – and sometimes several times – within their own country. Migration, in the nineteenth century, and possibly beyond it, is a gender-specific feature of social development.

Over the last few years efforts have been made to begin to redress the balance in migration studies. This early work has started, understandably, with the most visible, perhaps the most interesting, and unquestionably the best-documented activity of voluntary societies devoted to the promotion and reform of female emigration. A.J.Hammerton's *Emigrant Gentlewomen*[3] traces the growth of female emigration as a social 'cause' from 1830 through to 1914, with emphasis on how emigration came to be regarded as a 'solution' to the 'problem' of distressed gentlewomen. Amongst the many private societies established to promote female emigration was the Female Middle Class Emigration Society founded by Jane Lewin and Maria Rye in 1862 to provide assistance to educated impoverished gentlewomen who wished to start a new life in Australia, South Africa, British North America or New Zealand. The FMCES is of special interest in that it grew out of Lewin and Rye's involvement with the feminists of Langham Place. Unable to provide anything like sufficient employment for the women who approached the Langham Place Office of the Society for Promoting the Employment of Women (and the *English Woman's Journal*), they proposed emigration as a means through which women could earn an independent livelihood.

Canadian historians have taken up the subject from the vantage point of a country receiving some of the émigrées. One study[4] has placed the work of voluntary reformers on behalf of female immigration, over the period 1880–1920, within a context of social imperialism. Another examines the contribution female immigrants made to the labour force, particularly as domestic servants over roughly the same period.[5] Joy Parr's outstanding work on child migration from the British Isles to Canada deals with both the despatching and receiving ends of

the migration process, skilfully combining individual life histories with an overall account of what was a particularly piteous
episode in Atlantic migration.[6]

Australia's exceptionally strenuous and successful pioneer in
the field of female emigration, Caroline Chisholm, has been the
subject of two substantial biographies.[7] As well as this she gains
a mention in most general histories and has more recently
added to her fame as author of the term 'God's Police', adopted
by Anne Summers in her provocative exploratory study of
women in Australia, *Damned Whores and God's Police*.[8]

Fascinating and important as these studies undoubtedly are in
filling in some of the huge uncharted expanse in the history of
women, they do not tell us a great deal about the lives of
ordinary women. Hammerton devotes a whole chapter to Mary
Taylor's experience in New Zealand. Although he does not
represent her life as being in any way typical, the attention she
nevertheless receives is misleading. I am not suggesting that her
story should not be told, but she was an exceptional woman,
and a most unusual emigrant.[9] Few of the authors concentrate
on the large-scale working-class migration resulting from government initiative and sponsorship. If they do, the focus is on
the management and managers of the scheme, rather than on
the migrants themselves. They have tended to be most interested in the relationships and interaction between those
women who worked for the welfare of other women.

It is not easy to write the history of ordinary, working
women, let alone recover the experience of large numbers of
these individuals. The staple source material is missing since
few domestic servants wrote letters, diaries, journals, and little
of what was written has survived. There are only fragments of
records which testify to the feelings, thoughts, impressions,
attitudes and daily business from the women's own perspective.
Marriage registers, passenger lists, policy and other government records leave a trail which is possible to follow, if only to
recover in partial and skeletal form, the shape of individual
lives.

Young unmarried women were recruited as emigrants to
meet the demand for domestic servants and as the contempor-

ary discourse ran, 'to balance the disproportion of the sexes' in the colonial population. Within this dual intention lies a multitude of contradictions (between class and patriarchal interests), and a host of assumptions regarding sexual differences, many of which have carried over into the present day.

In this chapter I want to discuss three aspects of the study of women's migration which I feel deserve some critical attention. The first is the location of female emigration within the context of labour migration, in particular in the realm of domestic labour performed by domestic servants, as well as by women in their capacity as wives and daughters. Second, to look at what was meant by the 'disproportion of the sexes', its implications and significance; third, to put under scrutiny the notion that marriage acted as an incentive for women to emigrate. In the course of the discussion I hope to indicate something of the approach and some of the findings which have come from my attempt to recover the lives of one group of emigrant women.

Although my discussion focuses principally on the experience of people who migrated to New Zealand, in particular those who made their destination the province of Canterbury, the issues I intend to discuss are also present in the schemes of government-sponsored female emigration run by other British colonies in the same period. Agents for the Canadian and Australian governments competed (on a much larger scale), with New Zealand representatives in the British Isles to recruit prospective migrants. While the voyage was shorter across the Atlantic and the climate in each of the three countries different, the experience of the thousands who became new settlers was probably not too different for this to be read as a discussion of equal relevance to all three places.

The initiative and money for assisted emigration to New Zealand in the 1850s and 1860s, came from the colony rather than the Imperial government. The southern provinces of Otago and Canterbury, founded on Wakefieldian principles[10] and rich with gold and sheep, were most active in recruiting additional settlers by way of immigration. By 1865 over 2,400 young women had disembarked at the port of Lyttleton, their passages paid in part or in total out of public funds. A further

2,000 women arrived before the end of 1871. One of these was Sarah Greaves, a 28-year-old domestic from Yorkshire. On 18 October 1866, in the house of Mr William Thompson of Durham Street, Christchurch (NZ), Sarah was married to Stephen Simpson, a baker, also 28 years old. Sarah had disembarked from the ship *Blue Jacket* only four days earlier and had not paid a penny towards her passage; she went out as a 'free' migrant – totally sponsored by the colonial government.[11] How could this happen when women were supposed to be going out to meet the servant shortage? When the emigration advertisements called for 'competent domestic servants'? Sarah was by no means the only young emigrant to move quickly into marriage. Nearly one-third of the migrants who are known to have married in New Zealand[12] did so within a year of their arrival. Sarah was not obliged to pay anything towards reimbursing the cost of her passage, or to enter into any sort of contract whatsoever. There was never any form of indenture or contract for women going to New Zealand on assisted passage schemes. They were free to do what they liked once they disembarked; the only limitation imposed was that they should pay some token amount if they left the province, a regulation which was impossible to enforce. How could an operation run like this? How could public money be expended so liberally?

The demand for domestic servants in Canterbury was no figment of a colonial imagination; it was insistent and apparently insatiable. One of the greatest disincentives for the 'capitalist class' even to contemplate colonization was acknowledged to be the enormous difficulty in securing the services of household servants. The Immigration Officer at Lyttleton was constantly reporting that 'Good domestic servants are constantly inquired after'. Even the report of smallpox aboard a migrant ship did not deter prospective employers from flocking to the port to hire newly arrived migrants in December 1865.[13]

Sarah Greaves's marriage demonstrated the government's intention that female emigration schemes should introduce wives as much as servants. The difference between the two was not great in any case, and wife-labour was not only cheaper than servants' wages, but offered more, besides. Unpaid, undocumented, defined by affective relations and confined to a private sphere, the work women have done as wives has been ignored in studies of the development of a colonial labour force and economy. As servants women were expected to clean, cook, wash, sew, tidy, possibly milk cows, make butter, feed hens, draw water, tend fires, care for children – duties which were identical to those discharged by women as wives in charge of their own households. The vast majority of servants employed in New Zealand at this time (and throughout the servant keeping period in NZ history), were employed as 'generals' in single servant positions. Little specialization was possible under these circumstances, though some employers made special requirements of their hired help. Registering his name with the Immigration Officer in expectation of the next emigrant ship, K.M.Handyside requested a nurse-girl of the following specification:

> I want one about 18 or 19 years old who has been used to children is a Protestant & not Irish. Her duties w^d be to take care of three small children the baby 5 months old for which she would have to wash the napkins – to keep her two nurseries clean and sew a little in the evenings. Wages to start with 8/- per week.[14]

Many male settlers were well aware of the problems of womanless homes. Young Tom Arnold, an educated bachelor, discovered the problems of housekeeping in the colonies but managed to get himself

> a clean tidy upright – in the physical sense I mean – housekeeper, by name Mrs Curran, who will do the washing in the house, and the baking also – when I get an oven. I have to pay her £20 a year; but she will be quite worth that to me, if as I believe is the case, she really understands housekeeping . . . I should go on swimmingly if I had got a wife. But where is that necessary of life to be procured?[15]

One historian has even suggested that colonial working men showed particular tenacity in upholding the eight-hour day because they needed the time at the end of the day to do their *own* cooking, washing and cleaning.[16] But young men who took heed of the advice in most emigration pamphlets could obviate the need to do their own housekeeping. This advice recommended that young men take 'a wife' with them to the colonies, rather than going out alone in the expectation of marrying once established. With twenty-five years' experience of colonial life behind him, James Adam declared that 'every emigrant to New Zealand should provide himself with a *really useful* woman for his wife. Those who settle with such a partner are sure to succeed. Many who are now prospering there can trace a large amount of their prosperity to her diligent hands'.[17] Another source of advice put the services of a wife above those of a thoroughbred horse in the equipage of a masculine settler.[18]

The crucial difference between the work done by a woman as a wife and that done by a servant was in the beneficiary of that work. On the one hand, a husband and possibly children; on the other, an employer. As servants, women worked for wages and social superiors; there was as explicit a class relationship between master and mistress and hired help at an individual level, as there was between the social strata of wage workers and the middle class who employed servants (a class sometimes defined by historians in terms of individuals' ability to employ household servants). In the schemes of female emigration, as they operated to New Zealand at least, the interests of men as husbands were put above those of prospective employers. With no compulsion to stay within the pool of labour available for hire and no period of indentured service, men as husbands were given priority over middle-class masters and mistresses. The single women were to work as paid servants to the rich and unpaid house-workers to the not-so-rich. In this there is clear evidence of the intersection and collision between class and patriarchal interests, in which patriarchal interests are paramount.

Some of the beneficiaries of servant-labour were, of course, middle-class women. But they too were displaced in the priorities established for deploying young women like Tabitha Glassey, Julia Higgins, Ellen Glasspool and Betsy Webster. In so far as they were responsible for the management and execution of the work of their households their interests in gaining the assistance of paid help was placed second to the demand for women as wives. There is certainly an element of self-interest at work in the activities of some middle-class women, especially those in the colonies, who were promoting female immigration in order to enhance the supply of domestic servants.

It is clear from the criteria laid down for the selection of women for assisted passages that hard work was what was expected of them – whether as servants *or* wives. Education, gentility and refined accomplishments were not the requisite skills for pioneering housewifery: 'fine young ladies, who are unused to domestic work, and whose heaven of heavens is a drawing-room couch with the latest novel before them',[19] were not advised to think of emigrating. It is on this very point that Maria Rye's elaborate scheme for sending out to the colonies the educated but impoverished 'surplus women' of England foundered. There was no welcome and no place for educated or genteel independent women in colonial society. Even with the proviso that all women receiving assistance from the FMCES had to agree to undertake domestic duties in the households where they were employed as governesses (in effect a dilution of their skills and status), there was little demand for this sort of female labour. And it was on this very point that Maria Rye ran headlong into colonial disbelief and non-cooperation, not only in New Zealand but also in Australia where the Melbourne *Argus* wrote bluntly:

There is no market, perhaps, where the value of educated women is less appreciated than in Melbourne. That sort of genteel servitude which poor gentlewomen find so intolerable at home cannot but be greatly aggravated in a young country, where those who have the wealth have rarely the refinement, and those who have refinement have not much wealth . . . For an educated woman of high class who comes here to better her prospects we cannot conceive a more hopeless venture . . . She had better be a good plain cook or a pretty barmaid. There is not a housemaid who would not turn up her nose at her in any Melbourne labour-office.[20]

Gentility, particularly as represented by middle-class women, was not much in demand in the colonies whereas domestic skills and a capacity for hard manual work *was*. Where the prospect of large numbers of emigrant governesses was actively discouraged by the colonial governement, other female workers who were *not* domestic servants were granted assisted passages providing they professed or had demonstrated a readiness for steady physical work. Women from rural areas of Ireland comprised almost one-third of the single female migrants landing in Canterbury, few of whom would ever have served as household servants. Jane Whatmough worked as a jewel case liner in London before emigrating at the age of twenty-one in 1865, but more illustrative of the ways in which criteria were stretched in order to recruit prospective wife as well as servant labour was the selection exercised in the cotton districts at the time of the American Civil War. The Canterbury government offered assisted passages to several hundred people out of work as a way of providing relief which would also bring some direct benefit. Normally, manufacturing districts were regarded as highly undesirable areas for emigrant recruitment.

Factory operatives, lacking agricultural skills were never actively sought as settlers likely to excel in tending sheep, turning mutton chops over an open range, gathering the harvest, or coping with farmyard and orchard produce. In this instance, however, the usual rules of eligibility were suspended; those who were prepared to turn their hands to outdoor labour or 'to such work as would probably await them in a new country' were encouraged to apply. 'Married couples, with families, were to be discouraged; but single women, who knew their domestic duties, and were adapted for household work in the bush, would be accepted.'[21] How many young women in Manchester would have known what the bush was,[22] let alone have been able to demonstrate their suitability for life in it? The *British Crown* and the *Victory*, the ships which took the Manchester emigrants to New Zealand, carried a far larger proportion of single women than the regular emigrant ships. In this case youth, sex, and a willingness to try something new (or desperation in what faced them) counted for more than specific work skills. A selection for colonial domesticity and wifehood was preferred to a selection for wage work.

There was, however, no intention that the dispersal of young women into service or marriage should in any way lead to a blurring of class gradations in colonial society. There was no plan to work towards a situation in which all women would occupy the same station in society. Wives most of them might be, but presiding over household and hearth of entirely different dimensions. While the government imposed no barriers on women going from service into marriage, this was by no means a deliberate discouragement, or lack of support for domestic service itself. Assumptions of class differences were at the very basis of the colony's founding ethos, differences which were enshrined in the berthing arrangements made on board the ships which conveyed people to the colony, providing graded levels of comfort corresponding to position in the social hierarchy.

Passengers in the saloon (first class), had their own enclosed cabins, which were relatively spacious, well ventilated and lit, and ate at a table with the Captain where the food was fresh, cooked for them and served with generous quantities of wine and other liquor. The intermediate and steerage passengers had far less comfortable berths. The decks were usually poorly ventilated, there were no closed cabins in the steerage, the provision of water-closets and sick bay facilities were inadequate and the emigrants had to cook their own rations in extremely testing conditions.

Domestic labour and domestic labourers, whether paid or unpaid, have not been recognized as a major part of the nineteenth-century workforce or economy. As a consequence, the migration of women has not been placed within the context of labour migration. The demand for domestic labour in the colonies was a major feature of their early development, and one which was partly met by the introduction of large numbers of young working women. It is time for economic historians to take heed of women's work and to recognize their status as workers, in spite of the difficulties this may present.

Women were recruited to work as domestic labourers in the capacity of servants or wives but was this *all* that was encompassed by the phrase 'to balance the disproportion of the sexes'? What was this disproportion and what was its significance?

Emigration of all sorts, be it convict transportation, mining or gold booms, adventure, trade or pure fortune-seeking had always attracted more men than women. One of the common features of all British colonies last century was an initial period of male dominance in the first instance because there were more men than women. The dearth of women was conceived to be a problem of pressing moral and practical concern. In England in the same period quite the opposite imbalance was causing social anxiety of a different type. The number of women was greater than the number of men; the problem of what to do with 'surplus women' became a major social problem from which we have inherited the pining spinster as a stock figure of the late Victorian world. Whereas the surplus woman was an object of pity and the debate centred around the economic problems of women who would have to be supported in some way other than by or in marriage, the shortage of women in the colonies carried quite different connotations. To those people who were sufficiently aware of the colonial as well as the metropolitan sexual distribution, the solution appeared to be deceptively simple. Persuade the surplus women in Britain to emigrate to the colonies where there were people crying out for them (or so they were led to believe). This was indeed the reasoning adopted by many female emigration propagandists:

> We must not forget that our colonies are eminently in want of women of every rank, and that they are the natural destination of the great surplus which exists in England. If it were possible to plant those who are suffering and struggling at home . . . in useful independence or happy marriage over the broad fields of Australia and New Zealand, who among us but would say that it was by far the best solution of our difficulty?[23]

But female emigration made little impact in redressing the

sexual imbalance in British society. Contemporary and subsequent debates on the effects and significance of the sex ratio are important in what they reveal about assumptions regarding proper relations between men and women, and the prevailing sexual ideology. In colonial history the distinctive male dominance of settler society has long been recognized but never fully explored. What were believed to be the moral, social and economic consequences of such an imbalance for women, men and the development of society overall? How have late Victorian ideas concerning the effects of an inequality in the sexes carried over into modern historical writing?

It is hard to imagine that Bridget Madden (a 25-year-old domestic servant from Tipperary), Ann Ridley (a 22-year-old cook from Northumberland), or Gertrude Lawry (a 16-year-old domestic from Cornwall) or any of the other 4,000 Canterbury migrants who set off for New Zealand, did so with any esoteric intention to play a part in some global exercise of sex redistribution. Indeed, it has not ever been suggested that this *was* a reason why women did emigrate, although emigration propaganda was couched in terms of the abundance of young men just waiting for eligible young women to pick and choose from the available males at their whim and fancy.

While the emigrants themselves were not prompted by larger demographic considerations, the colonial reformers in England and sections of the New Zealand European community most definitely were. Most prominent among the former was Edward Gibbon Wakefield, who described the disproportion of the sexes as 'the greatest evil of all'.[24] An excess of men, it was argued, would spawn depravity and disorder. Significantly, the colonial sexual imbalance was usually described in terms of 'a shortage of women' rather than an excess of men, thereby denoting what women *represented* rather than what men *lacked*. In a male-dominant community it was believed prostitution would flourish, leading to general debauchery. This was bad enough, but an inequality in the sexes engendered a more general loosening of social cohesion, allowing men to drift about without the responsibility which came with having dependants to support. In this there is evidence of a further instance of overlap between class and patriarchal interests. Wakefield intended his ideal colony to consist of a hierarchical society, landowning capitalists at the top with labouring wage workers at the bottom. In order to ensure a good supply of wage labourers men had to be discouraged from dispersing all over the new land, and kept in sufficient poverty to be unable to buy their own land. The best way to make sure this happened – while at the same time guaranteeing a 'moral community' and the production of the next generation of the labour force – was to give every encouragement to people to marry. Within these married couples, the woman would be subordinate to the man, and beyond this the man would be at the disposal of the boss. The term 'settler society' (meaning one in which the men were 'settled') therefore acquired a new gender-specific meaning for women – economically, domestically, geographically and sexually. The women, meanwhile, were entirley oppressed and 'colonized' by men.

There is also an element of moral urgency in the discourse on the sexual imbalance. It is an imperative which goes beyond puritanical indignation at prostitution, and which arises from fears regarding the consequences of sexual expression and activity in 'unbalanced' communities. It is of course, extremely difficult to document an anxiety of this sort with any precision, but it undoubtedly existed. What else could the men who authored this report on immigration have meant by the following: 'not only is this inequality between the sexes, in an economical point of view . . . faulty, but that such a state of things is, upon infinitely higher considerations of *social comfort and progress*, extremely undesirable' (my emphasis).[25] What was social comfort? There is certainly a fear of men congregating in large numbers without 'access' to women. Given the assumptions current about men's uncontrollable sexual drive, the shortage of women forced men to find irregular outlets for their sexual energy – in masturbation, homosexuality or a prolonged state of continence which would be positively detrimental to health. It is interesting that the male-dominated society was conceived of as one predisposed towards depravity while the woman-dominated society invited pity. Jaunty appeals such as the one cited below were not uncommon in making an explicitly 'sexual' invitation to prospective emigrants:

> In Victoria [Australia], there are nearly three men to every female. Is that a healthy state of things? Morality must be at a very low ebb indeed. In England there are 2,000,000 marriageable young women pining in celibacy. Bring some of these out for mothers to Otago . . . Buxom English, Scotch, Irish girls let us have. The Irish are as good as the others. In some points better. Let it be known at home, that the swains of Otago want girls to enter on the matrimonial compact, and that they shall have free passages, and you will have abundance of virgins to bless your beds, grace your boards, and to rear offspring.[26]

One writer[27] has argued that the systematic colonizers regarded organized emigration as 'sexually therapeutic' for the 'uneasy classes'. By this he means that Wakefield saw colonies as providing the space in which capital and population could combine vigorously in a larger field for production. There would be none of the frustration of delayed marriage for men or celibacy for women in a society in which there was an equality in the numbers of the sexes, and in which a comfortable standard of living could be enjoyed without sexual abstinence.

It is impossible to know how great a following there was for these ideas, but the question of 'surplus women' and what to do with them gained very broad recognition as a social 'problem'. What is surprising is the lack of critical attention the very notion of surplus women has attracted subsequently. What, after all, is wrong with a society in which there is an abundance of women? Who or what are they surplus to? The notion of a 'surplus' of women seems to imply that women are only valid so long as they can be attached to a man. If there are more women than men then there are women 'left over', who are redundant in the coupling of members of society. There is implicit in the debate on the balance of the sexes, an assumption that it is 'natural' for there to be even numbers of women and men, and for this to be accommodated in heterosexual coupling in marriage. The corollary to this reasoning is that for every man there should be a woman. The problem was always discussed in terms of a stable number of men, women being the dependent variable to be added or subtracted where necessary.

How extensive was the imbalance in reality? Out of the total (NZ) European population in 1864 of 172,158, 62 per cent (106,580) were male. Looking more closely at the critical age range from twenty-one to forty years, there were 53,919 men to a mere 22,396 women.[28] The sexual proportion was not evenly distributed throughout the country, or between towns and more remote settlements, and females constituted a minority in the overall population until the turn of the century.

What was referred to last century as the 'balance of the sexes' has become for us in the twentieth century, the sex ratio (usually expressed as the number of males per 100 females in a given population), a low sex ratio indicating a preponderance of women, a high ratio indicating a surfeit of men. The effects of the sex ratio on society are as much the domain of historians as they are of demographers or sociologists. But it is a subject littered with confusion and rife with speculation, little of it with any factual or substantive basis. On the one extreme, Anne Summers argues that the small number of women in the early years of the convict colonies of eastern Australia resulted in women becoming whores, 'sexual fodder', 'distributed to the men almost as part of the daily rations'.[29] Another historian writing about colonial New Zealand, confidently asserts that not only was marriage an avenue of social mobility for women in New Zealand but that marriage prospects were 'doubtless better in New Zealand *if only* because of the numerical preponderance of men' (my emphasis).[30] The most extensive treatment I have encountered in a historical context, is in Roger Thompson's comparative study of women in Stuart England and America.[31] In this he steps right outside the seventeenth century to engage in a long digression about the effects of sex ratio on society. In his opinion a society in which there is a preponderance of women results in an upsurge of feminism, emphasis on careers for women, higher divorce rates and love triangles, concubinage, lesbianism, an increase in extra-marital fertility and all manner of other 'unbalanced sort of behaviour'.[32] Where there is a surplus of males, in contrast, the society is nasty, brutish, violent, though these features are moderated if there are a 'reasonable number of women', in whose presence 'uncouth and unkempt males would put away their guns and their decks of cards and use instead their combs and spongebags in order to attract not molls but wives,' though some 'might be driven to perversions by their plight, to sodomy or buggery, to miscegenation, or to rape or pederasty. Others might adopt different creative [sic] channels.'[33] In a situation of moderate imbalance, however, life for women 'though it might be materially hard, would hold many attractions. Not only would marriage be easy to achieve, but the marriageable girl [sic] could reasonably expect to be able to choose among rivals, and to make conditions before accepting . . . Widows could . . . expect to find themselves courted, and the poor or ugly or simple girl would have a chance.'[34]

We need to look a great deal more closely at exactly what effects an imbalance of the sexes actually did and does have. The shape of the population *is* important, and the proportion of the sexes is crucial, but it is not an explanation in itself. Demographic characteristics need to be examined in conjunction with other social factors, along with changes of a medical, legal, economic and political nature. We need to question the assumption that equal numbers of women and men constitute 'normality' from which everything else is a dangerous deviation. We need to look more closely at the characteristics of male- and female-dominant populations.

Studies of pioneer and frontier societies usually describe the preponderance of men in formative years of settlement, and sometimes this leads to consideration of the existence of a specifically male culture. Institutions of male preserve and power and the development of concepts such as Australian 'mateship' have been identified in this area. It is only very recently, though, that the study of colonial male culture has incorporated a question of how male dominance has shaped the position of women in those societies. An exploratory essay in male culture as it relates to women's experience declares its intention to break into the 'study of men as males'[35] (in contrast to the study of men as people, women as curious minorities).

The possibility of marrying, and marrying well, was held out to be the greatest single incentive for women to go to New Zealand and other New World destinations. Almost without exception historians have accepted this account without critic- ism, and have even extended it to argue that the primary motivation behind most women's decision to emigrate was a desire to marry. This has never been proposed as a reason why men emigrate. Many of these same historians accept marriage as unproblematic,[36] and representing an end in itself in the lives of most women. What this has meant is that married women rarely have received any serious attention from historians. They have been subsumed in discussion of the household, and disappear into the vast realms of unpaid workers and the private, undocumented world of domesticity. The rationale for female emigration which rested on the notion of an imbalance in the sexes contained a multitude of ideological assumptions as well as practical imperatives. Young women were introduced to channel the sexual energies of men and for procreation, be- cause this was, after all, a period of chronic colonial labour shortage, where an increasing population was equated with a flourishing economy. Belief in the normality of heterosexuality, and its institutionalization in marriage was implicit in the 'inequality of the sexes' discourse.

This section suggests that the impetus and pattern of women's migration springs from a much more complex set of circumst- ances than a simple search for husbands. Determining the motivation of individuals in the past is a treacherous area, and I make no claims to present a comprehensive account of why the many thousands of young women emigrated when, where and how they did. My intention is to raise questions which cast doubts on the accounts that have been presented to date.

Support for the idea that women emigrated in order to marry is grounded in two principal arguments. One suggests that emigration propaganda struck a direct chord in framing colonization in terms of likely matrimonial prospects. The other postulates that at a time when few economic opportunities were open to women to earn an independent living, marriage was perceived (by women themselves) as a means of survival in much the same way as men regarded a job or a piece of land. There are problems in establishing what lengths women were prepared to go to in order to secure a 'better' future, or indeed any future, by way of a husband, and to what extent marriage itself was regarded as security – it does tend to gloss over the fact that many women ended up supporting themselves or their children, or making substantial contributions to their subsistence. For the majority of working-class women, there was little expectation that marriage would free them from having to engage in some sort of paid work in addition to the usual load of domestic responsibilities.

Some writers have swallowed the demographic discourse whole – jumping from a recognition of the complementary sexual imbalances in England and the colonies, to attributing this very factor as the reason why young women contemplated emigration in the first place:

> In England there was a huge surplus of women; between 1851 and 1871 there was a 16.8 per cent increase in the number of single women of marriageable age and there was a surplus of over 125,000 single women. *Thus* a large proportion of the female immigrants were obviously in search of husbands [my emphasis].[37]

The idea that Isabella Hayes (a 21-year-old dressmaker from Sunderland) or Sarah Cain (a 24-year-old dairy maid from Co. Kerry) or any of the others went to the other side of the world on a long, hazardous and uncomfortable journey in order to get a husband is a wholly unsubstantiated view. Though as recently as 1981 the following account was proffered for their actions: 'it was the enrichment which colonial conditions could bring to home and family life which was the main inducement to women's emigration.'[38] These sorts of sweeping generalizations ignore the broader context of women's migration, especially the relationship between migration, domestic service and emigration.

In order to fully understand, or even to begin to understand the dynamics of women's migration it is necessary to look at why women moved at all – and why some (the majority), chose to move to a nearby town, and why others chose to leave their country altogether. Were there different motivations behind these two sorts of move indicating that the migrant and emigrant groups were essentially different? Was it the 'pull' factors – the magnet which the different destinations represented, which attracted different sorts of people, or was it the 'push' factors that were more important, and *where* people ended up was just a matter of chance? Comparing the pattern of women's migration with men's, opposite trends are evident. Fewer men moved about, but a far greater proportion of those who *did* ended up leaving their country altogether. Why should this be so?

The total picture of women's migration in the nineteenth centry reveals a pattern of movement from rural areas into towns and cities. Whether this was from Long Sutton to Somerton (Somerset), or from Boroughbridge to York, or several steps between these, or from Co. Cork to Bristol, the trend was the same. Young women in search of work, or a better sort of work took their chances in larger places. By far the most common means through which they made this move was by exchanging one position of domestic service for another. Situations in towns were more plentiful, more attractive, and often better paid. McBride, in a major survey of domestic service in France and England over the period 1820–1920,[39] declares that 'the history of domestic service in the nineteenth century is the story of urban migration.'[40] She argues that domestic service formed a transitional mode of occupation for women in an era when society was becoming industrialized. For women it served as an intermediary type of employment, facilitating their entry into urban life by combining a traditional occupation with innovatory long-distance migration. Rural areas were being depopulated disproportionately, the remaining inhabitants comprising more males than females while towns and cities were becoming increasingly female.

It would appear that in general, women were not making a

choice to move in search of husbands, they were not leaving areas where there was a shortage of men; but they were taking more direct steps to their own betterment by way of employment opportunities. I think this is a more realistic context in which to place expectations of marriage. Although we can never be sure of what people's expectations of marriage actually were – and whether people had conscious or even unconscious expectations at all – in so far as marriage was a consideration, I think few working women saw it as an end in itself. It may have been part of a larger goal of securing a better life for those who had aspirations to upward mobility. If marriage was a universal expectation for most people – men as well as women – then marriage itself recedes as a specific goal.

The age at which most people emigrated, in young adulthood, was also the age at which it was most common to marry and establish a new family unit. This coincidence of life-cycle stage (young adulthood), with emigration (an element of social time),[41] should not be confused with some form of *a priori* reasoning, which states that because a large number of women *did* in fact marry in New Zealand, *this* was the overriding consideration in their decision to emigrate.

The massive exodus of both women and men from the British Isles and much more dramatically, Ireland, during the last century, was of course an attempt to escape from poverty. Whether it was the poverty of actual starvation prompting the massive flood of famine migration in the 1840s, or the relative poverty of agricultural labourers in the 1870s, or the bleak prospects of Julia Burns, a charge on the parish of St Peter Cornhill,[42] or of the collapse of the means of subsistence in Cornwall prompting Emily and Mary Tregarnowarn [43] to take their chance in New Zealand, or any of the many other instances of severe distress, people were desperate for a way out. We can only surmise that this was why someone like Hannah Arthy left her position as general servant at Fenhouse Farm near Colchester, Essex, to go to New Zealand in 1855 at the age of twenty. She was one of a family of at least eight children born in the village of Ardleigh, Essex.[44] I would not like to leave the impression that all migration, especially women's emigration can be explained or understood simply in terms of a summation of a series of individual life histories. Or that it is a movement resulting from the convergence of a series of personal circumstances. Migration and emigration were part of larger and wider changes in society and economy brought about by the transformation of English society by industrial capitalism in the nineteenth century.

It is by no means satisfactory to dismiss the actions or experience of tens of thousands of young women with a single sweeping account which explains their behaviour solely in terms of personal goals. Until we know a great deal more about the lives of these women we can not put forward any single general answer to the question of *why* they emigrated. It seems to me altogether too hasty, and too easy, to assume that women risked their lives sailing from one side of the earth to the other, to find husbands.

How do we see emigrant women in a patriarchal past? Were they victims of oppression or heroines fighting against it? They were certainly brave and intrepid, worthy of admiration; heroines in their venturesomeness, but they were not feminist pioneers. They were not forging new ground for their sex. Most of them ended up in some oppressive sort of domesticity. But they stepped out in a positive way to escape what was a fairly bleak future. There is a tension in how they are remembered – and admiration mixed with disappointment in that their venture gained them so little. But at least they are remembered – Eliza Bealey, Margaret Ferguson, Martha Clark, Maria McGuinness, among the many.

5. 'Our women are expected to become . . .': women and girls in further education in England at the turn of the century [1]

Gill Blunden

I'm an historian by default rather than by intention. I started my research with an interest derived very much from my personal experience as a full-time lecturer in social studies at a college of further education in Lincolnshire. I enjoyed my work very much but could hardly fail to notice the rigid division by sex of the different groups of students that I was teaching. All my motor-vehicle engineering students were male; all my hairdressers (except one), female. Even amongst groups taking 'O' levels there were very clear student expectations about the 'sex' of the subject they were studying – 'But, Gill, economics, is really a fella's subject, isn't it?' So with the laudable aim of advancing a feminist understanding of this contemporary phenomenon I gave up a full-time, permanent, (relatively) well-paid, pensionable, rewarding, etc., teaching job to research into women and girls and further education by means of an SSRC studentship at the University of Bristol, department of social administration.

Why, then, am I contributing a paper on the further education of women and girls at the turn of the century? The answer is that the more I got involved in the topic the more I realized that I couldn't do what I had hoped to do without locating it within an historical framework. So, through using historical sources and becoming more fascinated by them, I decided to restrict the project to an historical one. In the light of this autobiographical introduction, it should come as no surprise that this paper is dedicated, as indeed is all my work, to my former students at Boston College of Further Education, who taught me much more than I ever taught them.

My aim in this paper is to take a particular issue raised at central government level and investigate how much notice was taken of it in each of three localities. The term 'further education' embraces all state-provided education that is not given in schools or universities.

I examine three case studies to substantiate the theoretical framework of my research: Swindon in Wiltshire, and Cinderford and Stroud in Gloucestershire. I look at the ways in which further education developed in each of these three areas and at the relative influence which local industrialists, the local state, educationalists and the 'clients' had on this development. In particular, I want to see what this can tell us about the growth of further education courses for women and girls.

At first sight, the relationship between the health of the nation and further education courses is hard to discern. However, the implied relationship was of real significance in defining the kinds of, and limits to, further education provision deemed appropriate to female students.

The problem was that if the health of the working classes was poor, Britain's imperial and economic aspirations would suffer. Unfit soldiers would not be able to defend and expand the Empire. And at this time the concern was particularly with Britain's ability to field a fit, fighting army during the Boer War. In some areas, as many as 40 per cent of applicants to the army had to be turned down as being physically unfit. According to the report of the Inter-departmental Committee of Physical Deterioration, 1904, the people to blame for this sorry state of affairs were women. The writers of the report argued that it was because women were ignorant of the ways in which a home should be run and children brought up, that the menfolk were so unfit. The problem could therefore be solved by educating girls and women in housecraft and child care. This was a national, rather than a local issue. However the report saw the solution in terms of *local* rather than national provision. The implementation of its recommendations was to remain with the initiative of local bodies.

In the case of the young girls who had left elementary school, their further education was to take the form of continuation classes which were to be compulsory and the instruction 'should cover every branch of domestic hygiene, including the preparation of food, the practice of household cleanliness, the tendance and feeding of young children, the proper requirements of a family as to clothing, everything in short that would equip a young girl for the duties of a housewife.'[2]

Working mothers, then as now, were identified as being particularly incapable of keeping a house properly and bringing up healthy children. Some women worked in factories because their husbands' wages were inadequate for a family, or because they had no husband. But they sometimes worked outside the home because they preferred that to devoting their whole lives to domestic chores. Although one of the witnesses giving evidence to the report found this surprising at first, on closer investigation it became understandable.

> At thirteen years of age the majority of these women would have begun to work in a factory, to handle their own earnings, to mix with a large number of people with all the excitement and gossip of factory life. They would thus in most cases grow up entirely ignorant of everything pertaining to domesticity. After marriage, therefore, it is hardly probable that they would willingly relinquish this life to undertake work of which they are in so large measure ignorant and which is robbed of all that is to them pleasant and exciting. Until as girls they have been *taught* [my emphasis] to find a pleasure in domestic work, and until there is a greater supply of healthy and suitable recreations and amusements in the reach of all women, to counteract the prevailing squalor and gloom of these Pottery towns, it is useless to expect them to relinquish factory life.[3]

What we might find surprising today, is this early recognition that girls and women do not naturally find their life's pleasure in washing dishes or darning socks. They have to be taught two things: how to *perform* these tasks and how to *enjoy* performing them so that they come to restrict their sphere of influence and expectations of fulfilment to those activities that are centred on the home. This is a recurring idea running through all the local and central government policy statements considered in this paper. Women are not 'naturally' competent cleaners, child nurses, home nurses, etc. They have to be taught that these tasks are properly theirs and taught the skills necessary to perform them successfully. The 1904 report recognized the illogicality of expecting girls to become, without example or teaching, perfect or even adequate wives and mothers. It is emphasized in the report that any classes or courses organized in pursuit of this goal were to be 'directed to the selection, economy and preparation of the material best suited to the needs of the poorer classes, including the requirements of young children'.[4]

Syllabuses were to be drawn up by people with intimate knowledge of the requirements of such households 'and care should be taken to use such apparatus and utensils as under favourable conditions are likely to be found in the houses of the poor'.[5] How this teaching was to relate to conditions found in the most deprived of homes was not made clear.

The three localities

I shall now examine the social and economic characteristics of the three areas which I'm looking at and then discuss the ways in which these recommendations were put into effect in these areas. One of my main arguments is that further education in domestic subjects for women was developed only where this was seen to be appropriate for the locality.

The three areas differed a great deal in the extent to which married women worked outside the home. In Stroud in 1901 around 45 per cent of all females over ten years old were engaged in full-time paid employment. Nearly 40 per cent of the workforce was female and over a quarter of all married or widowed women worked outside the home. This pattern of women's employment was unusual in the South West at the turn of the century. The Stroud area was an important centre for woollen and worsted production and clothing manufacture so that many of the women living there found employment outside the home. In 1901 nearly half of all women workers in the region were employed in dress and textile production. The local middle classes therefore found it difficult to persuade enough women to go in for domestic service.

Women's employment opportunities were changing in Stroud during this period. From 1880 the woollen cloth industry was declining and the economy was becoming more mixed. By the turn of the century people (generally men), were employed in engineering, dyeing, brewing, flour-milling, iron-working processes, as well as in the pin, umbrella and stick industries and in sawmills. The expansion of the clerical and business sectors meant that educated boys and girls were needed to work in offices and, as before, the middle classes remained keen to recruit suitable domestic servants.

In Cinderford and Swindon very few married women worked outside the home. In both these communities there was a dominant industry which demanded a wholly male workforce since much of the work required a great deal of physical strength which women were assumed not to have. In fact, in Cinderford, where the chief industry was mining, women had been legally excluded from underground work since 1842 and this legislation was generally enforced by the 1880s. In order to maintain a healthy workforce, women's work in the home was essential but this did not prevent women from seeking work outside the home when they could. As in Stroud, a high proportion of those women out at work were employed in domestic service.

Similarly, teaching was an occupation engaged in by women in all three areas. In fact, in Cinderford in 1905 these two occupations represented almost the entire range of options open to women and girls.

> Moreover, Cinderford is one of the best recruiting grounds for Female Teachers, as, mining being the chief industry of the locality, girls who do not desire to become domestic servants have but few means of earning a livelihood.[6]

Since there was no servant-employing class in Cinderford, many girls had to migrate to other parts of the county or country to find residential domestic employment.

Swindon, at this time, was also a one-industry town. The Board of Trade report of 1908 identified two social classes: one comprising employees of the Great Western Railway Company and the other consisting of shopkeepers, etc. It also noted that there was little scope for female labour. Female employees who were not teachers or daily domestics, worked in the dress and textile sector associated with the Great Western Railway – in uniform manufacture and upholstering – and in the production and serving of food and drink, possibly in the Great Western Railway refreshment rooms.

It was not until 1906 that women began to be employed in the various departments of the Great Western Railway although the possibility was discussed as early as 1876. However there is no evidence that women clerical workers were employed in any of the Great Western Railway's offices in Swindon before 1912. By 1917 there were at least 300 female clerical workers employed in the Swindon works.

Further education for women and girls

It is important to remember that each locality had already developed some form of further education for all kinds of students before the beginning of the century. This provision was suited to the needs of each locality. What I am now concerned with is whether the existing provision was modified in any way to take account of the recommendations of the 1904 report.

Gloucestershire
In Gloucestershire the early provision of courses in domestic economy had developed systematically and extensively since 1891. It is clear that the first funds allocated from the revenues derived from the 1890 Local Taxation (Customs and Excise) Act (known as 'the whisky money') by the Gloucestershire County Council, were in aid of the dairy and cookery schools in Gloucestershire. The instruction was to be given in the central institutions in Gloucester itself or on a peripatetic basis. The work of the Cookery Committee was concerned with both the Gloucester School of Cookery and Domestic Economy in the

city and with the provision of cookery, laundry and dressmaking classes in the county.

Twenty-four scholarships per annum tenable at the central institution in Gloucester, funded by the 'whisky money', were offered by the Gloucestershire County Council Technical Instruction Committee. Half of these were to be offered to elementary school pupils under fourteen years of age and the other half to pupils under sixteen from the county cookery classes. Each was tenable for a three-month course. In 1895 a residential house was opened for pupils attending the School of Cookery and Domestic Economy in Gloucester.

There were two types of pupil to be catered for: those intending to follow the two-year course of training with a view to becoming domestic science instructresses and those who followed the three-month course and who intended to go into domestic service. In 1895 it was recorded that a former pupil of the school had become the headmistress at the Woolwich Polytechnic. By 1905 there were sixteen students following the teaching course, thirty county scholars following the domestic course and other students taking a housewifery course. The training of domestic servants was seen as an important part of the committee's work, and the committee was committed to this 'necessary training for girls'.

> The importance of this training wants to be brought more
> before mothers of girls just leaving school. In no other
> profession, if we may so call it, is the work undertaken
> without preparation and yet our women are expected to
> become model house-keepers, cooks, dressmakers, sick-
> nurses, by intuition, an expectation hardly, if ever, realised,
> as all acquainted with domestic life among the poor, or
> indeed among all classes can testify. Mothers of scholars who
> are now engaged in domestic service speak highly of the
> benefits which their daughters received.[7]

However, even this kind of scheme was considered insufficient when the Gloucestershire Education Committee received and considered the report of the Inter-departmental Committee on Physical Deterioration, 1904. As a result of considering the recommendations embodied in the report, the Gloucestershire Education Committee obtained the Board of Education's approval to conduct, on an experimental basis, a two-year course of instruction in domestic subjects for girls aged twelve to fourteen years in certain schools in the county. One of these schools was at Badbrook in Stroud, where many married women were in paid employment and where there was an unsatisfied demand for domestic servants. In these circumstances the establishment of this school is understandable from the point of view of the local authority, acting in the interest of national efficiency and of the middle classes.

The Gloucestershire Education Committee opened the school at Badbrook in 1904. Initially, however, the experiment failed, probably because parents preferred their girls to be out at work earning money rather than staying on at school and because mill-owners and managers were so heavily dependent on girl-labour. The course was designed for girls over the minimum school-leaving age who had attended certain selected public elementary schools in the area. The school closed in September 1907 because

> in Stroud there was a prejudice on the part of some of the parents and teachers against this type of instruction. The attendance fell off, new recruits for the present year did not come forward, and it seemed the wiser course to close the School for a time.[8]

However, in order to effect the reopening of the school, an energetic and enthusiastic Ladies' Committee, under the Stroud managers, was delegated some executive authority in this matter. The school was reopened as a home-making centre on 1 September, 1909 for girls over twelve years old. The instruction offered was not supposed to enhance a girl's ability to sell her labour as a skilled cook or seamstress but to improve her capacity for homemaking and child-care. The 1904 report of the Inter-departmental Committee stated that factory operatives, such as many of the Stroud girls would become, 'make the worst wives' (Para 231). Nevertheless, the school's courses could and did equip girls to sell their skilled labour in the local labour market. As late as 1926 one of His Majesty's Inspectors was able to note with approval that 'a tribute to the teaching [of needlework] is the fact that the girls are eagerly sought after by the local dressmakers'.[9]

It might well have been the case that the appointment of the Local Management Committee of Ladies was seen by some girls and their parents as a way of making the school more commercially useful to them and thus enhancing their labour market prospects. To have followed a course at the school and be furnished with a 'reference' from one of the ladies on the committee might enable a girl to get a somewhat better domestic job than she might otherwise have done.

Yet this was not the main or declared reason for establishing either this or the short, residential, domestic courses in Gloucester itself. Both were ostensibly established to improve the ability of working-class girls as wives and mothers, at a time when the skills of the working class to reproduce itself adequately was in some doubt. Yet this is not to deny that there was no immediate gain to the interests of the bourgeoisie in the localities. Of course there was. Girls and young women so trained became a source of domestic servants that did not quickly dry up. How far, therefore, can one argue that the early articulated concern with the ability of working-class women to become adequate wives and mothers was no more than a justification to keep the local middle classes supplied with residential domestic servants?

Swindon

In Swindon the number of women employed outside the home was small. Some classes had been established during the 1890s by the Swindon and North Wilts Technical Instruction Committee to provide tuition for women in such subjects as artisan's cookery. Generally classes in 'women's subjects' (i.e. first aid, dressmaking, home nursing, hygiene and cookery) were established only if there was considerable demand for them and if the teachers' costs would be covered by student fees. In 1891–2 twenty-two students enrolled in the artisan's cookery classes, which consisted of ten demonstrations and ten practical lessons. The classes were held in the board room of the gas works, New Swindon. Exactly how much cookery could be learnt in the board room of a private firm is a question which indicates how useful the classes must have been to the sudents.

However, in 1898 a special subcommittee was set up to consider the whole question of tuition in domestic subjects. Its findings were that any additional costs involved in providing a greater number of classes would be off-set by a rise in income from student fees if attendance improved and also by increased government grants. In the light of that costing exercise and because the committee was convinced of the importance of domestic instruction for women, an increase in provision was sanctioned. The membership of this committee was exclusively male and representative of no local capitalist interest other than the Great Western Railway. Indeed, unlike the London School Board which Annmarie Turnbull examines in this collection, all the members of the Swindon and North Wilts Technical Instruction Committee were men. The important subjects which were taught were hygiene, home nursing and ambulance duties. The committee stated that the 'classes . . . are specially commended to Young Housekeepers and others. The Instruction will be practical and interesting.'[10]

It is noteworthy that the instruction offered was not in needlework or cookery but in subjects connected with health and cleanliness. This, presumably, reflected the opinion of the all-male Great Western Railway subcommittee as to what young women should be studying, rather than any demand from the potential students as to what their interest or needs might have been. Courses in 'women's subjects' developed from these and other rather *ad hoc* arrangements. Students were required to pay tuition fees and provide their own materials.

This not very systematic provision of courses in domestic subjects for women and girls continued throughout the first decade of the twentieth century. The authorities in Swindon were not concerned with problems of home-management and child care for married women at work since so few members of its workforce were married women. However, the comfort and well-being of the artisan in his own home was something that the Technical Instruction Committee felt it could support, particularly since it would be involved in little or no increase in expenditure by doing so.

In 1906–7 a subcommittee of the Swindon Education Committee, the Education Authority which was responsible for all education in the Swindon area from 1902 onwards, conducted an enquiry into the situation of girl school-leavers. This is an indication of its concern with an issue that recurs again and again in Swindon throughout the period under review: that of the predicament facing girl school-leavers in the light of their limited employment prospects in a town dominated by a company which only employed men, the Great Western Railway Company. Although the policy issues raised by this problem never totally informed the decisions of the Swindon Education Committee they certainly became prominent concerns with which the committee had to contend. It was impossible to ignore the situation and the problem did not just go away.

A cursory examination of the question, uninformed by a feminist perspective, would produce an explanation of the expansion of further education in Swindon solely in terms of the relationship between the college and the Great Western Railway Company, concentrating on the training and education of male engineers and clerks. Since my analysis identifies the sexual dynamics of the development of further education I am able to deal more adequately with the complexities of the situation. It is not inappropriate, therefore, to look at the development of further education for women and girls in a town such as Swindon, however odd this might appear at first sight. Part of my task is to uncover the reasons why the Swindon Education Committee found it impossible to ignore the position of women and girls in Swindon and to trace the history of such policies as the committee developed.

One of the strongest concerns of the committee was not to improve further education opportunities *per se* for women and girls but to provide a specific kind of further education for girls, as future, and women, as actual, wives and mothers. In this the committee was informed by the Inter-departmental Report on

Physical Deterioration, 1904. Domestic classes for adult women continued to be organized and in the early years of the century there was sufficient student demand for these classes to necessitate the employment of an additional teacher of domestic subjects from Trowbridge. These courses were not meant to enhance women's skills in the labour market but rather to reinforce their position as unpaid domestic workers in the marital or parental home.

A particular feature of this policy was that special classes were arranged for the factory operatives working for Messrs. Wills Clothing. The girls' employers encouraged attendance by paying the students' fees and by awarding cash prizes. Judy Lown has documented similar employer involvement in domestic classes in Essex. Although these classes generally filled up rapidly, the annual report of the Swindon Education Committee 1906–7 expressed disappointment at the 'want of persistence among the girls and young women who take these subjects'.[11] Presumably the initial demand of the students at the beginning of the session was not sustained and the committee was left with a number of unviable classes to administer. In fact, the Wills Clothing employees were often unable to attend as they were working overtime.

The Swindon Education Committee was keen to involve the ladies of the town in the building up of this aspect of its work 'which must have a notable effect upon the home life of our town'.[12] The delegation of this section of the Committee's work was because of its own inability to grapple successfully with these problems and to acknowledge that this was properly the work of women. As such it is not necessarily an indication of the lowness of domestic education for women on its list of educational priorities; on the contrary, it may be seen as an attempt to discharge its obligations more efficiently by referring them to a body of 'experts', i.e. 'ladies'.

Nevertheless, one of the results of this policy was that the domestic education of women and girls was removed from the centre to the periphery of the activities of the Swindon Education Committee. It did not develop in any systematic fashion and its effective functioning was dependent on the 'goodwill' of the ladies rather than the duty of the Swindon Education Committee. Between 1908 and 1911 extensive provision was made for the domestic education of elementary schoolgirls. The efforts of the committee were concentrated on the education of girls as *future* rather than as existing wives and mothers. Perhaps this policy can be interpreted as an attempt to universalize provision instead of leaving it to the non-compulsory sector.

In addition to these attempts to provide some form of domestic training for schoolgirls, there still continued *ad hoc* efforts to supply courses for women, often at the instigation of the Ladies' Committee. The general policy of the Swindon Education Committee seems to have been to establish such classes on an informal basis at the instigation of the Ladies' Committee or other body, provided there were sufficient students interested in enrolling so as to make the class viable.

Immediately prior to the outbreak of the First World War, the further education classes for women and girls in Swindon were organized into a separate department of the Technical Institution, the department for women and girls. The staff consisted of a superintending teacher and five staff teachers, together with additional staff. The department was organized into three sections: classes in cookery, dressmaking and first aid and home nursing held at the Technical Institution; general, domestic and commercial courses for young women held at the District Evening Schools; and special classes in health, first aid and home nursing, care of infants, cookery and dressmaking for adults and children, for adult women. No programme of grouped courses in domestic subjects was developed for adult women over eighteen partly because of the limited facilities available at the Technical Institution for such subjects and partly because many girls remained in the junior evening schools over the age of sixteen. Thus the proportion of adult women in the population who received such domestic instruction was small.

Conclusion

These case studies are important because they point out the

contradictions between the demands of the local economy, which required the labour of married women in factories in Stroud, and those of the central state, which acted to co-ordinate the needs of the economy as a whole, in this case in attempting to increase the efficiency of child-rearing practices amongst the working classes. Other conflicts of interest arose because of the requirements of the different classes within the same local economy. Yet others were manifest in the struggle between women's desire to broaden their employment opportunities and the widely held belief which was advantageous to both the central state and men in general, namely that a woman's place was in the home.

What I've been arguing is that in none of the areas studied did the central government concern raise issues that had never been considered in the localities. In none of the areas did national needs override, transcend or work in total opposition to those interests dear to the local dominant class. However, in the case of Stroud, these interests did appear to clash with those of the working classes, while the means of fulfilling *national* demand for an adequately reproduced labour force and healthy recruits for the army and *local* demand for domestic servants and seamstresses did coincide. How far was one set of interests used to justify the other? The conflict was resolved in so far as the home-making centre continued to turn out domestic servants and seamstresses, enhanced the young women's prospects in the local labour market, and in the long run was supposed to enable these young women to become better wives and mothers.

In both Cinderford and Swindon there were no servant-employing classes, and the development of domestic classes was consequently slower and less systematic than in Stroud, where there was a clear local demand for domestics. In Gloucestershire generally there was a demand for domestic servants, and girls left their rural homes in areas such as Cinderford to become residential domestics. Girls from such areas filled the residential courses in the central institution in Gloucester. Whatever their subsequent success as wives and mothers the immediate effect of their attendance at such a course was entry into domestic service, as an analysis of the annual reports of the Gloucestershire Education Committee reveals.

I shall make one final observation. It is interesting to see that both authorities eventually opted for a solution that tended to withdraw the issue from further education into the elementary education arena. Perhaps this was because the education of adult women was not seen to be in the immediate interests of the local economy, or in the immediate interests of a male-dominated society. After all, whilst married women were out at evening classes, albeit learning how to make children's clothes, someone had to stay in and look after their children. A husband might not have seen his wife's attendance at evening classes as being in his interest at all but rather as an activity which mitigated against his inalienable right to spend his (and her) leisure time as he chose.

However, in all three areas domestic education for adult women was allowed to continue on an *ad hoc* but certainly not the compulsory basis that the 1904 report of the Inter-departmental Committee envisaged. The training of girls to be domestic servants and seamstresses in the immediate future (and only perhaps incidentally to become more efficient wives and mothers), was maybe more visibly profitable in the locality than the training of adult women whose relationship to capital was obscured by their marriage relationship. Likewise, younger girls were probably perceived to be more malleable and responsive than adult women to the suggestion that it was 'natural' for them to restrict their hopes and aspirations to being wives and mothers. Adult women, grappling with the problems of child care, domestic work and income maintenance were less likely to accept either the suggestion that they were ignorant of their responsibilities to their children and husbands or that a course of domestic education would be the panacea to their problems.

One of my arguments has been that it was only in Swindon where the picture was not masked by the need of the middle classes to employ servants, that a direct response to the central state's needs for the reproduction of labour power can be seen. After all, the local dominant employer, the Great Western

Railway Company, needed a healthy workforce and it needed to ensure that there would be a continued supply of healthy labour for it to employ. Yet the Swindon example appears to reveal an inverse relationship between the provision of further education courses for women and their employment. It was the *unemployment* of women rather than their employment which influenced the Education Committee in its further education provision for women. The kind of further education offered did not appear to help women maximize their employment prospects but rather continued to confine them in their familial role.

I think that the fairest conclusion to draw from the evidence is that, however the policies were arrived at, one of their clearest results was to perpetuate and reproduce the sexual division of labour in society at the turn of the century, that is to say, to keep women and girls in the domestic sphere.

Part three

Women and public life

Introduction

The papers in this section examine the restrictions which women have to negotiate if they move out of the private world of domesticity and the home into public life, in particular the professions and in politics. By doing this, women are directly resisting men's domination and control of these areas.

Many forms of total control have operated to restrict women's participation in public life, most obviously in legislation. The local School Board elections were the first in Great Britain in which women were allowed to stand and to vote. Married women were excluded from the teaching profession in many places by local authorities' regulations. As treatment of the insane became medicalized, it was more difficult for women to practise in anything other than subordinate roles (e.g. as matrons), because they could not qualify as doctors.

Ideas about women's 'natural' role also operated to regulate their freedom in the public sphere on a more subtle level. Women have generally been permitted to do paid work only in those areas which are closely related to their domestic role – domestic service, teaching children, tending the sick – and in those areas of politics seen as legitimate concerns, such as those to do with children. For further general introduction to these issues see Patricia Hollis, *Women in Public* (London: Allen & Unwin 1979), Elizabeth Wilson, *Women and the Welfare State* (London: Tavistock 1977) and M.Stacey and M.Price, *Women Power and Politics* (London: Tavistock 1981).

These papers show how women have organized themselves both formally and informally, in order to get around these various forms of control. Women on the London School Board created complex supportive networks during the late nineteenth century. Some women teachers set up their own union to fight against the marriage bar and to achieve equal pay in the 1920s and 1930s. Women fought for the right to qualify as doctors, and so were able to continue running asylums. Later, the Medical Women's Federation had a special section devoted to psychological medicine.

Today women are still resisting and challenging male power in these areas of public life. In party politics the all-party 300 group aims to increase the number of MPs from its present miserable 3 per cent. A recent report on women teachers by the EOC with the NUT, *Promotion and the Woman Teacher* (1980), shows that they are still handicapped in the profession by their additional role as wife and mother, and their general position is no better than 50 years ago. However, within health-care feminism has raised the consciousness of some women mental health workers. For example, since 1976 the Women's Therapy Centre has offered feminist therapy to women in London on a pay-what-you-can-afford basis.

Campaigns being fought by women in trade unions, against low wages, against the concept of 'the family wage', and most recently against sexual harassment at workplace (see the NCCL report, *Sexual Harassment at Work*, 1982), show that in all areas of employment women continue to struggle for their rights.

6. Women and psychiatric professionalization, 1780–1914

Charlotte Mackenzie

The last ten years have seen a reappraisal of contemporary psychiatric practice and the history of medicine, from a perspective informed by the concerns of the Women's Liberation Movement. Feminist psychotherapists have criticized the quality (and biases) of treatment offered to women in mental distress,[1] and organized to provide alternative resources for treatment with a feminist orientation.[2] One reason for the observable male bias of established psychiatric practice may be the tenuous position traditionally occupied by women in the field of psychiatry, the history of which is the subject of this chapter.

Feminist historians of medicine have described the way in which the professionalization of medicine (and exclusion of women from qualifying exams) marginalized women's practice of the healing arts.[3] I want to look at the effects of this exclusion on women involved in the care and treatment of the insane, at a time when the appropriateness of medical treatment in cases of insanity was itself a contested issue.

Throughout the eighteenth century, women proprietored private madhouses. Full numbers of women involved in this capacity are difficult to ascertain, but women are named as proprietors in the *Town and Country Registers*, e.g. Esther Burrows (Hoxton), Mary Glenville (Kingsland), Ann Holmes (Islington) and Elizabeth Mullinger (Austin Friars).[4]

The roots of the private madhouse system lay in the seventeenth-century practices of boarding out pauper lunatics at the expense of the parish, and of accommodating more affluent lunatics with local clergy and medical men. Women might inherit houses from their husbands or fathers and some houses passed from mother to daughter, but owing to the system of patronymy such transitions are difficult to trace. Joanna Harris, for example, advertised in *Jackson's Oxford Journal* in 1778 that she had succeeded to the management of Hook Norton, in Oxfordshire, 'which her late mother (Mrs Sarah Minchin) kept with a distinguished reputation for upwards of half a century'.[5]

Ambiguity over whether or not insanity could be regarded as an illness, and a proper subject for medical intervention, facilitated women's continuing involvement in its treatment. Madhouse proprietors, hoping to improve the generally low reputation of private madhouses as places of brutality and corruption, frequently claimed exceptionally high rates of cure resulting from their system of management. But the systems they claimed to have instituted – of tenderness, sympathy and comfort – were calculated to reassure prospective consumers at least as much as to advance popular notions of genuine expertise. The resources needed to operate such a system were those of gentleness, homeliness and compassion – qualities entirely consistent with prevailing concepts of femininity.

Private madhouses, like other trade enterprises, were often family businesses, involving the participation of all members of the family. Thus Thomas Bakewell apologized to readers of his *Domestic Guide in Cases of Insanity* (published anonymously in 1805), for not giving full details of the pharmaceutical remedies he employed, 'consisting of a great number of articles which I am under strong family obligations not to disclose.'[6]

From the mid-eighteenth century onwards private madhouses enjoyed a boom. At the same time, medical men began advancing claims for a medical conception of insanity. These claims to a theoretical understanding of mental disorder challenged the empiricism of non-medical practitioners. Claiming 40 years' experience as a madhouse proprietor, Bakewell argued defensively that:

Some successful practice, and many sleepless nights, occasioned at one time by the noise of the maniac's chain, at another by my anxiety for his recovery, may entitle me to the privilege of giving my opinion, notwithstanding the knowledge and learning displayed in several recent publications on the subject . . . The reader had my full liberty to call me illiterate, provided he does not pronounce me ignorant.[7]

The period 1780–1830 has been described as one in which: 'the definition of masculinity and femininity, together with their social location in work and home, became an arena of conflict.'[8]

Catherine Hall has argued the importance of Evangelical opinion in the formation of a social ideology in which gender expectations became polarized between an outer, hostile masculine world, and an inner, protected, feminine home.[9] These gender expectations were not only proselytized in the writings of groups like the Clapham sect, but became embodied in reformist legislation, An example of relevance here was the passing of prison legislation in the 1780s which outlawed the practice of employing women jailers. Hitherto, women like Ann Wiseman in Reading had succeeded their husbands as prison keepers.[10]

During the early nineteenth century, the proportion of female proprietors fell, although owing to the continuing boom in trade their actual numbers increased (see Table 1).[11] This decline paralleled increasing endorsement by the state of medical claims to expertise in the treatment of insanity. The Madhouses Act of 1828 required medical visitation of all private asylums, and medical superintendence of those with more than 100 patients. As medical training at this time was closed to women, the medicalization of insanity led to a restriction of their role.

Table 1

	Proprietors				Total number of madhouses
	Male		Female		
	no.	%	no.	%	
1807	39	84.78	7	15.22	45
1819	78	85.82	13	14.18	86
1830	110	89.43	13	10.57	107

Historians preoccupied with increasing medical involvement in the madhouse business have paid little attention to the role played by women at this time. Parry-Jones dismisses women's involvement by saying that those women who were involved were generally 'the widows or daughters of former proprietors'.[12] But given the greater longevity of women, this did not necessarily render their contributions negligible. At Witney in Oxfordshire, for example (one of the two houses looked at in detail by Parry-Jones), it meant that for 26 of the 34 years the asylum was open, it was operated by women.[13]

Despite the odds, some women pursued prosperous careers as madhouse keepers during the first half of the nineteenth century. Mrs Mary Bradbury claimed 20 years' experience when she moved in 1836 from Hollywood House, Chelsea (listed in 1830 as having sixteen patients), to the former home of anatomist John Hunter. Here she opened Earl's Court House 'for the recovery of ladies labouring under affections of the mind', an upper-class institution for 25–30 ladies.[14]

Although a visiting physician was appointed (William B. Neville, author of a medical textbook *On Insanity*), the system of treatment was 'moral'. Inmates were encouraged to participate in a varied routine of 'calisthenic exercises': archery, donkey-rides, a mock-fort, see-saws, shuttle-cocks, skipping-ropes and swing-boats were all employed to distract inmates from their mental distress. Henry Halford, then president of the Royal College of Physicians was amongst those who praised the establishment, and Michael Ryan, editor of the *London Medical and Surgical Journal* commented that:

> The greatest praise is due to Mrs. Bradbury for having expended a large amount of capital on this complete and unequalled establishment, and for having devoted it to ladies exclusively.
>
> I can also conscientiously add, that the kind and gentle treatment invariably practised by that lady on her unfortunate inmates is entitled to the highest commendation, which with the advantages of her judicious system of treatment, tend to the restoration of health better than any private abode, however excellent.[15]

Discretion for the upper-class inmates was assured by a private road to Kensington Gardens, and a 14ft wall. The house remained consistently full until Mrs Bradbury's death in 1852, when it was passed to her niece Miss Elizabeth Burney.

One problem in assessing the role played by women in private madhouses is that the name of the licensee does not necessarily indicate the person with greatest responsibility for the day-to-day running of the asylum. Early returns frequently distinguish proprietors from superintendents, but in the reports of the Commissioners in Lunacy, both are listed as 'licensees' without their actual roles being distinguished. Thus, following the death of her husband in 1852, Mrs Newington is listed as the proprietor of Ticehurst Asylum in Sussex, although two of her sons who were medically qualified were responsible for the running of the establishment. More frequently, medical men proprietored madhouses for women, but employed a female superintendent. This pattern was already well established by 1830, when four madhouses in the metropolis are listed as being proprietored by women, and seven more as being proprietored by men, with a female superintendent. Many prominent 'mad-doctors' proprietored more than one house in this way, e.g. Alexander Sutherland (Blacklands House, Chelsea, and Fisher House, Islington), and John Conolly (Wood End Grove, Hayes and Lawn House, Hanwell).[16]

In county asylums, the division of authority between the medical superintendents and matrons was not clearly demarcated, and some women were able to assume positions of influence. Thus Mrs Ellis at Hanwell Asylum in Middlesex was responsible for instituting a policy of employing patients whilst they were confined. Women patients at Hanwell worked in the kitchen, dairy and laundry, cleaned, spun, knitted, sewed, made straw baskets and picked coir. Their products were sold at bazaars, and raised money for an organ for the asylum chapel. Men farmed, gardened, laid bricks, carpentered, painted, made shoes and string, and sewed their own clothes. The visitors were pleased to report in 1835 that 'The inducement to these patients to work is a little indulgence in tea, tobacco and extra diet, but

the value to the institution is more than ten times the cost.'[17]
And a year later they commented that patients were able to
take 'in a great measure the place of servants in the
institution'.[18] This can clearly be seen in the context of 'industrial training' recommended by many middle-class lady philan-
thropists for working-class women: Hannah More (education),
Elizabeth Fry (prisons), Mary Carpenter (ragged schools),
Louisa Twining (workhouses) and Octavia Hill (housing and
charity reform) all recommended such labour.[19]

William Ellis[20] pays many tributes to his wife's skill in handling
patients. Confronted once by two male patients, one of whom
was threatening the other with a knife, she told him:

> she was surprised to find a man, of his talents and under-
> standing, so far forgetting himself as to dispute with the
> other, who, as he knew, had been insane for several years.
> This gratified his self-esteem. He said 'You are right, ma'am;
> I shall take no further notice of him' – and he at once became
> quiet.'

In advocating education for those employed in asylums Ellis
argued that:

> in order that the insane may really be placed under the most
> favourable circumstances, the instruction ought not to be
> confined to our sex . . . I do not mean that females should
> attend a dissecting-room, or enter upon a course of study of
> medicine, but it would be most desirable that they should
> have an opportunity of obtaining a sound and fundamental
> knowledge of the various modes in which diseased action of
> the brain exhibits itself in the conduct, and of the dangers to
> be guarded against, and of the moral treatment which ought
> to be adopted.[21]

But increasingly, matrons came under attack, as medical
superintendents attempted to extend their authority. In 1847
John Conolly argued that:

> where the matron of an asylum is not the wife of the
> superintendent, it would generally be productive of har-

mony to have no matron, but in her stead, a nurse and an assistant nurse in each ward, superintendents in the different workrooms, the storeroom, and laundry; and perhaps a chief nurse overall, whose duty it should be to carry the superintendent's plans into effect on the female side of the house, reporting to him alone all circumstances to call for his attention. The government of the female side of an asylum would then be assimilated to that of the male side, where certainly more order generally prevails, fewer complaints are made by patients, fewer changes take place in the attendants, and fewer disagreements among the officers.[22]

The Commissioners endorsed this in their next report, recommending that matrons should obey all directions given by the medical officer, and vesting sole power of dismissal of both male and female attendants with the male medical superintendents.

Both Conolly and John Charles Bucknill favoured the appointment of superintendents' wives as matrons; incumbent matrons restricted superintendents' occupational mobility, and personal authority could supplement formal powers. Although the Commisioners recommended in general that matrons should be single women or widows of the middle class, they also conceded that, 'where the Medical Superintendent or the Steward is married, it may sometimes be convenient to assign to his Wife (if not incumbered by a family, and supposing her to be *otherwise peculiarly eligible*) the whole or part of the Duties of the Matron.'[23]

Where this was the case, wages were not always paid separately – the matron's salary at Derbyshire County Asylum is listed in 1852 as 'Included with Superintendent's Salary and Allowances'. In general, matrons' wages were far lower than those of the superintendents. The Commissioners recommended that they should be twice the highest wage paid to other female attendants, thereby encouraging matrons to view themselves in relation to other female employees, rather than administrative staff. They recommended matrons' wages should range from £40 to £100 per annum, in contrast to £150 to £500 per annum for superintendents.[24] In practice, yearly wages ranged from £25 to £150 for matrons, and (as the Commissioners recommended) from £150 to £500 for superintendents.[25] The only exception to this was at Hanwell, where both the matron and superintendent were paid £200 per annum.

Mid-century it appears to have been the practice for superintendents of public asylums to manage private madhouses when they retired. William Ellis, Samuel Hitch, John Harris and Thomas Prichard are examples of county asylum superintendents who prospered sufficiently to do this. Not surprisingly, medical officers in public asylums were amongst the most zealous opponents of non-medical proprietors. 'If insanity is a disease requiring medical treatment,' argued John Charles Bucknill, then medical superintendent of Devon County Asylum, 'ladies cannot legally or properly undertake the treatment . . . If private interests are to over-ride public ones, the widow of a clergyman ought on the same principle to hold the rectory of her departed husband, and manage the parochial duties by means of curates.'[26] Increasingly, the Commissioners endorsed this point of view; in 1859 they considered limiting new licences to medical proprietors, and although this plan was rejected, they introduced a rigorous list of questions to be put to prospective proprietors which would favour those applicants with a medical background.

Except for those houses which women inherited from their husbands (like Mrs Allen at High Beech, and Mrs Newington at Ticehurst), houses proprietored by women tended to be small. Warwick House for example, a metropolitan asylum run by Mrs Fleming (and from 1856 by her daughter Mary), was licensed for six patients, and often had only three patients resident at any one time. Few women could afford the large financial outlay required for a larger house, and smaller houses also went some way towards filling what was generally regarded as the greatest gap in institutional provision for the insane – low-cost, genteel treatment for lower-middle-class patients.

In a different context, houses such as these may be seen as one of the many 'surrogate family activities' undertaken by unsupported middle-class women at this time.[27] Like opening a small private school, keeping a madhouse had the advantage that it offered women a chance to retain their own homes, in contrast to some of the other activities open to them (e.g. becoming a lady companion or governess). It is striking that the author of *Familiar Views of Lunacy and Lunatic Life* (1850) uses the analogy of a school to capture the ethos of a small private madhouse.

The experience of women involved in the running of small private madhouses is largely undocumented. The Commissioners comment primarily on cleanliness, order and facilities provided for the patients. Yet running houses of such a small size must have required considerable personal involvement and emotional resources. It was the policy of the Commissioners to restrict the intake of houses run by women to quiet, chronic cases. As John Charles Bucknill and Daniel Hack Tuke[28] commented:

> Some small private asylums with few inmates are well adapted for the continued residence of chronic lunatics needing more care at less cost than can be provided in private dwellings. Such asylums are excellent for the care and detention of chronic lunatics who are not fit for the enjoyment of domestic life, but they do not and cannot offer the means and appliances for the curative treatment of recent cases.

Patients thus remained in the same houses over considerable numbers of years, many of them in need of constant physical care. And women who ran these asylums can seldom have had the satisfaction (and kudos) of sending a patient home.

The Commissioners preferred to restrict houses owned by female proprietors to women patients, However, in 1860 they agreed to allow a male patient to stay at Derwentwater House with Miss Benfield, as he had been under her care for many years, and friends were anxious for him to stay with her.[29]

In the county asylum system, comparable houses existed in asylums which operated the 'cottage system'. Quiet, chronic cases would be boarded out with women in the village, often former nurses and the wives of male attendants. This system enabled women to combine earning money with other responsibilities, such as child care. (John Arlidge notes that 7s–8s might be paid for lodging a patient; female attendants were paid £8–£14 a year, plus board and lodging).[30] But whereas for middle-class women opening a madhouse might be a strategy to maintain their independence, for working-class women and their husbands, lodging lunatic paupers meant their homes became subject to the scrutiny and inspection of the medical superintendents. And whilst female proprietors might leave many of the day-to-day problems of physical care to the attendants, it was to deal with these that working-class women were asked to board patients, and without the protection of the shift system operated inside the asylums.

Throughout the second half of the nineteenth century the trade in lunacy declined. Growing concern over allegations of wrongful confinement put pressure on the government to legislate for the closure of private madhouses. The Lunacy Act of 1890 forbade the Commissioners to issue any new licences.

In a different context, Sally Alexander has argued that an increase in the number of women involved in a trade may indicate its down-grading.[31] Throughout this period the number of women named as licensees of private madhouses increased. In 1855, about one-fifth of all private madhouse proprietors were women, but by 1900 this proportion had risen to nearly half.

This increase does not indicate improved status or greater authority. Increasingly, women found it difficult to operate madhouses on their own. Elizabeth Burney (who succeeded Mrs Bradbury as proprietor of Earl's Court House) had begun to lose patients before Robert Gardiner Hill (a prominent mad-doctor) became co-proprietor in 1865. The Commissioners recorded in 1884 that a Mrs Bishop who had been granted a licence had to return it because she could not find any patients. Lists of licensees indicate a steady increase in the number of houses with mixed proprietorships (see Table 2).[32]

Many licences from the later period contain four or five names. In a climate of growing insecurity, proprietors attemp-

Table 2

	All male	Mixed	All female
1860	85	8	18
1870	71	11	22
1880	66	15	16
1890	49	21	19
1900	35	24	11
1910	33	25	9

ted to ensure a smooth transition of the licence to other members of their family by naming them on the licence. Multiple proprietorship meant each partner invested less in the success or failure of the madhouse. Within this structure, women licensees were subject to the authority of (medically qualified) male partners, much as matrons in public asylums were subject to the authority of medical superintendents.

Only by becoming medically qualified could women begin to regain authority in asylums. The history of women's entry into the medical profession is well known. Here, I am concerned only with women's entry into the field of psychiatry. It is worth noting, however, that the opinions of asylum doctors had been used as authorities to oppose women's entry into the medical profession. *The Journal of Mental Science* frequently carried articles warning of the dangers of mental exertion in women. More famously, Henry Maudsley's article on 'Sex in Mind and Education' in the *Fortnightly Review* (1874) was sharply rebutted by Elizabeth Garrett Anderson.

Favourable articles on work done by female physicians in American asylums in the mid-1880s may have gone some way towards modifying opinion. In 1888 Jane Elizabeth Waterson became the first woman to be granted the Certificate of Psychological Medicine. Women doctors were already employed in asylums (at Holloway Sanatorium, Surrey, and Richmond Asylum, Dublin) when the subject of their right to membership of the Royal Medico-Psychological Association came up in 1893, and members voted 23:7 to admit women.[33]

Local factors seem to have affected whether or not women were employed in county asylums. Thus the LCC, who had difficulty in recruiting staff to their over-full asylums, paid equal wages to women doctors from 1888. Elsewhere, the presence of a superintendent who was sympathetic to women's employment affected appointments. George M. Robertson, of Stirling Asylum wrote several articles in the *Journal of Mental Science*, calling for the employment of female nurses on male wards. In 1905 Stirling was the first asylum to employ two women doctors and Williamina Shaw Dunn, writing in the *Journal of Mental Science* in 1916 thanked Dr Robertson for encouraging her to write.

In county asylums, women remained in the lower ranks of the profession. Where employed, they supervised the female wards, and promotion to more senior positions was barred by their lack of experience on male wards. In private asylums, women doctors had more autonomy. Mary Edith Martin (resident licensee of Bailbrook House, Bath, in 1907) and Constance Charlotte Robertson (assistant MO, Tue Brook Villa, Liverpool, 1905–6) are the first two women doctors I have been able to locate working in the private sector. Two sisters, Bertha May and Annie Mules, who were both medically qualified, became the first women to have independent control of a private asylum when they succeeded their parents to the proprietorship of Court Hall, Kenton, in South Devon.

At least some of these early women psychiatrists identified themselves as feminists. Alice Helen Boyle, for example, acknowledged only the help of two other women doctors – Mary Edith Martin and A. Gertrude Grogan (assistant MO at Fulbourn, Cambridge) – when she published an article in the *Journal of Mental Science* in 1905. She called for the treatment of women by women, although this was only the sixth of seven recommendations concerning the early treatment of nervous and mental cases. She also argued that there should never be so many patients that the medical staff could not know them personally, and for getting rid of red tape. In 1907 Helen Boyle became the first woman to hold office in the Royal Medico-Psychological Association as, ironically, librarian.

Whilst some women psychiatrists may have favoured the treatment of women by women, their psychiatric theories do not appear to have differed radically from those of their male colleagues. Articles by women in the *Journal of Mental Science* reflect a search for somatic explanations for mental disorder which is in keeping with mainstream Edwardian psychiatry. In an article on 'Menstruation in its relationship to Insanity', Sheila M. Ross draws conclusions which are very similar to those drawn earlier by Dr Sutherland in the *West Riding Asylum Report*[34] that disturbed menstruation should be seen as a sympton rather than a cause of insanity.

By the early twentieth century, women had regained some of the ground lost through the professionalization of the treatment of the insane. Yet they worked within a profession, and body of psychiatric theory, which had been constructed by men, and from which it was difficult to deviate at a time when their professional status and respectability were so newly acquired. It is this heritage which feminists working within the psychiatric professions today are struggling to overcome.

7. 'So extremely like parliament': the work of the women members of the London School Board, 1870–1904

Annmarie Turnbull

In 1928 women finally achieved suffrage on the same terms as men. This did not mean, however, that they had not played a part in the political arena prior to that date. Women have always, to a greater or lesser extent, wielded some degree of political power, either formally or informally. But by 1980, more than 50 years later, we had 635 honourable members elected to govern on behalf of us all – of these 615 were men, a mere 20 women. How women have progressed in 50 years!

I will examine the work of the women members of the first elected public body to admit women on the same terms as men, and suggest some of the reasons why our progress has been so slow.

In 1870, as a result of that year's Education Act, local school boards began to be formed to supplement the existing inadequate schemes of voluntary elementary schools, and to set up and administer our new system of elementary schooling. The boards' responsibilities were great: the establishment of a state-financed system to educate Britain's children. As *The Times* commented on the formation of the London School Board, 'No equally powerful body will exist in England outside parliament, if power be measured by influence for good or evil over masses of human beings.'[1] Election to the board was open to women as well as to men. This was the first opportunity ever for female citizens to wield political power officially, and in an area where their expertise was acknowledged and their influence already in evidence.

Yet women did not flock to serve during the 30 years of the school board's existence. Below I consider the work of the 29 who did, and who, along with 302 men, laid the foundations of our educational system, in Britain's most influential school board. By understanding who they were, why they stood for election, what they did, and, perhaps most importantly, what constraints they found in the male political world, we can begin to see why, over a century later, very little has changed.

Women and party politics

As Britain's first woman doctor, Elizabeth Garrett was already a well-known public figure when, on 12 October, 1870 she received a deputation asking her to stand at the forthcoming elections as a candidate for the Marylebone Division of the school board. The deputation comprised the fathers and sons of her patients at the Marylebone Women's Dispensary.

Having already started to chip away at the foundations of one male citadel, she was keenly aware of the significance of what they asked. It was one thing to have proved your ability to minister to the sick in the privacy of a consulting room or hospital ward, but quite another to compete directly with men on public platforms. 'Platform women' were a quite new phenomenon for the people, and besides, Elizabeth dreaded having to make public speeches. She wrote to her friend Emily Davies:

> I dare say when it has to be done I can do it, and it is no use asking for women to be taken into public work and yet wish them to avoid publicity. We must be ready to go into the thing as men do if we go at all, and in time there will be no more awkwardness on our side than there is on theirs.[2]

Emily, already known for her work on behalf of girls' education, was also asked to stand, and the importance of these two women's decision can be seen from the tone of her letter to another friend:

> I am torn in two between rival advisers. My mother and Miss Garrett urge that if a woman is wanted to try it, I ought not to lose time by holding back. My brother insists that it would be *too* audacious to offer to stand for 'the greatest constituency

in the world' without *more* invitation. What do you think? If one could be tolerably sure of a respectable failure, it would be enough. An ignominious and ridiculous defeat would do harm . . . It strikes me as preposterous to think of. But preposterous things sometimes get done.[3]

Preposterous it seemed and newsworthy. The press lavished attention on the 'lady candidates'. As is still common today, their personal appearance, dress, voices and mannerisms were given considerable press coverage.

November and December 1870 were devoted to the elections, and on the day of the polls the results were encouraging: Elizabeth Garrett and Emily Davies both stood at the top of their polls in their divisions (Marylebone and Greenwich). Indeed Miss Elizabeth Garrett MD received the largest number of votes of any candidate: 47,888, to her nearest rival's poll of only 27,858. Thus the two friends joined the 47 men as the elected members of London's first school board. Subsequent elections were held triennially and although the boards were comprised overwhelmingly of men, from the first to the eleventh and final board there were always at least two women members.

From the second board two broad political parties emerged. Members identified themselves, or were identified with, either a 'moderate' or a 'progressive' policy. These labels were in fact only cemented after the creation of the LCC in 1889 but throughout the period two parties did, in reality, operate. Those members who identified with the Tories in parliament and with the protection of voluntary – mainly Church – schools were variously described as the Church, Economical or Moderate Party. Their opponents comprised non-conformists and moderate liberals and were styled the Board or Progressive Party. Additionally there were always a number of independent members. One striking feature of the female board members was their tendency to initiate and support progressive policies. Only three women sat as moderates, the remaining 26 supporting the progressive wing.

The women who sought this public work had already served lengthy apprenticeships in politics. Some, like Elizabeth Garret, Emily Davies, Helen Taylor, Florence Fenwick Miller, were well-known campaigners for women's rights. None were complete novices to the world of committees, debates and public speaking. Prior involvement in a wide range of formal organizations, both political and philanthropic, was a characteristic all shared.

The women's candidatures always had the backing of political organizations. They were generally asked to stand as candidates by an all-male committee, and from these organizations at least, there appears to have been little opposition to them on the grounds of their sex. Indeed, many of the men argued that being female was an asset to their campaigns. Certainly, women candidates were popular with the voters, and were often returned at the top of the polls in their divisions.

Not only could women stand for election, but, if they were ratepayers, they could vote. One London vestry clerk noted that, 'Ladies vote at the school board elections, and they come up in shoals and ask a great many questions.'[4] We don't know how many eligible women used their votes or for whom they voted, but the feminist journals (like *The Englishwoman's Review, Women's Suffrage Journal* and *Women's Penny Paper*) encouraged women to take their responsibilities as electors seriously, regularly covering school board elections and the work of women members. In 1888 an ediortial in the *Women's Penny Paper* pressed the need for women's involvement:

> The London School Board has under its immediate care hundreds of thousands of little children; two-thirds of the whole number are girls, who need a woman's teaching, and infants, who need a woman's care. It has in its pay a vast army of teachers, two-thirds of whom are mistresses of the girls' and infants schools. It is quite impossible for anyone who is unacquainted with the working machinery of the Board to realize how great and how urgent is the necessity for electing members who are just to women.

> Our advice to women electors is, give all your votes to the lady candidate; when there is none, give them to the man who is in favour of Women's Suffrage – it is a tolerably safe test.[5]

Indeed, it was not only party political support that provided the opportunity for women to stand for election.

Women's political networks

Participation in organized feminist activity was a crucial factor in the basic grounding in political work for most of these women. Membership of Women's Suffrage Societies and/or experience in arguing publicly on women's rights was a background shared by at least 15 of the women.

All the female members belonged to the middle or upper classes, as indeed did the vast majority of all school board members. In terms of the school board electorate, managers, members and increasingly teachers, the running of the London education system was firmly dominated by a class that did not use it themselves. However, the spectrum of social origin was nonethelesss quite broad. A former board school teacher (Mary Bridges-Adams) and a titled 'gentle-woman' (Hon. Maude Lawrence) both sat on the final board. Furthermore their own social origin did not necessarily determine the politics of the women. Although middle class themselves, Helen Taylor, Edith Simcox, Alice Westlake and Annie Besant were radical supporters of socialist ideals.

There was no uniformity in their ages or marital status. Many women were in their thirties and forties when they served on the board, but Florence Fenwick Miller was only twenty-two and the youngest ever member when she took her seat, whilst Rosamund Davenport-Hill was seventy-two when she retired after 18 years' continuous service.

Prevailing conventions as to the employment of married women may have some bearing on the marital status of women members. Only six women were married when they took their seats. Of the remaing 23, five were widowed and 16 were single (I've been unable to establish the marital status of two). The antagonism to married women holding responsible positions outside the home was seen when in 1871 Elizabeth Garrett annnounced her engagement to John Anderson. *The Times* suggested that on marriage she should resign from the school board, 'Since a conflict might arise between the right of the husband and the duties of the wife.'[6] At her wedding Elizabeth refused to be 'given away'. Her refusal to bow to convention continued. She remained on the board. Only five years later Elizabeth Surr and Alice Westlake, both married, took their places on the board, apparently with no opposition. Nevertheless, the predominance of single and widowed women suggests that a commitment to the private sphere was still a priority for the married women at least.

It would be misleading to see these women as 29 completely independent and self-sufficient individuals. Gradually during my research I discovered the existence of an important support network amongst the women. They were frequently united by their feminist and party political politics, and also by close friendship.

Once members themselves, women encouraged other women to stand. Alice Westlake and Helen Taylor suggested the idea to Rosamond Davenport-Hill and Elizabeth Garrett encouraged her sister Alice Cowell, Emily Davies and Rosamond Davenport-Hill to stand. Similar examples abound, and it is clear that throughout the 1870s and 1880s, and well into the 1890s this complex support network existed amongst the women members. They often argued, but their shared ideals meant that it was rare for a woman to attempt election without the support and encouragement of past or serving female members. In fact, so keen were the women members to ensure that their sex's interests would be represented on every board, that they trained possible successors before retiring from office. Discouraged with the work herself, Edith Simcox noted in her journal:

> I have almost made up my mind not to stand again for the School Board. The remaining year and a half that one has to serve in it I want to spend in quite mastering the work, training a successor, practising speaking on subjects I care about much.[7]

Emily Davies noted bitterly after the defeat of the woman standing as her successor, that, 'It is vexing to have lost

Greenwich, Isa worked very hard for Miss Guest, and heard a great deal of talk – among other things that I did not fight enough for needlework but left it to an old bachelor.'[8]

What was the contribution of these women to the work of the London School Board? There is every reason to believe that women took their responsibilities on the board very seriously. One historian's comments are misleading. Peter Gordon writes:

> A characteristic of all types of female participation in this work was its short-lived and spasmodic nature . . . to take one example, during the thirty three years of existence of the London School Board, only half the lady members served for more than a term of three years.[9]

What he fails to point out, however, is that three years' service was also a characteristic of half of the male members.

The demands of school board work were great. Weekly attendance at the afternoon meetings at the board's headquarters, first at the Guildhall and in later years at offices on the Embankment, were the minimum. During her nine years' service Helen Taylor scarcely missed a meeting whilst Rosamund Davenport-Hill never once missed a meeting in 15 years. Their conscientious attendance was frequently cited by the supporters of women members during their re-election campaigns.

As the scope and range of elementary schooling grew, so did the work for board members. The ever-increasing sub-committees demanded much time. Margaret Eve, for example, was a member of eleven such committees. Additionally, there were managers meetings, 'B' meetings (for consulting the parents of truanting children), and school visits. There was often much extra work. Helen Taylor held four public meetings a year to keep her constituents informed of her school board activities. She and many other members organized and ran committees for feeding, clothing and arranging outings for local children, and there were interviews with local teachers and heads to hear their troubles. Reports in Edith Simcox's journal reveal the time she spent involved in school board activities. Her rare mention in the official board minutes and reports belies her true commitment to the work. On 9 March 1880 she

> reached Mortimer Street at 9, looked round, then to Hart St
> to see about Pupil and Assistant teacher, then to Vere St for
> drawing examination – surprised to find that the second step
> included geometry: then saw the Visitor and received report
> of street cases caught by other visitors, Managers' Meeting,
> made Mrs Buxton's acquaintance, then set off for the Rota,
> Works Committee and Educational Endowments Etc. –
> home reading Blackwood en route, wrote several letters and
> read beginning of Froude's History of Henry VIII for another
> Club Lecture.[10]

There was no payment of any kind, not even expenses, for this work, and although many of the women had no worries on this score, it is still a point of significance not only in explaining the predominance of wealthy men on the board but also the absence of working-class members. Edith confided to her diary her disappointment at having some articles refused by a journal: 'I wanted to earn money for the Notice B meetings and other necessary expense that comes from being on the board.'[11]

Sexual politics on the board

That the women members found life on the board with their male colleagues difficult emerged again and again during my research. Women were outsiders and had to adjust to a male-created political world, an adjustment that was not easy, and which some of the women did not finally want to make. When Elizabeth Garrett and Emily Davies arrived to take their seats at the first board meeting they were asked to sit apart from the male members. This they refused to do, and sat instead with the main body. Elizabeth noted:

> The new chairman recognised us, no one else had done, by
> begining Ladies and Gentlemen. I felt the atmosphere to be
> decidedly hostile, but of course that is not surprising, and it is
> not a bad discipline to find it so after the intoxication of one's
> 47,000.[12]

That this antagonism was purely on the grounds of their sex is obvious. In his recollections of the London School Board one member, Thomas Gautry, reports an exchange between Helen Taylor and a fellow member John Rodgers, 'She exclaimed "So Mr Rodgers, you would not allow us poor women any sphere". He retorted "Oh yes, I would; get a house full of children, then stay at home and mind them".'[13] Her uncompromising adherence to her ideals, for example in the question of the proper use of endowments, and the abolition of school fees and corporal punishment, made life difficult for her on the board. She referred to this in election addresses. On one occasion in 1882 she is reported as having declared that in her 6 years on the board, by standing firm on her principles, 'She had had to bear a great deal of what was not pleasant for a lady to bear, both from her colleagues on the Board and on the occasion of her last election.'[14] In another speech she declared her belief that no woman 'with womanly feeling and a comfortable home of her own' would stand for the board if she knew what she must face on it.

In contrast to the assertive Helen Taylor, Rosamond Davenport-Hill never spoke during her first 6 months of board meetings, and was always an infrequent contributor to debates, which she often regarded as useless and time-wasting. Yet she too recalled the hostility towards the nine women of the 1879 board and the scant respect shown to their opinions. Her habit of sitting quietly knitting during meetings annoyed some of her male colleagues, one of whom tried to have her actions moved out of order. When the subject was raised at an election meeting she retorted that it was the first time she had heard a woman complained of for using her tongue too little and her hands too much.

Florence Fenwick Miller and Elizabeth Surr were also members of the 1879 board. Like Helen Taylor they stood firmly by their personal principles, and would not adhere strictly to progressive party line if they did not consider that doing so was in the best interests of London's children. For this they were repeatedly chided in the *School Board Chronicle*. In one editorial it commented:

Mrs Surr takes an exaggerated view of the seriousness of the difficulties she has encountered. We wish she could find herself able to go on with the battle. This excellent lady, and some of the other lady members of the Board, have shown much lack of appreciation of the true elements and conditions of warfare in public life.[15]

Florence Fenwick Miller had taken her seat on the 1879 board in a flurry of publicity. On marriage to a Mr Ford, in 1877 she had decided to keep her name, a move unprecedented in Britain (except in occasional cases amongst the peerage). The board's chairman took legal advice before he would call out her name on the division lists as Mrs Fenwick Miller, and an attempt was made to upset the following election which she fought using that name. In school board matters also she was never afraid of standing by her own ideals. Her actions moved the *School Board Chronicle* to comment: 'Mrs Fenwick Miller can see no struggle going on in School Board world, worth a moment's consideration, except the comparatively trivial matters in dispute between herself and what she describes as the "official ring".'[16]

Helen Taylor, too, was single minded in the face of what she saw as wrong-doing, and her persistent agitations about the appalling mistreatment of children in some industrial schools brought her to the centre of a scandal. In 1882 she was sued for libel by Thomas Scrutton who chaired the Industrial Schools Committee. On the fourth day of the trial she agreed to pay him £1,000 rather than withdraw what she had said, or apologize for saying it. Emma Maitland (a member for 9 years) believed 'men look first to what is expedient and then to what is right, while women look first to what is right and then to what is expedient.'[17] This was simplistic, certainly, but, viewing these women's actions from a feminist perspective, the rejection by some women of the accepted rules of male-dominated politics required great courage and persistence.

That they were sometimes victimized because of their sex is indisputable. Despite the overall acceptance of the prevalent male-defined system by women like Margaret Eve and Rosamond Davenport-Hill, it nevertheless did not exclude them from male hostility. Even towards the close of the century women's presence was still sometimes openly resented. Visiting Christ's Hospital School on board business, Margaret Eve was refused admittance by the Almoners on account of her sex. When she reported this to the board several of her male colleagues supported the Almoners. A majority of the members voted to persist with their chosen representative, but not before Ruth Homan had denounced the objecting members for their conduct.

Even after 30 years of being in the public eye, women continued to be seen as anomalies. The final board was as rigid in its adherence to a sexual double standard as the first had been. When it was reported that Honnor Morten had been observed walking down Fleet Street smoking a cigarette, she was forced to resign her seat.

Women's work for women

These women made a large contribution to the moulding of a school curriculum that was acknowledged as the most progressive and adventurous in Britain. But here I want to show their involvement in other issues – issues that directly and indirectly concerned the status of women, and challenged male power. Whether women chose to try to ignore the structures of gender altogether, to actually fight against sex roles, or indeed to support them – these actions were always made against a background where men firmly held the balance of power. They could only react to an educational framework already created by men. It is important to bear this in mind when examining the variety of methods and tactics women used in the political arena.

Questions involving the principle of justice between women and men, girls and boys, were inherent in much of the work tackled by the board. Inequality was apparent at every turn. Women members repeatedly argued for parity of treatment between females and males as pupils, pupil teachers, head teachers, managers, clerks, inspectors, school cleaners – in short, at every level of school board activity. They were not often successful in such attempts, but it seems likely that without the presence of women on the board the questioning of sexual differentiation would rarely have occurred at all. Below, I outline a number of the cases that arose during the board's history.

On the second board Jane Chessar and Alice Cowell, the only female members, intervened when the Lawrence scholarships were established to allow a number of board school pupils the opportunity to continue their education. It was proposed that whilst boys winning the scholarships should receive £7 each, it was appropriate that girls should be given only £6. The women's opposition to this groundless anomaly was successful, and the scholarships were equalized.

Women members sought to protect and promote the employment of their sex in educational work. Alice Westlake ensured that women doctors would be present at the medical examinations of school girls. On the third board Elizabeth Surr, Helen Taylor and Alice Westlake all supported Florence Fenwick Miller's motion that no male teacher should be appointed as a head teacher in charge of a girl's department. Although the motion was carried, the actual success of these women must be judged against an incident of the fifth board. Florence Fenwick Miller brought it to the board's notice that a male head had been appointed to a girls' school and attempted to have the place filled by a woman. Her move failed.

In 1881 an attempt was made to remove married women teachers with children under two from the board's employ. The move failed this time, but was a frequent tactic in education, as Alison Oram's chapter shows. As a result of this threat to women, Florence Fenwick Miller and Helen Taylor helped found the 'Metropolitan Board Mistresses Association' to protect women teachers' interests.

In December 1883 Henrietta Muller proposed that the board employ women clerks. Cleverly, she argued that women, being traditionally paid less than men, would be cheaper to employ. Her mixture of justice and economy found much sympathy and her motion was carried by 27 to 6.

In reality, she, along with many other women members, supported equal pay. Only 2 weeks after her success in getting women clerks employed by using an argument against equal pay, she unsuccessfully moved a motion (seconded by Helen Taylor) that female junior teachers should be paid the same as males. Women's wages on the board were only two-thirds of men's wages and the equal pay issue was returned to again and again in the board's history – but with little success. Honnor Morten, a campaigner for equal pay declared herself 'not prepared to wait until the river of man's wants dried up'.

In 1886 whilst serving on the sixth board Rosamond Davenport-Hill opposed another injustice to women teachers contained in the board's pension scheme. Being liable to leave the board's service earlier than men, in order to have children, women stood to lose all their contributions to the superannuation scheme. As a result of her objections a clause was added to the effect that women might be awarded something if they left on the grounds of ill-health, but not otherwise, 'For it was agreed, when they left to be married, which was frequently the case, they would not require a pension, their position having been on the contrary improved.'[18]

Whilst the women accepted much of the contemporary social order, and to some extent the traditonal archetype of women as pacifiers and supporters, they nevertheless added a new dimension – a notion of the maturity and responsibilty of women. They therefore fought consistently for improvements in the social conditions experienced by females. Some were also impassioned feminists and/or socialists, rejecting many aspects of the Victorian social world, at the level of both working-class life, and middle-class conventions. They spent their time on the board attempting to change both spheres.

These were all atypical women seeing themselves as exceptional path-breakers in a traditionally male field, and regarded as such by their contemporaries. A woman clerk writing to the *Telegraphist* in 1885, after an attack on women clerks, commented, 'We are not Amazons, nor yet Miss Helen Taylors, and most of us do not claim to be strong willed.'[19] But – and the but is crucial – she had been moved to write a letter arguing her right to fair treatment as an employee. The very fact that women could be seen to openly challenge the male political monopoly must have been a subtle, but significant inducement for some women to re-evaluate their own social position and its possibilities, and to start to resist the accepted patterns of male dominance in their own lives.

Recalling the first meeting of the school board, Elizabeth Garrett wrote:

> I was sorry afterwards I said so little, but I was really a little awed by the whole thing being so extremely like parliament, and by having to spring up so quickly to get a hearing after someone else had finished. The whole difficulty of speaking is concentrated in that moment of swift self-assertion.[20]

Henrietta Muller also was keenly aware of the extent of women's silence and the necessity for ending it.

> Women must learn the difficult and disagreeable task of saying fearlessly what they think, even if it is not very welcome, men must learn the equally disagreeable task of hearing it.[21]

Some women board members succeeded in that task, but women today still have only a small voice in political decision-making. Many successful women politicians deny that being female has posed any particular problems for them. 'It's not because of your sex you get anywhere, it's because of your ability as a person,'[22] said Margaret Thatcher in 1979. Whilst Shirley Williams's comment on being the only woman member of the last Labour cabinet – 'I'm just one of the boys'[23] strikes a note of complacency that would make at least one of the London School Board members turn in her grave. 'Bless us! It's a tough and toilsome business,' exclaimed Elizabeth Garrett during her election campaign. It is still so tough and so toilsome to challenge male power that very few women even make the attempt.

8. Serving two masters? The introduction of a marriage bar in teaching in the 1920s

Alison M. Oram

The problems women workers face today – public spending cuts, mass unemployment, opposition to married women's employment – are not new. During the economic recessions of the 1920s and 1930s there was a huge reduction in government spending, widespread unemployment and an outcry against married women working. In many occupations married women were actually sacked, just because they were married, or else lost their jobs when they got married.

In the present economic recession women have suffered particularly badly from unemployment. Between 1974 and 1978 the official rate of unemployment in Britain increased three times faster for women than for men.[1] Married women have fared worst of all. They are not acknowledged as proper workers by the government or by employers and are being pushed back into the home which is seen as their first responsibility.

How does this happen? Why are married women always the first to lose their jobs? In this chapter I am going to answer this question by looking at married women teachers in the 1920s, showing why local education authorities introduced a marriage bar and why they thought they were justified in doing so.

In the early part of this century it was not usual for middle-class women, or even working-class women, to be employed outside the home after marriage. Despite this, a significant minority of women elementary school teachers were married – 12 per cent before the First World War – and married women were encouraged to return to teaching during the war, so that by 1921 more than 15 per cent of women teachers were married. Some local authorities operated a marriage bar before the first World War, but it was only in the early 1920s that the vast majority of education committees clamped down on the employment of married women. The regulations which were introduced differed slightly from one area to another, but they generally combined a ban on appointing married women to teaching posts with a rule providing for the resignation of women teachers on marriage. Many local authorities also dismissed married women teachers who were already employed.

The immediate cause of the widespread introduction of a marriage bar was the economic crisis of 1921 which enforced cuts in public expenditure. LEAs, who wanted to create jobs for unemployed training college leavers as well as reduce expenditure, thought that a marriage bar would serve both these purposes, although they usually alleged that married women teachers were less efficient when they passed the legislation. Public opinion, as expressed in the press and in letters from ratepayers to the local authority, also encouraged action against married women teachers. These factors were reinforced by the prevailing patriarchal belief that a married woman's place was at home, not out in paid work; a belief which gave men greater control over women and consequent material benefits. I am going to go on to discuss each of these influences in greater detail, but first I want to introduce the underlying ideas which I use to explain this complex situation.

It is evident that married women teachers were used as a reserve army of labour[2] by the education authorities – that is to say, they were a group which were easily brought into employment when there was a shortage of teachers and dismissed without much difficulty during a period of recession and over-supply. Their particularly vulnerable position was due to the pre-existing male domination of women in the family, and particularly the notion of the man as breadwinner earning a family wage.

The attack on married women teachers in the 1920s was also the beginning of a series of measures carried out by men in response to feminist gains during and just after the First World War. As a result of feminist struggles women had obtained the vote, access to the universities, a Sex Disqualification (Removal) Act which allowed women to enter all the professions except the civil service on the same terms as men, and wider opportunities in the labour market generally. The anti-feminist backlash of the 1920s and 1930s was a renewed attempt to assert male power and restrict women's independence. The marriage bar is a concrete example of male power operating through overt restrictions on women's activities. How were the local authorities able to bring in such regulations?

It is important to emphasize that education committees were overwhelmingly male political institutions. Although one or two women were normally elected, they had difficulty in making their presence felt.[3] LEAs had quite a lot of freedom to organize the staffing of their schools as they wished, and did not need the approval of the Board of Education (central government) to introduce a marriage bar. In any case there is evidence to show that in 1922 and 1923 the Board also believed that the exclusion of married women was the best way of solving economy and staffing problems. In an internal note a top official observed that 'It is common ground that the elimination of married women teachers whose husbands are able to support them is the most obvious and natural way of mitigating the extensive unemployment of young teachers which is almost inevitable this autumn.'[4] In public, however, the board took a neutral stand on the question, and in doing so was able to avoid criticism.

The Sex Disqualification (Removal) Act of 1919 should have protected married women teachers from dismissal. It stated: 'A person shall not be disqualified by sex or marriage from the exercise of any public function or from being appointed or holding any civil or judicial office or post or from entering or assuming or carrying on any civil profession or vocation.' However, in a series of court cases brought in the 1920s by married women teachers claiming unfair dismissal, this Act was almost totally disregarded. The main argument in these cases concerned the proper 'educational' grounds for dismissal. The Sex Disqualification (Removal) Act was not considered to be relevant by the male judiciary, and so was even less effective than today's Sex Discrimination Act. After a case brought in 1922 by a group of married women teachers in the Rhondda,[5] it was established that married women teachers could be dismissed if the reason was to promote the efficiency of education in the area. Further test cases in 1925[6] confirmed that LEAs were quite free to dismiss married women employed in their schools, unless the LEA had acted in a particularly corrupt or unorthodox way. Married women teachers in Church (voluntary) schools had slightly more protection since LEAs did not directly control their staffing

So local authorities had almost complete powers to bring in a marriage bar if they wanted to. Although in theory women's jobs were protected by the law, in practice the law was interpreted in the interests of the local authorities. Thus, the local state (the LEAs), the national state (the Board of Education) and the legal system were all working against married women teachers and indirectly in the interests of men by strengthening their position in the household and in the labour market.

If we look closely at the most commonly used justifications for the exclusion of married women from teaching, it is clear that from the local authorities' point of view, a marriage bar was not even a particularly effective way of saving money or reducing unemployment.

The financial collapse of 1921 followed the short-lived post-war boom and there were huge cuts in public expenditure, including education. There was a halt to the reduction in class sizes and LEAs were put under considerable pressure to reduce spending in other ways. Staffing standards were reduced, with few or no vacancies for college leavers, so that a whole generation of newly trained teachers were without job prospects. This climate of economy and the fear of unemployment led to demands that married women should be sacked because they were in jobs which other people 'deserved' more.

The most immediate and pressing problem for the local authorities, and the issue which the general public felt most strongly about, was the unemployment of young teachers fresh from training college. It is important to point out here that most of the unemployed teachers were young women – married women teachers were *not* accused of taking men's jobs. In the civil service, for comparison, women workers were bitterly attacked – as women – by unemployed ex-servicemen. The oversupply of newly qualified teachers was first felt in the summer of 1922 and continued in the following years. It was alleged that in London alone there were 800 certificated teachers without work, and letters and articles in the national press complained of the disgraceful situation in which young people were encouraged to train and then could not find jobs. A letter in the *Daily Mail* suggested, 'If there are 800 certificated teachers unemployed it is time that all married women teachers whose husbands have employment should be forced to resign.'[7] This was a common reaction by both press and public. Press cuttings and letters were collected, filed and discussed by local education officials, showing that these views were taken very seriously. LEAs were considerably embarrassed by the problem of a large number of unemployed teachers who originally had been encouraged to enter the profession, and the immediate solution was to compel married women to make way for them.

The attempt to eliminate one group of teachers in order to create jobs for the unemployed disguised the lack of long-term planning of the supply of teachers. It was a short-sighted policy, a once-and-for-all measure to cope with the crisis and in fact might well discourage young women from entering the profession. Basically, the debate was about whether one group of teachers had a greater right to employment than another group. The married women were already employed, sometimes for a considerable time, but due to the prevailing ideology of a married woman's lesser right to work they were still more vulnerable than the group of inexperienced young teachers.

By reducing the number of married women teachers, local authorities thought that as well as creating vacancies for unemployed college leavers, they could also save money on staffing costs. Public criticism of the cost of employing married women centred on absenteeism caused by pregnancy and looking after sick children and husbands. Critics argued that the cost of supply teachers and sick pay was excessive. In London the provision of paid maternity leave (unique among local authorities) was also attacked.

> For reasons of economy her services should be dispensed with, at the present time . . . Each maternity case alone costs the LCC nearly £100. There is corresponding expense when the teacher mother is absent through illness of her family.[8]

Education officials were also conscious of the higher salaries paid to married women, who formed a group of older, more experienced and senior teachers. However, they generally did not stop to work out the financial costs and benefits of a marriage bar, and where they did do so, as in London, their findings were ignored by the full council, anxious to bring in a marriage bar because of political pressure.

Even in those areas where many married women teachers were employed, the savings to be made by dismissing them were negligible. If senior married women teachers were sacked, other teachers would eventually have to be promoted to take their place – it was inevitable that some teachers should be older and more highly paid. Furthermore, a 1920 report on London teachers showed that married women were only marginally more likely to take time off because of illness than single women.[9] Only about one married woman out of 33 was absent for confinement per annum and married women teachers had very small families.

It was roughly estimated that the employment of married women teachers cost the council £10,000 a year more than single women because of absence and maternity leave. Against this, however, has to be set the cost of introducing a marriage bar. In London the average service of women who did resign on marriage was 8 years and of those who did not, 17 years. If women were required to retire on marriage the value of their training and extra years of service would be thrown away and to compensate for this more teachers would have to be trained every year. The cost of these factors generally outweighed the cost of the absenteeism of married women teachers.[10]

Although the pressures of teacher unemployment and public

spending cuts were the real catalyst for the widespread introduction of a marriage bar in 1922, local authorities frequently
alleged that married women were less efficient teachers, since
this was a more acceptable reason for dismissal, both legally
and morally.

It was said that the school could not be the chief centre of
interest for a married woman in the way it was for an unmarried
teacher, and she could not devote as much time to her
profession. However, this charge of inefficiency could not be
supported. London school inspectors who were asked to report
on the efficiency of married women teachers, pointed out that
married women were more experienced, had a wider view of
life and probably a greater knowledge of children. On the other
hand, family ties meant married women could give less time to
their work out of school, and their attendence was less regular –
especially during the childbearing period. The general feeling
among the inspectors was that marriage was irrelevant to the
ability of women teachers.[11]

Even from the local authorities' point of view, the marriage
bar was not justified in terms of the problems it was intended to
solve. It did help to ease the immediate problem of teacher
unemployment but only by throwing another group of teachers
out of work. Why then, were such widespread regulations
introduced against married women teachers?

Economic causes alone are not an adequate logical explanation for the introduction of a marriage bar. Public pressure,
based on the prevailing ideology of a married woman's proper
place, which was shared by education committees, the educational press and the general public alike, forced the local
authorities to take action in this way. The above arguments
against the employment of married women teachers were taken
up in letters from the general public to the press and the LEAs,
and tended to escalate into a general attack on married women
teachers. It was argued as a self-evident truth that married
women should not work outside the home and this provided a
context in which the abrupt dismissal of long-serving teachers
could be seen as natural, justified and even praiseworthy. If we
examine more closely the different strands of these assumptions

about women's 'natural duties' then it becomes apparent how the dismissal of married women teachers provided advantages for individual men in the home as husbands, as well as in the school as teachers.

In these letters it was assumed that for women, marriage was a job in itself, and that they should not have another job outside the home.

> If marriage as a profession does not appeal to a woman she should remain single.[12]

> the married woman teacher whose place is home and who ought to make way for the single girl who has to fight her way in the world.[13]

The housewife's position also entailed financial dependence on the husband.

> No injustice will be done, because the men who married them should be made to do their duty as 'men' and 'citizens' and maintain their wives in their proper sphere – the home.[14]

> The husbands should be compelled to keep these women not the public.[15]

The immorality of two incomes going into one home was condemned, and women teachers were accused of greed and selfishness.

> Many have incomes which together with their husbands' amount to nearly four figures.[16]

> There is little doubt that the love of a double income is at the bottom of the desire of women teachers not to resign their posts when they marry.[17]

The idea that a wife could earn a salary undermined the husband's ability to claim a higher 'family wage' in order to support his wife and children, and also eroded the advantages which this gave him in the home.

If married women were forced back into the home as full-time housewives, then men – their husbands – stood to gain more and better personal services from them. Of course the loss of the woman's job did mean a sharp decline in income for the married couple. Against this, however, should be considered the changing power relation of husband and wife. With the loss of her job, the married woman lost status and autonomy and became financially dependent on her husband, and more personally identified with him and the marriage. It is significant that in the debate, the married woman's function as housewife was emphasized at least as much as her role as mother, showing the importance that was attached to the relationship of wife to husband.

There was, however, considerable emphasis on the married woman teacher's role as actual or potential mother. Doubts were cast upon the character of married women teachers unless they became full-time mothers.

> After the birth of the child, the woman teacher, if she resumes her duties, must forgo the happiness of looking after her baby and entrust it to another – either this or the couple must agree not to have children. A woman who is content to adopt either of these alternatives cannot be said to have a real love of children.[18]

Widespread alarm at the falling birthrate, especially in the middle class, fostered this prescription of women's role as mothers. It was pointed out in the press that married women teachers had very small families, although physically and mentally they were said to be 'the cream of British womanhood'.

Restrictions on the employment of married women teachers meant that their husbands received more services in the home and also the basis for more personal power in the relationship. Only the single woman had the right to work; in marriage she had to depend on a man, with an identity restricted to wife and mother. This attack on women's financial independence from men was particularly significant in the case of teachers since they did earn relatively good salaries. These factors were not necessarily consciously in the minds of the men who decided policy, but the prevailing set of ideas about women's place being in the home which influenced them in their decisions was based on actual benefits to men.

In the face of this attack on their right to work, how could married women teachers respond? Most women teachers belonged to the National Union of Teachers, then, as now, the largest and most powerful teachers' union. Although the union was against the marriage bar and did take action to help married women teachers, it was unable to properly challenge the policy, because it did not want to alienate its male members. We can see how the male-controlled NUT sidestepped the issue by comparing its actions with those of the National Union of Women Teachers, the union which identified itself as feminist.

The NUT helped married women teachers threatened with dismissal in three ways. It made representations on behalf of individuals to their local authorities; it took or threatened to take legal action against LEAs in cases where this was likely to be successful; and it gave very limited support to efforts in the House of Commons to get legislation passed to protect married women teachers.

The national machinery of the NUT enabled local associations to exert pressure on behalf of individuals threatened with dismissal. Action was taken in many districts, but it is impossible to estimate how many married women were helped in this way. The NUT felt there was a greater chance of success if they intervened on moral grounds where a teacher had given long service and had only a short time to go before being entitled to her pension, or on compassionate grounds where the husband was unable to support the family.[19] However, there were cases of the local NUT official actually supporting the marriage bar.

The union was prepared to bring a test case in defence of married women teachers if this was likely to be successful. The NUT investigated the case of the 64 Rhondda married women teachers but refused to help them because they were advised by lawyers that there was little chance of success. The Rhondda women were very angry about this lack of support. They pointed out that the union normally used all its legal resources in tenure cases, but despite the fact that they had been union members for many years and their posts and pensions were in danger, protection had been withheld.[20] The women themselves thought their jobs were important enough to take the case to court at their own expense but they lost. The NUT did support the Poole married women teachers in 1925 as a test case, but although the teachers won initially, the case was lost on appeal.

Obviously the NUT was justified in only supporting cases which had a chance of success, but despite these legal defeats the union was reluctant to push for fresh legislation. The NUT gave limited support to the Married Women (Employment) Bill sponsored by NUSEC (the National Union of Societies for Equal Citizenship) in 1927 which failed. The NUT also took part in a deputation to the Board of Education later in the same year, but only after considerable pressure from its London members, a high proportion of whom were married women.[21]

Although security of tenure for teachers was one of the main aims of the NUT, the union never fought the marriage bar as a matter of principle, and it was seen as a peripheral problem affecting only a few members. Some action was taken to defend married women teachers' jobs, but the leadership crucially failed to challenge the view that married women had a lesser right to employment. The union Executive, composed largely (around 80 per cent) of men, said they were afraid that any wholesale commitment or intervention might arouse divided opinion among the membership. However, resolutions were passed at conferences every year between 1924 and 1927 condemning the dismissal of women teachers on marriage,[22] so it seems that the rank and file (two-thirds of whom were women) were firmly against the marriage bar.

While a lot of men teachers did oppose the marriage bar there were undoubtedly many who were not sorry to see women teachers' professional sphere restricted since it meant less competition for them. Some individuals and groups of men teachers, especially the National Association of Schoolmasters, were actively attacking women's position in teaching during the 1920s, by campaigning against equal pay, against women heads in mixed schools and against women teaching boys over 7. The exclusion of married women teachers would not directly benefit men by providing more jobs, since most of the unemployed teachers were young women. But the higher posts, the headships of mixed departments or schools, would be filled less often by women if they had to resign halfway through their careers, and this, combined with the reorganization of the schools, did provide more opportunities for men. Throughout the 1920s and 1930s there was a small but steady increase in the proportion of men teachers generally, and of men in the senior posts. The general status of women teachers as professionals was also diminished by the marriage bar – they were seen as having a fill-in job, rather than a life-long career like men. Men teachers did not neccessarily calculate the benefits which they would gain by a marriage bar. But they did have an interest in supporting it in order to enforce the continuance of male domination – within the profession, in the household, and more widely in society.

Women teachers' attempts through the NUT to resist men's restrictions on their right to work, were thus thwarted by the male-orientated structure and aims of the union. During the early 1920s many active women unionists broke away from the NUT (originally over equal pay), in order to fight with other feminist teachers in the National Union of Women Teachers. Despite a very small membership, concentrated mainly in London, the NUWT was actively involved in the campaign to defend married women teachers' rights. Some of its activities were similar to those of the NUT, on a smaller scale, but it was much more concerned to press its members' views on the policy-making institutions.

The NUWT tried to help individual women teachers in cases of dismissal, but it did not have the resources to make much impression on the problem. The union sent a deputation to the Home Secretary in 1923 and prompted the questions which were asked in the House of Commons.[23] They also worked with other feminist organizations to publicize the arguments in favour of married women teachers' employment and tried to influence central government. One particularly important activity of the NUWT was to sponsor the election of a representative, Agnes Dawson, to the London County Council in order to work for the removal of the marriage bar and generally watch over the interests of women teachers. Her efforts eventually helped to get the bar abolished in London in 1935.[24]

The NUWT argued against the bar from both a feminist and professional point of view. It emphasized the fact that the marriage bar was an encroachment on individual liberty, something the NUT was not concerned about. The NUWT also argued that the dismissal of women on marriage was a waste of their work experience, as well as the expense of their training. It also robbed the children of the invaluable contribution of teachers who had experienced a wider and fuller life.

Despite the small size of the NUWT, its energetic campaign did make some public impression out of all proportion to its size, by getting the question raised in the House of Commons and at the London County Council. The NUWT made the marriage bar into a feminist issue and upheld women's right to work and to financial independence.

So far I have looked in detail at the ways in which a marriage bar aided LEAs and indirectly gave more power to men, particularly to husbands and other teachers, but also generally. Now I want to fit this into a broader framework to explain why this attack on married women teachers took place in the early 1920s.

Married women teachers did act as a reservoir of teaching power which was used by the state in periods of shortage and dispensed with when there was an oversupply in times of economic recession. During the First World War large numbers of married women were encouraged to re-enter the teaching service to ease the shortage of teachers, and existing marriage bars were relaxed in many areas. The Board of Education recognized the contribution of married women teachers by making special provision for them in the Superannuation Act of 1918.

But within a few years the elimination of married women teachers was seen by local authorites and the Board of Education as 'the most obvious and natural way' of dealing with the problem of unemployed young teachers and the economic crisis of 1921–2. Married women teachers formed a more disposable group than even young inexperienced teachers.

During 1922 and 1923 many LEAs either reintroduced regulations against married women teachers or passed them for the first time. By 1926 about three quarters of all local authorities operated some sort of marriage bar, providing for the resignation of women teachers on marriage and in many cases involving the dismissal of serving teachers. In Durham, for example, 300 married women teachers were dismissed before the beginning of the new school year in September 1922. In England and Wales as a whole, at least 2,500 married women had been sacked by August 1922, and their numbers fell from 18,600 in 1921, or 16 per cent of all women teachers, to 14,400 or 12 per cent in 1927.[25] So, although the marriage bar did not eliminate married women teachers, it did mean that they were less likely to be able to continue in employment. However, many local authorities soon found it necessary to continue to employ married women as supply teachers, work which was intermittent, without prospects and without security. Thus, the marriage bar made the position of all married women teachers much more precarious and marginal.

In 1929 the new Labour government proposed to raise the school leaving age, and efforts were made to expand training facilities to meet the need for extra teachers. In a 1929 circular the Board of Education suggested that LEAs should 'temporarily at any rate' suspend their marriage bars and that married women teachers who had been forced to resign should be invited back into teaching.[26] In a letter to *The Times* the London Teachers' Association attacked this arbitrary treatment of married women teachers.

> It has become the custom of LEAs to regard married women teachers as the means whereby they can solve staffing difficulties, dismissing them when there is a surplus of available teachers and re-engaging them when there is an insufficiency of supply.[27]

The local authorities were able to get rid of married women teachers so easily because their unemployment was hidden by their 'return to the home' – which was the place they really should be according to patriarchal ideology. Very much the same thing is happening today.

During and just after the First World War, women, especially middle-class women, had made many important economic and political gains. Women had entered new occupations in large numbers, particularly office work and the civil service, and had gained some access to the professions. The Sex Disqualification (Removal) Act promised to safeguard their position. The divorce laws were being reformed and contraception was more freely available. Older women had of course won the vote. There was still a strong feminist consciousness and women were obviously more independent than before the war.

The reaction to this began soon after the war when the conditions for men to reassert their power were established. This was done through some very overt restrictions, like the introduction of a marriage bar, which operated not only in teaching but also in the civil service and many commercial firms. The laws which protected married women's rights, were simply disregarded, as today. The gains which men stood to make fed the powerful and pervasive ideas which told women that marriage – looking after a man – and motherhood – looking after their children for the state – was the highest occupation to which they could aspire. Women were told that it was psychologically unhealthy to reject this role, and to want to work outside the home – especially if they acquired status and a good salary with the consequent challenge to male power.

Part four

Sexuality

Introduction

As feminist historians our attempts to uncover the origins of our oppression have led us to see all areas of our lives as worthy of investigation. We have accordingly taken up the challenge of the Women's Liberation Movement's slogan that 'the personal is political' and looked at that most intimate of all areas, sexual relations. Our investigations show that sexuality is a major arena in which the subordination of women is enacted. Indeed, in her paper in this section Sheila Jeffreys argues that the maintenance of heterosexuality is a crucial strategy which male supremacy employs to continue the oppression of women.

Current feminist work on the history of sexuality has covered such areas as prostitution, lesbianism, abortion and birth control, rape and sexual violence. Our disparate theoretical approaches and subject matter are united by the view that the form which our sexual behaviour assumes is determined by a conglomeration of social factors. We do not believe that we are born with a fixed amount of 'sexuality' which is then allowed a greater or lesser amount of expression depending on the degree of repression or permission of the society we live in. The belief that there exists a more or less fixed amount of sexual energy has dominated discussions of sexuality currently and historically and has led to historians being principally interested in the role of the family and the state in regulating sexual behaviour. Feminist historians are opening up the issue and looking into the many layers of historical baggage attached to our sexual expression.

So insidious are the means by which patriarchy impinges on our perceptions of sexual desire that we cannot assume we know yet what our sexual lives will be like once we have rid ourselves of all patriarchal influence. We do know that in our sexual relations feminists are pioneers in exploring new ways of giving and receiving the nurturance, love and sexual pleasure we need. Historical work has been crucial in revealing the social origins of sexuality. We have learnt of the appalling sexual suffering women have undergone and of the inspiring forms of resistance women have devised. Lillian Faderman's *Surpassing the Love of Men*[1] is a particularly valuable contribution to lesbian history; lesbians have felt a tremendous sense of power on hearing at last the silence of our past being broken.

The three papers in this section consider ways in which women's sexual integrity has been invaded and colonized by men. The basic structures of male supremacy are reinforced by control of sexual relations; the papers point to ways in which this is done through the institutions of prostitution and marriage and the control of reproduction. Myna Trustram's paper shows how prostitution was regulated and made legitimate for soldiers in the Victorian army through the Contagious Diseases Acts. Regular genital examination of soldiers for venereal disease gave way in the 1860s to regular examination of women, as officers and the ranks united to protect their own interests. Sheila Jeffreys's paper discusses the attempts by the sex reform movement in the 1920s to smash militant feminism's challenge to the heterosexual couple and marriage. Barbara Brookes considers how women in the 1920s and 1930s used abortion as a survival strategy in their attempts to maintain their reproductive autonomy.

Sexuality is an area in which our historical interests are especially intermeshed with our current feminist concerns. Women's position in the military, not just their sexual role but as combatants and in non-uniformed support services, is becoming of vital interest to feminists, especially in response to the current nuclear debate.[2] Abortion and prostitution are the focus of campaigns, consciousness-raising and discussion and are issues which the media has taken up in the face of the Women's Liberation Movement's challenge. Heterosexuality and lesbianism are discussed at length within the movement, such discussions being stimulated by Adrienne Rich's article,

'Compulsory Heterosexuality and Lesbian Existence' and the collection of papers, *Love Your Enemy*.[3] Judith Walkowitz has pointed to the parallels between feminist actions to curb male sexual power today and those of the nineteenth century. In a controversial article in *History Workshop Journal*[4] she compares the ninteenth century campaigns around prostitution with today's campaigns on pornography and thereby underlines the unique contribution which historical understanding can give to our current actions.

Further historical readings on the areas discussed in this section tend to be scattered in not very easily available journals. But we would recommend Judith Walkowitz's *Prostitution and Victorian Society*[5] and Sheila Rowbotham's life of Stella Browne,[6] the socialist feminist campaigner for birth control.

9. Distasteful and derogatory? Examining Victorian soldiers for venereal disease

Myna Trustram

Why choose the army as a subject for feminist historical research? I grew up in a village on the edge of the military network of Salisbury Plain and my mother was a teacher in a garrison school. A vivid adolescent memory is of catching the last bus home from Salisbury on a Saturday night. From the top deck came the shouts and songs of the drunken 'squaddies'. I would sit downstairs, as near the conductor as possible, frightened of these unknown, dangerous men. Then later, whilst an undergraduate, I did a study of prostitution in Colchester in the 1870s. Colchester being a garrison town, the study raised many questions about the treatment of women by the army. As perhaps the most highly male-defined institution of Victorian Britain the army highlights in an acute way many issues which affect women of both yesterday and today. The offer of three years' research money enabled me to undertake a study of this unexplored area.[1] My research was to show that my early experiences of the army and my mother's experience – apparently so different – were part of the same continuum of experience which all women who come into contact with the army, undergo.

My initial approach sprang from the 'filling in the gaps' enthusiasm which informed our feminism of the mid-1970s. I wanted to find out about the lives of the women who trudged around behind the regiments. It did not take long, however, to realize that the experiences of women at the hands of the Victorian army could not simply be slotted into the framework of our existing knowledge of the social history of the army. Nor could the treatment of soldiers' wives and prostitutes be looked at in isolation from that of soldiers themselves. The actions of the men had to be considered – not in the name of redressing any imbalance nor in the name of seeing men as passive victims of a sexist society – but in order to shed light on the oppressive relationships women were forced into having with the men. The approach had to be broadened out to one which saw the army as a male institution in a patriarchal society. My aim, therefore, is to draw out the specificity of male behaviour in a world where male supremacy passes as the unquestioned norm, and where woman remains as 'other'.

I shall look at one strategy adopted to deal with one particular consequence of soldiers' sexual behaviour: venereal disease. Regular genital examination of prostitutes, as established by the Contagious Diseases Acts (1864, 1866, and 1869), was the favoured method of dealing with the problem of venereal disease and hence indirectly with prostitution. However, regular examination of men did also take place: this paper considers the discussions which took place over the desirability of this practice.

The Victorian army

The mid-Victorian period was a formative time for the modern army which by then had become a crucial branch of the nineteenth century state, defending and extending the Empire. The lessons of the Crimean War (1854–6) brought home the need for reform in the administration and organization of the army and in the terms and conditions of service of the men serving in the ranks. The 1850s to 1870s saw reforms covering the health, housing, recreation, punishment, education and pay of the rank and file.

Underlying the post-Crimean reforms was a shift in attitude to the soldier. The long-standing view had been 'the worse the man the better the soldier'. Soldiers were cannon-fodder, mindless brutes to be bullied into obeying orders; strong discipline and brutal punishments, whoring and drunkenness were the order of the day. In the course of the century this attitude to the soldier became increasingly at odds with the social, sexual and moral norms of the 'Age of Improvement'.

By the 1850s and 1860s the ruling moral code, determined by and large by the influence of the Evangelicals, had reached its zenith. Duty, self-restraint and the sanctity of the family were its central values.

From the middle of the nineteenth century attempts were made to narrow the gap between military morality and that of the rest of society. There was a growing appreciation of the influence the 'moral discipline' of the ranks could have on the maintenance of morale, efficiency, discipline and good relations with civilian society. Just as the men's physical welfare was being considered, so was their moral and domestic welfare. Accordingly, moves were made to instil Christian beliefs into the army. Recreational facilities were improved with a view to keeping the men away from the temptation of the brothels and beerhouses of the nearby towns: reading rooms, libraries, sporting and educational facilities were extended.[2] Provision for married men was improved. An altered approach to soldiers' sexuality was a central feature of this shift in attitude.

It was a proverbial fact that brothels and drinking places sprang up in the vicinity of any army garrison or camp. Soldiers' desire for prostitutes was seen to be based in men's involuntary sexual drive which made liaisons with prostitutes an inevitable, if unfortunate, necessity. The structure of military employment, with its delayed marriage and deliberate maintenance of a transient male population, was thought to exacerbate this need for sexual gratification. Soldiers were mere slaves to their passions and victims of the military life-style.

The immorality of the larger garrison towns was thought to be particularly bad. In 1856, shortly after the arrival of the troops at the newly formed camp at Aldershot, the syphilitic patients admitted into the workhouse increased from two in the preceding year to 21 in 1856.[3] In 1861 Captain Pilkington Jackson visited Aldershot and Portsmouth to report on Soldiers' Institutes. Speaking of Portsmouth he reported:

> The temptations leading to intoxication and lust are very great at Portsmouth. To the large military force which is permanently established there is added a large naval force;

combined, the number of men stationed there at all times is
larger than at most garrison towns, and in the same proportion is the number of brothels and public-houses . . . Those
parts of the town in which these places of resort are principally situated, are about the worst in the country. Vice in its
most offensive forms revels and thrives there. The utmost
that can be done by the military and civil police to preserve
the appearance of decency in the principal thoroughfares, is
to try to keep the prostitutes and their companions within
certain boundaries.[4]

This widespread prostitution around army camps resulted in
a particularly high rate of venereal disease amongst soldiers.
The Army Medical Department report for 1859 claimed that for
every 1,000 men there were 422 admissions into hospital for
venereal disease. It was calculated that the inefficiency arising
from the loss of the services of these men was equal to the loss
of nearly three regiments (or 2,417 men), for a whole year.[5]

The Contagious Diseases Acts attempted to reduce the loss
to the services which this high rate of venereal disease brought
about. They marked a significant period in the history of
attempts by the state to regulate sexual behaviour. Early
Victorian Britain had seen an effervescence of both popular and
official interest in prostitution as a social problem. The licence
which Victorian sexual ideology gave to male sexual profligacy
was not a new feature of the mid-Victorian period. The new
departure one sees in the period was a growth of concern for the
causes of this profligacy and its medical and social results. By
the early 1860s belief in the need for some form of regulation of
prostitution as the only way to ensure the health of soldiers and
sailors was common. Thus, it was the confluence of the
mid-Victorian sexual ideology whereby male sexual licence was
tolerated, with the administrative and medical apparatus necessary for regulation, which contributed to the passing of the
Contagious Diseases Acts in the 1860s.[6]

The three Contagious Diseases Acts introduced a system of
regulation of prostitution similar to that which already existed
on the Continent. They established a system of compulsory

periodic genital examination, and, if diseased, detention of prostitutes in 18 naval and garrison towns. The Acts were not originally conceived as a method of moral reform for the women or the men concerned, but were seen to be a purely pragmatic response to a situation where the efficiency of the army was imperilled. Nevertheless, they embodied a range of ideological assumptions based on class and sex exploitation; specifically, they were a clear illustration of the double standard of sexual behaviour. It was the ideological roots of the Acts which the feminist repeal campaign was to reveal so effectively. The repeal campaign was successful in getting the Acts suspended in 1883 and repealed in 1886.

Examining men

Studies of the Contagious Diseases Acts have concentrated on their administrative and legislative history and their impact on the women involved. As measures designed for the military, discussion of the military origins of the Acts is essential for a complete understanding of their impact and significance. Since the Acts were based on the view that it was legitimate to examine women and not men, it seems appropriate to look at the attitudes which contributed to this belief.

Regular genital examination of unmarried soldiers – married men were exempted – was general throughout the army until 1859. In 1869 Dr T. Graham Balfour, the Deputy Inspector of Military Hospitals, told the Select Committee on the 1866 Contagious Diseases Act that

> It [i.e. examination of men] was given up on the recommendation of the Committee appointed to enquire into the Sanitary Condition of the Army, presided over by the late Lord Herbert because it was, I may say, the general opinion of the medical officers of the army, that it was extremely inefficient in reducing the amount of venereal disease; it was unpopular with the men; and it was very much objected to by the medical officers.[7]

After 1859 it was left to the discretion of the Commanding

Officer of a regiment as to whether men should be examined on a regular basis.

Examination was not an effective measure against venereal disease; it was cursory and men could easily hide any sores they might have. Besides, there was no known cure for the disease. George Blenkins, Surgeon-Major of the Grenadier Guards, examined his men every week. Asked how the examination was carried out he explained:

> There are different ways of doing it; but the way in which I think it is generally done is, that the men come into a large room, in companies, they pass the examining surgeon in single file, and as each man comes opposite him, he raises his shirt for the moment for the surgeon to make his examination. If he sees there is no venereal, he passes him; if he fancies that the man has been concealing it, he examines him more minutely.[8]

Other regiments examined the men on parade. Men of the Coldstream Guards were examined every seven to ten days. Their Assistant-Surgeon, John Trotter, claimed to be able to examine from 500 to 600 men in half an hour![9]

Regiments varied as to whether they examined married men and NCOs as well as the single rank and file. The assumption amongst officers was that married men were less likely to use prostitutes and so less likely to contract disease. There was also a belief that married men deserved more dignified treatment than single ones. NCOs were viewed similarly in that their higher rank and greater age demanded better treatment.

The question of the desirability or not, of regularly examining the men arose during the discussions in the 1860s on the merits of regulation of prostitution. The Skey Committee of 1864, for instance, discussed this issue. The committee consisted of eight medical men and was set up to report on the medical treatment of venereal disease and on preventive measures.[10] They recommended an extensive system of compulsory periodical examination of all known prostitutes and believed examination of soldiers should be universal throughout the army:

without such a regulation, the proposed periodical examination of women must lose half its value. They [i.e. the committee members] have no doubt that, as formerly carried out, personal inspection, en masse, was very offensive both to medical officers and men, but they have as little doubt that it can be done with such decency and privacy as to lose that offensive character.[11]

The committee claimed to be following the views of some of the highest military authorities. At the same time, they acknowledged that many of the medical officers who gave evidence were not in favour of examining the men.

William Perry, a surgeon in the Royal Artillery, had such an objection. When he first joined his regiment he was sent to examine some 1,500 men:

I can assure you that I left that room with feelings of the deepest degradation. I considered that my professional status was altogether sacrificed, so much so, that I rued the day on which I had entered the service. I thought that I was placed in an utterly false position as a gentleman and as a medical man.[12]

The Director-General of the Army Medical Department and other army and naval medical officers all objected to examination of the men on the grounds that it was 'distasteful to the men and derogatory to the character of the medical officers'.[13]

William Acton, a particularly influential commentator on prostitution and venereal disease, agreed with the Skey Committee's recommendations on examination of men. Acton's *Prostitution*, published in 1857, became the principal pro-regulation document.[14] He argued that prostitution might be engaged in by a woman in a particular stage of her life and that the popular image of a woman being on the quick road to ruin once she started to engage in prostitution was incorrect. He argued for state regulation of prostitution to ensure that this period of a woman's life left her and society with as little permanent injury as possible. Acton urged that the old public method of inspection of soldiers be replaced by fortnightly examinations performed in private 'in a decorous and decent manner'.[15] This was based on his view that prostitution was inevitable when restrictions on soldiers' marriages were enforced; the state was obliged to regulate prostitution since it made it a necessity.

By and large examination of the men was argued for on pragmatic, medical grounds – it was pointless to examine only one-half of the venereal partnership. It was not suggested that it was the soldiers' sexual behaviour which lay at the root of prostitution and hence they who deserved the 'punishment' of examination. In contrast, the justification of examination of women was based on the argument that guilt lay with the women; they were responsible for immorality and hence they should be examined. The more logical health argument, that one woman could infect many men, was not greatly evoked. Hence, ideology was called upon to argue for the examination of women, whilst those who supported examination of men did so on more rational, common-sense grounds.

An article in the *Westminster Review* in 1870, whilst not actually stating that it was soldiers' sexual behaviour which was to be questioned, did point out the injustice of examining the women and not the men. It argued that on enlistment, soldiers entered into a particular relationship with the state which justified intervention into areas of a man's life which, in the case of a civilian, would be considered a violation of liberty. Unlike soldiers, women entered into no such contract with the state and were therefore not liable to have their constitutional and moral rights abused by such legislation as the Contagious Diseases Acts. Therefore examination should be of the men and not of the women:

Though the soldiers are rightfully under the personal control of the Government, whereas the women have not voluntarily surrendered their personal liberty at all, yet, by a strange perversity of judgement, the self-respect of the women has been ruthlessly disregarded, and they are forcibly submitted to a repulsive examination, the soldiers being allowed to escape meanwhile! In short, the self-respect of the men may be saved – a kind of justice which, unhappily, has been meted out to women throughout all the ages during which men have exercised their dominant power.[16]

The 1871 Royal Commission

The 1871 Royal Commission, the major investigation into the Acts, marked a departure from previous discussions on the subject of examination of the men. Evidence to the commission illustrates the shift in the debate on the Acts, away from the condition of the army and the medical benefits which could be expected from regulation, to the details of the enforcement of the legislation and the moral and constitutional implications of the Acts. By the early 1870s the Acts were being both attacked and defended as far-reaching legislation which raised crucial issues covering the moral and social well-being of the nation. Regulation was seen to have the potential either totally to subvert the morality of the nation or to be its salvation.

The inability of the commissioners to agree led to an ambiguous and evasive report. It recommended that regular examination of women be discontinued but that detention of diseased women be retained and police powers against prostitution be increased. The failure of the report to uphold the regulationists' cause marked the downturn in their ascendancy and the growing influence of the repeal campaign.[17]

To counter the growing strength of the repeal movement a strong statement and reaffirmation of the double standard – the ideological basis of the Acts – was made by those in favour of regulation. In a classic exposition of the double standard the commissioners stated:

Many witnesses have urged that as well on grounds of justice as expediency, soldiers and sailors should be subjected to regular examination. We may at once dispose of this recommendation, so far as it is founded on the principle of putting both parties to the sin of fornication on the same footing by the obvious but not less conclusive reply that there is no comparison to be made between prostitutes and the men who consort with them. With the one sex the offence is committed as a matter of gain; with the other it is an irregular indulgence of a natural impulse.[18]

In order to explain this apparent about-turn in the official attitude one needs to remember that in the mid-1860s the Acts were seen as a rational health measure in the tradition of the mid-century sanitary movement, employed to prevent venereal disease amongst the military. In this spirit the examination of men was a logical concomitant to the examination of women. The aim of the repeal campaign was to expose this claim that the Acts were a rational public health measure and to reveal the wealth of oppressive attitudes and behaviour towards women which lay behind the Acts. Any defence of regulation needed to protect its ideological base – the double standard. Pragmatic arguments that both men and women should be examined, fell by the wayside in the face of the polarization between repealers and regulationists which had set in by the early 1870s; hence the vehemence of the commissioners' statement on examination of men.

Male sexuality

How do the debates on the relative merits of the examination of men or women fit into the general shift in attitude to soldiers during the period, from seeing them as mindless, amoral brutes to seeing them as Christian noble men?[19] The original purpose of examination was certainly born of the concern to improve the health and social standing of the army. It is ironic though, that the method chosen to improve the men's health betrayed a basic belief that they were slaves to their animal passions and had to be protected against the worst consequences of this. The thrust of the army's approach was to recognize prostitution as a necessity and to use measures to reduce venereal disease. While provisions were being made to 'civilize' the men, the view was never really relinquished of them as sexual brutes. Hence the fears amongst the military in 1883 that a great increase in disease would occur with the suspension of the Acts.

Typical accounts of nineteenth-century prostitution and sexuality are couched within a discussion of the Victorian domestic ideal. The definition of sex roles embodied in the ideal are seen to determine the bounds of what was considered to be the proper form of sexual behaviour. Under this view prostitutes' clients in the nineteenth century were by and large middle-class men who, in order to preserve the purity of their wives and homes, used working-class prostitutes to fulfil their less honourable sexual demands.[20] Whilst this was undoubtedly one theme of nineteenth-century prostitution, an explanation centred on the domestic ideal does not account for the widespread use of prostitutes by working-class men, or in this case, by soldiers. Prostitution is presented as essentially a class issue: the exploitation of working-class women by middle- and upper-class men. It hides the fact that all women suffer sexual exploitation from men of all classes.[21]

What we see in the discussions and actions concerning examination of men is a bonding together of men across rank and class boudaries to protect the interests of all men. Officers, rank and file and other interested men literally closed ranks and argued that examination was degrading and offensive, not only for the men examined, but also for the officers who had to perform the inspection. Whereas examination of women was thought to be legitimate and, unlike the examination of men, not considered a slight on the examining doctor's professional or moral standing.

Prostitution and venereal disease were seen by both the army's critics and supporters as problems linked with the general conditions in the ranks and in particular the severe restrictions placed on a soldier's opportunity to marry. Removal of these restrictions does not lead to the disappearance of prostitution, as the case of today's army testifies. In order to understand prostitution it seems necessary to look further afield and see it as one aspect of male sexual behaviour in a patriarchal society. The army within this perspective is more accurately seen as an extreme case on a continuum, illustrating not a unique problem caused by particular conditions of military service, but exemplifying commonly held Victorian attitudes which still persist today.

10. The illegal operation: abortion, 1919–39

Barbara Brookes

In February 1920, Lillian Matilda Arthur, a married woman and mother of a small child, was found dead. She was, the judge pronounced, guilty of 'self-murder'. Yet it was far from Lillian Arthur's intention to commit suicide. She had sought to induce an abortion by a hot-water douche and did not survive the attempt.

For this one case with tragic results there were undoubtedly many that were successful, but just how many will never be known. Because she died, Lillian Arthur is an atypical representative of those women who chose abortion as a solution when faced with an unwanted pregnancy. Her situation, however, was common. Married at 22 in 1918, Lillian's first child was born in July 1919. She became pregnant again soon after the birth but did not tell her husband. Instead, she turned to her sister for sympathy and, with the latter's help, Lillian carried out the fatal douche.[1]

The themes of Lillian's experience – of apparently ineffective or non-existent contraception, frequent pregnancies, and the support of other women – are common to women who resorted to abortion in the inter-war years. Abortion was a subject of controversy at this time because of the contribution made by deaths from abortion to the high maternal mortality figures. Proscribed by law, and by medical and religious assumptions about women's health and the sanctity of life, abortion was nonetheless an important measure for women who wished to control their fertility. This chapter will explore the legal, medical and governmental strategies which controlled access to abortion in the 1920s and 1930s. It will also examine women's resistance and challenge to these strategies, particularly that posed by the Abortion Law Reform Association which was founded in 1936.

Abortion law became increasingly restrictive throughout the nineteenth century. The first civil proscription of abortion was introduced in 1803 and it followed ecclesiastical tradition in distinguishing between abortion before and after quickening. This distinction was lost in 1837, and in 1861 the woman herself was specifically named, along with the abortionist, as being liable for prosecution.[2] The aim of the original law was essentially paternalistic, to protect women from enforced abortion and from the dangers of abortifacient drugs or instrumental interference in pregnancy. It also incorporated religious views on the sanctity of foetal life. This legal strategy to protect women and infants became more and more oppressive as the desire to limit family size increased.

Families in the 1860s, when the abortion law was formalized, generally consisted of about six children. Queen Victoria's family of nine was by no means unusual. By the 1920s, however, the average family consisted of only two or three children. It was in the 1920s that the birth control movement gathered momentum and at the same time it appeared that induced abortion had reached epidemic proportions. A Ministry of Health committee, investigating the causes of maternal deaths, collected figures which revealed that the percentage of deaths due to septic abortion rose from 10.5 per cent in 1930 to 20 per cent by 1934.[3] By the end of the 1920s, the medical press claimed that there was a 'fashion' in abortions and noted their 'appalling frequency' while Marie Stopes publicized the 'holocaust of embryos.'[4] Women clearly wished to limit their families and, in the absence of efficient contraception, abortion provided one method of birth control.

The law, as Lillian Arthur's case demonstrates, was unenforceable. There was no means of policing private acts carried out by women in their own homes. Moreover, most women did not regard 'bringing on' their period as an abortion. Abortion was thought of as a surgical procedure which bore little relation to drinking herbal teas or inserting a seaweed pencil into the mouth of the uterus – both common remedies for a delayed period. This gap between the medical and popular view of abortion is illustrated by the case of a criminal abortionist who, the judge stated, 'objected to things being called what they were'. The defendant believed that if pregnancy was terminated 'by some other means than using a sharp instrument, then it ought not to be called an abortion'.[5]

Such contemporary debate over even the *definition* of what constituted an abortion demonstrates the difficulty of the historian's task when she tries to establish the incidence of abortion in the past and it serves to obscure the reality of women's experience. Patent medicine manufacturers captialized on the illegality of abortion and advertised potions and pills to 'restore regularity' or to 'remove obstructions'. Abortion cases reported in the press appear under the heading of 'illegal operations'. In contrast to the euphemisms of popular advertisements and the conservative press, is the language of women themselves. In letters to Marie Stopes, individual women requested means to 'bring me round'. to 'put me on my way' or to 'put me right'. Stopes, anxious to make birth control a respectable cause, shied away from any public association with the 'illegal operation'. Requests for abortion were denied but she did counsel women to 'make every effort to keep their periods regular'. To do this she suggested taking a dose of quinine 2 or 3 days before the period was expected and a hot bath the night before it was due.[6] These means to ensure 'regularity' were also well-known abortifacient measures.

There was, it appears, a 'freemasonry amongst women'[7] in which they exchanged information on abortion. Gin and hot bath, pennyroyal, saltpetre, carbolic lotion and Beechams Pills were among the remedies discussed. In 1924 a nurse noted that gunpowder had become a popular abortifacient in a certain district of London.[8] Names of abortionists were 'bandied about by married woman to married woman'. When Mary Moulder, a professional singer, found herself pregnant, she asked her friend Mrs Brewer for help. Mrs Brewer put her in contact with Emma Cole. The latter performed the abortion that caused Mary's death. In her defence Mrs Cole said 'what I did I only did out of kindness'. Many other women engaged in similar illegal and compassionate acts, but it was only the unsuccessful cases that came to court. Minnie Roberts received a 7-year sentence for procuring an abortion that ended in death. She had, she claimed, treated over 800 cases in 25 years, and this was her first fatality.[9]

Because abortion was illegal, women such as Minnie Roberts, found guilty of performing the operation, could receive very heavy sentences in comparison with other crimes. Attempted rape, for example, merited a maximum penalty of a 7-year sentence whereas the maximum penalty for attempted abortion was imprisonment for life. The law did not prevent the operation but drove it into undesirable channels. Women were open to exploitation by patent medicine manufacturers and to the trade in backstreet abortion. A London shop, ostensibly for hairdressing, did a heavy trade in abortifacient pills. The pills were bought at 10 shillings for a dozen boxes and sold to customers at 10 shillings per box. When these failed, customers could get an amateur surgical abortion for £30 or less, depending on their circumstances.[10] Extortion and blackmail were other unpleasant aspects of the abortion trade.

What led women to possibly risk their health, if not their life, by seeking 'criminal' abortions? Each woman had her own reasons, whether of an economic, physical, or psychological nature. She may have been, like Miss O.D., unwed and afraid that the pregnancy would reveal her 'unpardonable crime'. It was more likely that she was married, already had some children, and did not think she could provide the 'everyday comforts of life' for another.[11] For those who had access to, or could afford contraception, it was a disaster when the sheath burst or the cap failed. In the absence of birth control, women became exhausted by close-interval pregnancies. Mrs E.S. wrote to Stopes begging for help: 'I am only 36 and have had 10 children. I am 2 months overdue and am nearly off my head, I can tell you I'd rather die than have another which will probably kill me anyway.'[12]

Many women wished to determine their own family size and were prepared to take the risks an abortion might entail. By the inter-war years, therefore, the original intention of the abortion law (to protect maternal health) had been subverted by the resort to criminal abortion which contributed to the maternal death rate. Changed expectations of family size and women's determination to control their own fertility transformed a protective law into a form of control over women's reproductive autonomy. At a time when family size reached its lowest level ever, women who attempted to terminate pregnancy were, if caught, branded as criminal and deviant.

The medical profession reinforced the view that women who wished to terminate pregnancy were selfish and irresponsible. By 1930 it was clear that, as a cause of maternal deaths, abortion had become 'more important than delivery at term'.[13] The medical response to this problem was informed by contemporary views of women's role and state population problems. Doctors regarded health for women as synonymous with marriage and children. Spinsterhood thwarted 'natural instincts' and a marriage without children was unfulfilled. A standard medical text warned of the dangers of the 'maternal instinct driven inward' and exhorted the practitioner 'to do all in his power to counteract the modern tendency to curtail families for the sake of the State as well as for the sake of the woman's bodily and mental health'.[14] 'The key' to the abortion problem, according to a leading obstetrician, was 'education'. Women should be made aware of the dangers of abortion. Doctors noted, however, 'the pertinacity' of married women who wanted to terminate pregnancy and realized that little could be done to stop them.[15]

Doctors performed legal abortions in cases where pregnancy was a threat to the mother's life. The interpretation of this phrase was left to individual practitioners, most of whom interpreted it narrowly as they had no wish to be associated with a criminal act. A woman aged 39 with severe Parkinson's disease and chronic depression was refused a therapeutic abortion. She had a son of 15 and was barely capable of looking after her house but, although she had attempted suicide, the doctors decided that the pregnancy should continue.

Some doctors ignored the law at their own peril. Dr Laura Sanders-Bliss was sentenced to 3 years' imprisonment for terminating pregnancy in cases where she believed abortion was 'the only successful treatment that could be given'.[16] For a doctor, a conviction for abortion usually resulted in being struck off the medical register, a risk few were prepared to take and only for a lucrative return.

Legal and medical strictures on abortion were regarded as safeguards for national population requirements. Mr Justice Darling made this clear in the trial of a criminal abortionist in 1920. Speaking of 'race suicide', the judge went on to say:

> A country which permits its population to be dealt with in this way [abortion] is bound to decay. Those who have as many enemies as the British Empire must for their own safety have plenty of children to meet those enemies in the gate. We have many gates to defend, therefore it is that the law for that and other reasons makes these practices penal and awards a heavy punishment for them.[17]

Such arguments multiplied in the 1930s when studies of population movements predicted the demise of the British race. Enid Charles's significantly titled *The Twilight of Parenthood* caught the mood in which the low birth rate (the net reproduction rate was 0.75 in 1933) created fears of national extinction, particularly in the face of growing militarism in Europe. In fact, the medical profession feared that the publicity given to the high maternal mortality rates had made women afraid of childbirth. To counter this trend doctors were encouraged to offer reassurance to women 'whose duty it is to go on producing noble Britons'.[18]

The government never articulated a formal population programme but its reluctance to sanction state provision of contraceptive services or legalized abortion served to limit women's options. When Nancy Astor took up the plea for birth control in the House of Commons, Dr O'Donovan replied that the 'trilogy of birth control, abortion and sterilization', if imposed by the government, would turn the Ministry of Health into a 'Ministry of Death'. Instead, the government was willing to support policies such as maternity benefits and child allowances which upheld women's maternal role. Neville Chamberlain made explicit his pro-natalist intention in his proposal to raise child allowances in 1934. The increase was designed to encourage maternity and would therefore, Chamberlain hoped, counteract the continued decline in the birth rate which he viewed with 'considerable apprehension'.[19]

Even those working to make contraceptive information available were careful not to undermine motherhood. Marie Stopes was at pains to counter the opponents of birth control who considered it 'only as a negative measure designed to *prevent* births'. She stressed its 'positive' side which by allowing child spacing, enabled mothers to be considered 'not only as the producers of mere babies, *but as the creators of splendid babies*'.[20]

What were the responses of women to the pervasive ideology of motherhood in the inter-war years? Few women chose to have more children. They did, however, put more time into raising their smaller families. 'Scientific' child-care and higher standards of housework demanded just as much attention as the larger families of the previous century. Local authority policies, such as the marriage bar discussed by Alison Oram, reinforced the prevailing notion that a woman's place was in the home. Clearly, governmental, legal and medical norms limited women's options, but for most women, decisions about fertility were made for personal reasons without reference to the dictates of national needs. Abortion, as we have seen, was a survival strategy discussed by women and used when necessary. Marie Stopes highlighted the extent of the practice. In 1929 she revealed the 'staggering facts' that had come to light at her clinic:

> In three months I have had as many as twenty thousand requests for criminal abortion from women who did not apparently even *know* that it was criminal . . . In a given number of days one of our travelling clinics received only thirteen applications for scientific instruction in the control of conception, but eighty demands for criminal abortion.[21]

For Stopes, as for Labour Party women and others in the birth control campaign, the answer to the abortion problem was to make contraception readily available. The campaign for 'constructive' birth control, emphasizing child spacing for healthier infants and mothers, could only lose support if allied with the seemingly 'destructive' advocates of abortion.

Other women active in sex reform and the birth control movement were not so reticent. Stella Browne, Dora Russell, Janet Chance and Alice Jenkins, all active in the birth control campaign, went on to challenge the abortion law. Public discussion of birth control, provoked mainly by Marie Stopes and the new 'science of sexology' discussed by Sheila Jeffreys, brought the subject of abortion to the fore. The sex reformers argued against any state intrusion into private morality (except to protect the young and the weak) and called for reform of the abortion law. Stella Browne was the first to argue against the English law in a paper delivered to the British Society for the Study of Sex Psychology in 1915. As a feminist and a socialist she criticized state demands for population as both 'imprudent and inhuman'. Women required birth control information and the abolition of the abortion law to avoid coercion into motherhood and establish 'absolute freedom of choice'.[22]

In 1925, Dora Russell declared that the task of modern feminism was 'to accept and proclaim sex; to bury forever the lie that has too long corrupted our society – the lie that the body is a hindrance to the mind, and sex a necessary evil to be endured for the perpetuation of our race.'[23] Dora Russell was drawn into the birth control campaign by the trial of Rose Witcop and Guy Aldred in 1923. The trial was over the publication of a pamphlet written by Margaret Sanger instructing women in matters of sex and contraception. The seizure of the pamphlet by the police roused her anger 'for I could not see why information which a middle-class woman could get from her doctor should be withheld from a poorer woman who might need it far more.'[24] Dora Russell then became a founding member of the Workers' Birth Control Group and when the major battle with the Ministry of Health over birth control had been won, she went on to demand reform of the abortion law to give women complete control of their fertility.

Janet Chance was another woman whose activities in the

birth control movement convinced her of the need for abortion law reform. Her early experience as a lay worker at the Walworth Birth Control Centre led her to the belief that sex education was needed at all levels of society. As a consequence she opened a Marriage Education Centre in the East End of London in 1929. The Centre provided sex education for children and instruction in sexual satisfaction for women. In her report on the centre, given to the World League for Sex Reform in 1929, Janet Chance criticized the lack of hospital facilities for either sterilization or termination of pregnancy. 'More than one woman,' she stated, came to ask for an abortion and had to be told 'the legal and health aspects of that common practice'.[25]

Perhaps the clearest statement of the progression from involvement in the birth control campaign to advocating abortion law reform came from Alice Jenkins. Having helped establish a birth control clinic in her local area, she was dismayed to find

> A curious result – a certainty that contraception was *not* a
> complete defence against an unwanted pregnancy; for
> amongst the arguments used on the platform and in the press
> against the clinic were the following:
>   a) Contraceptives were neither reliable or cheap;
>   b) Privacy to adjust the appliances was almost impossible
>   in overcrowded living conditions.

When Alice Jenkins learned of the possibility of safe surgical abortion, this seemed a revelation, a 'way of escape from that welter of maternal suffering' which led to more deaths from illegal abortion than from full-time confinement.[26] The experiences of Stella Browne, Dora Russell, Janet Chance, and Alice Jenkins were shared by other feminists in the birth control movement, and in the mid-1930s, these women grouped together to promote the issue of abortion law reform.

It was difficult to speak publicly of abortion, let alone to suggest that it should be freely available. The Abortion Law Reform Association, formally convened in February 1936, set out to challenge 'the almost complete press censorship' of the abortion problem.[27] The association was formed by women (the executive was limited to women only) to give voice to 'opinion inarticulate in the lives of women'. The Women's Co-operative Guild had already demanded revision of the abortion law in 1934. The women in ALRA hoped that a single-issue organization would help to change public opinion and bring pressure to bear on parliament which would result in a change in the law. ALRA members organized conferences, wrote to the press, and raised the issue of reform in party and non-party organizations in an attempt to win support for the cause. In spite of the small size of the group (at most about 10 women were actively involved) they managed to address 57 meetings from 1 May to 30 September 1937. Members helped sympathetic MPs, such as Mavis Tate and Robert Boothby, to draft questions to raise in parliament about the relationship between abortion and maternal mortality. ALRA also stressed that women's groups should be represented on any governement inquiry into abortion law reform.

The feminists in ALRA were mainly middle class and they regarded the abortion law as a class law, pointing out that the difference between a therapeutic and a criminal abortion was usually a matter of the ability to pay specialists' fees. They were much influenced by the example of the USSR, both because of their political leanings and the freedom for women that the liberal Russian law seemed to imply. When the USSR reversed its law in 1936 the feminist sympathy of the ALRA members overrode their party politics and they condemned the restriction of women's rights. Women, they believed, could never 'trust to the gratitude of groups of men'.[28] Men's refusal to consider women's demands seriously had been clearly demonstrated in the fight for birth control. In the face of overwhelming support by Labour Party women for contraception, the party refused to consider birth control to be a political issue. It was left to voluntary organizations to provide birth control advice. Abortion, however, was prohibited by statute and its political relevance, therefore, could not be denied.

The feminist argument for abortion law reform was put most forcefully by Stella Browne. A restrictive abortion law denied women full humanity. Such a law was 'a survival of the veiled face, of the barred window and the locked door, burning, branding, mutilation, stoning, of all the grip of ownership and superstition come down on women, thousands of years ago.'[29] To Stella Browne and the other members of ALRA, sexual reforms could not be divorced from political and social change. If such reform was overlooked, it was women who suffered.

The ALRA women were unsuccessful in their challenge to 'compulsory maternity'. They represented their case forcefully before the government committee (the Birkett Committee) which had eventually been appointed to investigate the abortion problem. The committee heard numerous submissions from women's organizations which made it clear that abortion was widespread. The request by ALRA for 'safe surgical abortion on humanitarian grounds' appears startlingly radical when compared to the final report issued by the Birkett Committee. This group of upper-class doctors and titled women failed even to unanimously support contraception as a means to enable women to control their fertility. Only Dorothy Thurtle, who issued a minority report, made constructive suggestions for relaxation of the abortion law and greater access to contraception.

The challenge to the abortion law in the 1930s was unsuccessful in the face of apparent population decline and the imminence of war. The feminists in ALRA were claiming a right for women which threatened accepted gender roles. To escape maternity by destroying the product of conception was to deny the sanctity of motherhood. It was not until 1967, in an era of progressive liberal legislation borne on a wave of economic prosperity, and in the face of threats of over-population, that the abortion law was liberalized. And ALRA was instrumental in lobbying for this reform.

Women's right to safe legal abortion, denied in the inter-war years, has been a central claim of contemporary feminism. No feminist regards abortion as pleasant, but most see it as a necessity for survival in a society in which contraceptive methods are inefficient or hazardous to health, and where heterosexual relationships mirror the imbalance of power between the sexes in the society at large. A sense of autonomy for women requires freedom from the physical and psychological demands of an unwanted pregnancy, and freedom from coercion in sexual relationships. With Stella Browne we believe that 'our bodies are our own'. From the past, however, we can see that state, medical, legal and religious norms attempt to manipulate women's fertility. Like the founders of the Abortion Law Reform Association, feminists must ensure that the voices of the inarticulate are heard, whether in Britain or abroad, so that national policies do not operate at the expense of the individual.

11. Sex reform and anti-feminism in the 1920s

Sheila Jeffreys

'To be roused by a man means acknowledging oneself as conquered.'[1]

In this chapter I will look at the work of those involved in the sex reform movement in the 1920s, and suggest that it represents a backlash against the gains of the last wave of feminism and a response to the challenge posed by feminists to the institution of heterosexuality. Wilhelm Stekel, the author of the epigraph to this chapter, made it clear that he saw heterosexual sex and specifically sexual intercourse, as a necessary and appropriate regulatory mechanism in the maintenance of male dominance and female submission. Historians of sex have approached the development of the sex reform movement from the standpoint of 1960s sexual revolution ideology. They have seen sex as an area of personal and private concern. This has enabled them to pose the tremendous battle of ideas which was being waged in the first three decades of the twentieth century between militant feminists who advanced a critique of male sexuality, and the men and women involved in the sex reform movement, in terms of the advocates of puritanism versus the advocates of sexual pleasure. Few of those involved in the debate saw sex as private. Both feminists and anti-feminists at all points on the political spectrum shared an interest in eugenics which made it impossible for any of them to see sex as merely a matter of private and personal concern. More importantly, in the context of this chapter, they shared a conscious and articulated understanding of the significance of sexual activity in the power relationship between the sexes – an awareness which is not overt in most contemporary writing about sex. Some feminists argued that the sexual colonization of women's bodies was the very basis of men's domination over women and must be ended.

From a feminist perspective sexuality cannot be seen simply as an area of personal and private concern. The heterosexual couple is a political relationship within which the woman's labour is extracted and the woman's life is controlled and harnessed to the satisfaction of the man's needs. The sexual activity which takes place within this relationship represents an area in which man's power and control can be reinforced, and woman's subordination reproduced.

During the late nineteenth and early twentieth centuries social, economic and population changes, as well as feminist campaigns, brought about great shocks to the traditonal Victorian structure of heterosexual relationships. The sex reform movement developed against this background. There were many different currents and concerns within sex reform but the unity which existed between those of widely differing political views can best be explained as emerging from a common desire to shore up the heterosexual couple, and challenge militant feminism through the conscription of women into heterosexual intercourse. This chapter will concentrate on the development of the concept of the 'frigide' in the 1920s The 'frigide' who has marched through the pages of sexological and sex advice literature as a problem of major concern throughout the twentieth century, was 'invented' in the 1920s to explain the phenomenon of women rejecting marriage altogether or sexual response within marriage. The 'frigide' became the focus of attention, not because of concern for her individual sexual rights but because she effectively blocked the use of sex as a regulatory mechanism in the relations between the sexes.

The background to the sex reform movement

The primary works which laid the foundations for the creation of the science of sexology at the beginning of the twentieth century were those of Havelock Ellis, Iwan Bloch and August Forel. The sexologists of the next three decades continued to acknowledge their debts to these progenitors and to maintain their international links, formalized in the 1920s into the International Society for Sex Research and the World League for Sex Reform.

The sex reform movement in Britain developed from the work of Edward Carpenter and Havelock Ellis in the 1890s and reached its height in the Sex Reform Congress in London in 1929. Until recently the sex reformers have been represented by historians as making a positive contribution to the greater happiness of men and women or even as a progressive, socialist, pro-feminist force. In fact, both 'progressive' sex reformers and outright anti-feminists (some of whom were overtly fascist in sympathy) were united across the political spectrum by their alarm at militant feminism and its critique of male sexual behaviour, and particularly at what they saw to be the threatening withdrawal of women from heterosexual relations. What was it that united these proponents of sex reform whose differences on such matters as infanticide, birth control, abortion, marriage and homosexuality were often very large? Their common aim was to promote the value and necessity of sexual intercourse. There was a mutual understanding that the enemy of 'puritanism' and Victorian sexual attitudes had to be attacked, and that the chief culprits in the propagation of these attitudes were spinster feminists. The execration of the spinster is a theme common to the works of all those considered here.

Another common theme was to promote the active participation in sexual intercourse of *all* women. All the sex reformers saw the non-participating woman, whether married and resisting, or determinedly unmarried, as undesirable or positively dangerous.

It is clear from the works of the sex reformers that they were conscious of and reacting to, the development of a feminist critique of male sexual behaviour and of heterosexual relationships. The significance of the sex reform movement can only be understood in relation to the feminist campaigns of the period.[2] In the late nineteenth and early twentieth century there was a massive campaign by women to control and set limits to male sexual behaviour and assert a woman's right to control access to her own body. Those women who campaigned around the issues of sexual abuse of children, prostitution and venereal desease proclaimed that the form taken by male sexuality was a social and not a biological phenomenon and that male sexuality did not have to take a form which was dangerous to women's interests. Some feminists, like Elizabeth Wolstenholme Elmy and Francis Swiney, were saying that the sexual control of women's bodies was the basis of men's domination over women. They undertook a critique of male sexual behaviour within marriage and questioned the necessity of sexual intercourse as a sexual practice. Before the First World War feminists like Christabel Pankhurst launched a critique of heterosexuality itself and withdrew from sexual relations with men. Women's determination to transform male sexual behaviour provided a strong uniting and motivating force for pre-First World War feminists.

There were other factors which helped to shape the social and political climate in which sex reform developed. In the period before the First World War, the 'surplus women' problem was beginning to cause acute concern, particularly amongst anti-feminists and the popular exponents of sex reforming ideas. From the earliest years of the women's movement the fact that there was an excess of women over men in the population had contributed to the alarm of anti-feminists. In the 1911 census it was revealed that the excess of women had reached an all-time high. At the same time it was becoming clear that some women were actually choosing to remain single and the rate of marriage was low. Changes in the pattern of employment were making it slightly easier for women to support themselves outside marriage. Increasing opportunities for women in education were contributing to this process. Some women were stating that remaining celibate was a political decision made in response to the nature of male sexuality, the conditions of marriage and the necessity of a large class of spinsters to fight for women's emancipation. Such a debate was conducted in the pages of the *Freewoman* magazine in 1911 and 1912.[3] The First World War helped to increase the 'surplus' of women, though the popularity of marriage increased after the war.

New opportunities for women in education and work combined with developments such as the Married Women's Property Act, passed in 1882 and for which feminists had campaigned, had been eroding the foundations of marriage, at least for the middle classes. The total dependence of women in marriage upon their husbands and the total authority of the husband had suffered some diminution. The relative freedoms enjoyed by some women, particularly those who engaged in war work during the First World War, appeared to many writers in the 1920s – including many of the proponents of sex reform – to pose a serious threat to the maintenance of male power and domination. It is in this context that women's frigidity was posed as a problem by sexologists and the writers of sex advice literature.

The dangers of frigidity

In several important ways the sex reformers can be seen as contributing to the undermining of feminism. Havelock Ellis and others undermined the feminist critique of male sexual behaviour by defining, with the authority of science, male sexuality as active and female sexuality as passive and submissive.[4] They developed their own definition of feminism in which the glorification of motherhood replaced the struggle for women's emancipation.[5] They categorized women's passionate friendships with each other as lesbianism and thereby set limits to the intensity and depth of acceptable women's friendships.[6] They also invented the category of the 'frigide' to account for all those women who were refusing to engage enthusiastically in heterosexual intercourse, either by avoiding marriage or by remaining resistant to sexual intercourse within it.

During the years of the First World War the question of woman's right to sexual pleasure was raised by some of the foremost proponents of sex reform. In *The Erotic Rights of Women* Havelock Ellis asserted that women had erotic rights which had been largely ignored in the nineteenth century. He prescribes how these erotic rights should be claimed, and this, in the form of an active male who gains pleasure through the infliction of pain and a passive female who gains pleasure through masochism, is consonant with the ideology of male and female sexuality he propounds in his other writings.[7] In a 1915 pamphlet Stella Browne launched a broadside attack on the conventional assumptions about women's sexuality and, in particular, the idea that women's sexuality was devoid of a 'strong, spontaneous, discriminating . . . sex impulse'.[8] In Marie Stopes's book *Married Love* (1918) care for the woman, both her right to sexual pleasure and her right to bodily integrity, forms the central motif.[9]

In contrast, the sexological literature of the 1920s locates women's frigidity as a problem, not for the woman herself, but for men, for marriage, for 'society' and 'civilization' in general. Woman's sexual pleasure becomes, for these writers, a means to an end rather than an end in itself. These writers included the sexologists themselves, both doctors and psychiatrists, their popularizers and those ardent anti-feminists who employed the arguments of sex reform. They viewed the problem of women who were not participating in sexual intercourse with men, within marriage or outside, with a consternation verging on panic. By frigidity they clearly did not mean the absence of sexual response since in the causes of frigidity, as we shall see, they included lesbianism and masturbation. Frigidity meant the refusal of women to see sexual intercourse as desirable, vitally necessary or pleasurable. Underlying the arguments about the drastic effects of non-participation in sexual intercourse ran the idea that lack of sexual response in that act could make women dangerous, to other women, to children or to the fabric of society.

The idea of dangerousness developed from theories of repression constructed by the psychoanalysts, particularly by Freud. A.M.Ludovici, in his anti-feminist classic *Lysistrata*, employed this idea.[10] Ludovici is clearly fascist in sympathy and propounds the necessity of destroying democracy to substitute the rule of the 'superman'. Like other anti-feminists of the period, he found sex reforming ideas useful. He also had connections with the more 'progressive' ranks of sex reform.

The foreward to the book consists of a letter of congratulation from Norman Haire, founder in 1921 of the Walworth marriage advice centre, and organizer of the 1929 congress of the World League for Sex Reform. The central 'problem' of Ludovici's book is that of 'surplus women', the two million women in the population in excess of the number of men. He claims that the reason for his concern is that the women's 'thwarted instincts' would find some destructive outlet since 'a thwarted instinct does not meekly subside. It seeks compensation and damages for its rebuff.'[11] The danger was exacerbated by the fact that these women were spreading the doctrine that 'human beings can well get on and be happy without sexual expression' even to married women, and their numbers were steadily increasing. Ludovici makes it clear that his fear stems from the threat which he sees these women as posing to the maintenance of male power. The dangerous effects of 'thwarting' the 'instincts' were that women would compensate with the 'lust of exercising power' and alongside that there would be a 'bitter hatred of men'. He pointed out that there was a 'note of hostility to the male' in woman movements, since these movements were 'largely led by spinsters or else by unhappy married women'.

Ludovici paints an illuminating picture of the future he envisaged if the 'disgruntled females' should be successful. His anxiety stemmed from the idea that male dominance would be overthrown, the exercise of male sexuality severely curtailed and, eventually, the numbers of men in the population drastically reduced. His predictions about restrictions on male sexual behaviour are based upon the demands of feminist campaigners of the day, though much exaggerated.

> Congress of male and female will have begun to seem much more guilty and disgusting even than it is today, and as the male will still be looked upon (as he is now) as the principal culprit in the matter, the age of consent will probably be extended to 35 or 40, if not to the menopause. Seduction and rape will be punished brutally, probably by means of emasculation; and men of vigorous sexuality will be eliminated in order to make way for a generation of low-sexed, meek and sequatious lackeys.[12]

Women would go even further than the above, he claimed, and take to extra-corporeal gestation, cease to cohabit with men and, at length, 'the superfluousness of men above a certain essential minimum (about 5 to every 1,000 women) will have become recognized officially and unofficially as a social fact'. There would then, he conjectured, be an annual slaughter of males, or at least vigorous males, and if sex choice were developed, only 0.5 per cent of males would be reared yearly.

Weith Knudsen's *Feminism – The Woman Question from Ancient Time to the Present Day* was translated into English in 1928. Weith Knudsen was a professor of economics and judisprudence in the Norwegian Technical College, Trondheim, and a committed anti-feminist. His work, like that of other European anti-feminists and sex reformers, was fed into the British debate through quotations in the works of British writers and the translation of his books. He believed firmly in the rule of men over women and when he describes frigidity grandiloquently as a 'threat to civilization' his anxiety is about a threat to male dominance. He asks rhetorically why 'psycho-erotic' deficiency is worth making such a fuss about and what it has to do with feminism and replies:

> it is not possible to dismiss the lurking social-biological danger that this sexual anaesthesia, so prevalent among civilized women, will intensify the misunderstanding between the sexes and contribute to make them even greater strangers to each other than Nature has already made them. Thus this (relative or absolute) feminine erotic insensibility actually reinforces the threats to our civilization, which in a higher degree than in any former culture is based on the assumption of mutual understanding and co-operation between the sexes.[13]

Weith Knudsen's conclusion is that allowing what he calls 'erotically impotent' women to have any political power would be dangerous to other women and to men. No political power could be given to women since it would be impossible to separate off 'erotically impotent' women from those who were potent. If women were allowed any political voice he considered, the decisions would

> depend pre-eminently on the hyper-feministic, anaesthetic minority among the women. For it would not be unreasonable to assume that hyper-feminism has its most numerous, most ardent and most fanatical adherents among the erotically anaesthetic, neurasthenic women. Many of its monstrous assertions and proposals are simply only to be explained by an inborn and incurable blindness to all erotic phenomena.[14]

The argument that it would be dangerous to give the vote to spinsters, if not to all women who refused to show enthusiasm for sexual intercourse, was proclaimed by many anti-feminists in this period. Some posed the danger as the fact that spinsters would use the vote in their own interests, which would be opposed to the interests of the happy wife and mother. Some simply argued that the women's 'thwarted instincts' would make them dangerously unstable and destructive and so unsuited to the exercise of political responsibility.

Walter Gallichan, a popularizer of sex reforming ideas, shared all the alarms of previous writers. He also saw 'frigid' women as dangerous in provoking antagonism between the sexes, posing a 'menace to civilization' and wrecking conjugal happiness. In his 1929 book, *The Poison of Prudery* he writes:

> The erotically impotent women have an enormous influence upon the young, the conventions and regulations of society, and even upon sex legislation. These degenerate women are a menace to civilisation. They provoke sex misunderstanding and antagonism; they wreck conjugal happiness, and pose as superior moral beings when they are really victims of disease.[15]

In his book *Sexual Antipathy and Coldness in Women* (1927) Gallichan describes a formidable array of other dangers which he saw as arising from women's frigidity. A most serious one was, in his opinion, the effects of a mother's frigidity on her children. He wrote, 'the children of sexually cold mothers generally show signs of emotional and neurotic disturbance at an early age'. Much of the disturbance, he claimed, came from the domestic disharmony and disappointment of the parents which stemmed from the wife's frigidity. He separates out the specific and different effects on sons and daughters but one effect to which both fall victim, apparently, is the development of antipathy towards the opposite sex.

> Her sons frequently develop cynical ideas upon married life when they reach adolescence. They distrust women; they tend to be sensual but anti-feminine in their opinions [16]

> Many daughters of cold mothers die spinsters. They imbibe the maternal prejudices and ideas at the school age or earlier, and they grow up with a smouldering antipathy towards men. They are often disappointed with love, and if they marry they develop shrewishness, and become naggers or termagants. [17]

Wilhelm Stekel, a psychoanalyst in the Freudian tradition, contributed an article entitled 'Frigidity in Mothers' to a collection called *The New Generation* (1930) which contained articles from many well-known figures in the sex reform movement, and was introduced by Bertrand Russell. Stekel's article detailed the dire effects of frigidity in mothers upon their children. According to Stekel, frigidity meant 'repressed sexuality'. The effect of the repression was 'a division of the psyche' which caused a 'split personality', with the result that the frigid woman 'will never be able to create the quiet atmosphere children need to avoid the dangers of nervousness. She may have lodged in her soul the contrary tendencies of a Holy Mary and an unholy Magdalene' [18] She was likely to both love and hate her children. He states categorically that 'frigid women are not fit to be mothers. They should first get rid of their frigidity.' The children born into a marriage which was unhappy because of the wife's frigidity, developed an 'unhealthy condition – which is so frequent today – the fear of marriage'.

Gallichan considered that frigid mothers were likely to put their children off sex by their attitudes and to hinder the children's healthy sexual development by refusing to allow sex instruction. Stekel also makes this point and the result he foresaw was the creation of psychopaths.

> Frigidity in women is by no means an insignificant phe-nomenon. It is a social disease that can take on the propor-tions of an epidemic. The offspring of frigid mothers are exposed to the greatest dangers. It is their fate to swell the infinite host of psychopaths, of those who are ill-equipped for life.[19]

Both Gallichan and Stekel point out the danger that frigidity might lead to feminism or man hating. Stekel notes that most frigid women were either militant suffragettes or, surprisingly enough, 'outright woman-haters'. Gallichan was determined that the 'cold' woman was likely to be hostile to men, and that this was particularly dangerous if she was a teacher since,

> as a teacher, the frigide wields considerable power over the unformed minds of her pupils. She rarely takes pains to examine the justice of her indictment of men, and her bias is obvious to those whom she instructs.[20]

Sex and submission

There was another result which the anti-feminists, marriage advice writers and the psychoanalysts saw as very serious. They considered that frigidity in woman was likely to lead to the breakdown of marriages through the discontinuance or unheal-thiness of the marital sexual relationship. Behind the concern over sex in marriage lay two assumptions. First, that the sexual relationship was the fundamental basis of marriage and, second, that marriage was the fundamental basis of society, or, as seems clear on close examination, male dominance. Thomas Van de Velde, in his best-selling manual *Ideal Marriage* (1926) which was still being reprinted in 1977, postulates four corner-stones to marriage, but concentrates on that which he consi-dered most important, 'a vigorous and harmonious sex life'. He wrote that 'sex is the foundation of marriage'.[21] In a marital advice book entitled *The Hygiene of Marriage* (1923), by Isabel Hutton, the same message is put over forcibly. The foreword argues that sex problems will damage marriage because sex is the basis of marriage. She enjoins active participation in sex upon women to avoid 'infidelity' (presumably that of the man) and 'the divorce court'.[22]

This was a new role for sex in marriage, very different from the Victorian ideal. The anxiety about the popularity of marriage which had been voiced before the war had greatly increased as a result of women's new occupations and independence in the war. An important motivation of sex reformers in the 1920s was the need to shore up marriage. This was to be done partly through recognizing woman's right to sexual pleasure and thereby slightly decreasing one of the grossest inequalities of marriage. It was also to be done by introducing a new binding ingredient into marriage to compensate for the lost legal and economic restraints. But this new ingredient, active sexual response from women, was enjoined upon women not as a joy but as a duty.

Gallichan described the seriousness of frigidity and its connection with marital breakdown thus:

> Frigidity is not simply a question for the pathologist and the student of morbid psychology. It is a matter of serious social importance. Conjugal calamity being so fequently brought about by the coldness of one of the pair, it is necessary that the idiosyncrasy should be reckoned with.[23]

The crucial importance of sex in marriage did not simply depend upon the fact that an unsatisfied woman or her disappointed man might grow discontented with her or his partner. The importance of a 'satisfactory' sexual bond went far beyond the mere question of a frustrated desire for pleasure or response. There was a general understanding amongst this group of writers that sexual intercourse served a fundamental purpose in regulating the relations of the sexes.

Ludovici, who was writing not just of sex in marriage, but of the surplus-women problem, saw sexual intercourse as the factor which prevented sex antagonism. The feminists who rejected it had unleashed this antagonism.

Neglect and degeneration of the body were bound to lead to a loathing of the body and the wish to be emancipated from its thraldom. This, however, necessarily destroyed one of the chief bonds between man and woman, and left the natural and radical hostility between the sexes naked and unconstrained. This is one side of feminism.[24]

Sexual intercourse, particularly intercourse in which women engaged actively, was seen by many writers to prevent women from developing resentment of their oppression and struggling against it. Some made the connection between the subjection of women and women's experience of sexual pleasure very clear.

Ellis, Bloch, Forel and other sex reformers before the First World War proclaimed that female sexual pleasure involved the necessity of subjection to the will of the male during sexual activity, but made little comment on the way in which this would affect the wider relationship between men and women, in marriage or out of it.

Freud made illuminating revelations about his views on the importance of sexual intercourse for wives in his 1918 essay 'The Taboo of Virginity'. Ellis was a much more significant influence on British sex reforming writers of the 1920s than Freud, though occasional reference was made to Freud's work. I include Freud's comments here to show that the idea that female submission and sexual intercourse were inextricably linked, was quite general.

Freud describes the meaning of the expression 'sexual bondage', as used by Krafft-Ebing, as 'a person's acquiring an unusually high degree of dependence and lack of self-reliance in relation to another person with whom he has a sexual relationship', a phenomenon which could extend as far as 'the loss of all independent will and as far as causing a person to suffer the greatest sacrifices of his own interests'.[25] Freud declares that 'some measure of sexual bondage' is 'indispensable to the maintenance of civilized marriage'. He makes it clear that 'sexual bondage' is a phenomenon experienced almost entirely by women and not men, for obvious reasons:

the decisive factor is the amount of sexual resistance that is overcome and in addition the fact that the process of overcoming the resistance is concentrated and happens only once. This state of bondage is, accordingly, far more frequent and more intense in women than in men.[26]

Some writers in the 1920s, notably Stekel and Van de Velde, took up the idea of the importance and necessity of the subjection of women during sexual activity and showed how this could help solve all the problems which exercised them most, such as feminism, man hating and female resistance to male domination. They gave a new significance to heterosexual activity. Sexual intercourse became both a metaphor for the subjection of woman and a method of effecting that subjection.

Wilhelm Stekel's *Frigidity in Woman in Relation to her Lovelife* was published in two volumes in New York in 1926. It was one of many studies of 'sexual impotence' or 'deficient sexual sensibility' in woman published in the second decade of the twentieth century. Many writers before Stekel had alluded to the connections between feminism, man hating and frigidity. Stekel's unequivocal proposition was that female frigidity was a form of resistance to male dominance, a weapon to be used against men in the battle between the sexes. He writes:

> We shall never understand the problem of the frigid woman unless we take into consideration the fact that the two sexes are engaged in a lasting conflict . . . The social aspect of the problem, too, unveils itself before our eyes. We recognize plainly that dyspareunia (frigidity in woman) is a social problem; it is one of woman's weapons in the universal struggle of the sexes.[27]

Stekel considered that a woman must submit herself to her husband in order to experience sexual pleasure. He saw woman's refusal to experience pleasure as an unconscious or conscious refusal to submit to be 'conquered'. He states that 'two bipolar forces struggle for mastery over human life: the will-to-power and the will-to-submission (or the self-subjection urge).' It is no surprise that he expects the subjection urge to conquer the will-to-power in women but not in men. He argues that all lovers must yield in love but continues to speak in the same breath only of women being 'conquered'.

> A secret (unrecognized) notion of all persons who love is that to make another person 'feel' is to achieve a victory over that person. To give one's self to be 'roused', means self-abandonment; it means 'yielding'! This act of submission is expressed symbolically even in woman's position during the sexual embrace. Alfred Adler very properly lays great stress upon the symbolisms of 'above' and 'below'. Indeed, certain women feel roused only if they are 'on top', i.e. by clinging to the fantasy that they are males and that they are the ones to 'rouse' their sexual partner, who is thus relegated to the passive or feminine role. To be roused by a man means acknowledging oneself as conquered.[28]

It is clear that he does not see the submission as being something biologically ordained but as related to the very material power relationship between men and women. He describes with great scorn women who find it easier to experience sexual pleasure with partners who are not obviously in every way their social superiors; women who are in fact healthily rejecting masochism. Any man who is not in total control in sexual activity he describes as being 'possessed' by the woman.

Submission in sex signified that a woman was prepared to submit in her total personality to her husband. He was indignant at the general 'obstinacy' of the women he treated, their refusal to submit and the fact that they wished to be personalities in their own right. Such a wish he associated with the 'will-to-power' and it becomes clear that to Stekel the 'will-to-power' meant the desire of a woman to survive as a self-respecting, independent human being who still had some conception of herself as a person not subsumed into her husband. According to his analysis, a woman's capacity for sexual pleasure depended on the extent to which she was able to embrace joyfully the reality of her inferior status. Her resistance to the happy acceptance of male dominance had to be broken down before she would respond correctly. Stekel's conclusions illuminate Ludovici's statement that sexual inter-course was the 'bond' which regulated sex antagonism. Stekel saw women's frigidity as a mass phenomenon and as a weapon used by women in the general war of the sexes. Curing 'frigidity' on a mass scale would aid the end of women's resistance to men in the battle of the sexes and ensure male dominance, not just on an individual but on a societal plane.

Thomas Van de Velde's *Ideal Marriage* was his first book in a trilogy on the relations between the sexes. It was translated into English by Stella Browne and was, to judge from the way that it is quoted and referenced, considered by the sex reformers to be an important contribution to the debate. His second work, *Sex Hostility in Marriage*, was published in Britain in Heinemann's Medical Books Series in 1931. In this book he shows that he considered the correct form of marriage to be male dominance and female submission, and that this power relationship was not only symbolized by, but reinforced through, sexual activity. 'Hostility' in marriage was caused by the woman's refusal to submit to her husband. He describes woman's 'dependence' on man as natural and biological and notes that 'numerous power-ful influences making for submission to the man are present in sexual connection, the sexual impulse is associated in the woman with a tendency to submit herself.'[29]

Weith Knudsen, the Norwegian anti-feminist, also saw woman's subjection to be necessary to her sexual pleasure.

> It is therefore only to be expected that a mental atmosphere like that of present-day feminism, which in a number of women actually precludes the psychical submission, aban-donment and self-effacement under the man's will – one of the most important requirements for the woman's attaining maximum erotic gratification with all that follows therefrom – should of itself be calculated to increase the already large number of white women who are erotically impotent from other causes of a more physical nature.[30]

He speaks specifically of white women because he was con-vinced that women in the East would 'squeal with delight' simply at the touch of a white man's hand. Such racist sexual stereotypes of women of colour are, of course, still common today.

The size of the problem and its causes

There was disagreement over the size of the problem of frigidity, and over the question of whether frigidity was curable or had a biological basis. Stekel estimated that 40–50 per cent of women were frigid and considered that the problem particularly afflicted women of the 'higher cultural levels'.[31] He asserted that there was no such thing as an 'asexual' being. Frigidity was the result of repression and therefore curable. Weith Knudsen quotes estimates from various sources which place the percentage of women who are frigid at between 40 and 60 per cent. He claimed that the first 20 per cent of frigid women were incurable.[32] Van de Velde estimated the number of women who were at least temporarily 'anaesthetic' in marriage at 100 per cent.[33]

The reasons offered for women's frigidity were many and various and included both physiological factors such as constipation, psychological factors and even social ones such as the spread of feminism. Stekel, Gallichan and Charlotte Haldane (wife of the biologist whose *Motherhood and its Enemies* was published in 1927), suggest homosexuality or intersexuality as one explanation, though at other times they cite it as the result and not the cause.[34]

There are similar confusions around feminism and man hating which are cited as both cause and result. Weith Knudsen attributed 10 per cent of frigidity to feminism and the rest to cerebral defects, defective secretion of the sexual glands and nervous disorders. Gallichan cites masturbation as one of the causes of frigidity in women. Apparently, women who masturbated sometimes preferred this activity to sexual intercourse. He also cited masturbation as a result of frigidity since some women were said to take to it in order to avoid sexual intercourse which they disliked. One frequently mentioned cause of the phenomenon of frigidity was 'puritanism'. The attack on puritanism was dear to the hearts of those 'post-

Victorians' of the early twentieth century who aimed to disman-
tle what they saw as repressive Victorian ideas on sexuality. The
pre-war feminists who had launched a swingeing critique of
male sexual behaviour were characterized as representatives of
puritanism and attacked in books such as Walter Gallichan's
The Poison of Prudery.[35]

Two much favoured explanations for frigidity were ignorance
due to lack of sex education and the trauma of the first night.
Most sex advice writers of the period wrote about defloration as
a fearful ordeal to be got over as swiftly as possible – like a visit
to the dentist. Behind the concern over defloration lay the idea
that women could not be expected to have a satisfactory sexual
response at the outset of married life. Not only were women
expected to be slower to arouse on each occasion on which
sexual activity took place, but they were expected to take
months or even years to learn to respond sexually to their
husbands. Van de Velde, in *Ideal Marriage,* quotes two experts
who considered:

> inadequate sexual sensibility in coitus at the beginning of
> sexual life, must be accounted physiologically normal in
> women: they have to learn how to feel both voluptuous
> pleasure and actual orgasm. The frequency of temporary
> anaesthesia, these specialists estimate as absolute, 100 per
> cent.[36]

Sexual pleasure in intercourse was to be learnt by women,
often with considerable difficulty, but was presumed to be
pleasurable from the start for men who were not expected to
undergo lengthy distress and pain. This did not cause the
experts to pause in their assumption that submission to the
male in sexual intercourse was natural and inevitable for
women. Seldom can anything natural, healthy and instinctive
have required such intensive training. Isabel Hutton in *The
Hygiene of Marriage* writes, 'It is quite normal, however, for
a woman not to experience in any way the feelings of sexual
excitement, even towards the man she loves, till some time
after the marriage has been consummated.'[37]

The result of this 'temporary anaesthesia' was that the

wedding night was likely to be a frightening and painful experience for the bride which could have a profound influence on the whole of the rest of her married life. The advice books therefore recommended consideration and tactfulness on the part of the husband to avoid alienating his wife. Van de Velde enjoined tact upon the husband to reduce the trauma of the first night because,

> Normal defloration, too, on account of the elements of subordination, injury, pain and disappointment involved, arouses a certain (of course, mostly unconscious) feeling of hostility towards the man who performs the act.[38]

Woman's pleasure does not seem to have been the aim of this procedure which need only be entered into for the purpose of reproduction as far as many earlier feminist writers on sexuality were concerned.[39] Its purpose was the man's pleasure and the woman's subjection. Hutton shared the anxiety over the first night. She wrote, 'if the man is not especially gentle and considerate in the early days of his marriage he is endangering the happiness of the whole of his married life.'[40] Van de Velde, who describes the penis on the wedding night as the 'invading organ' was determined that the husband should not wait around any longer than four nights but must consult a gynecologist/psychologist if his wife showed resistance for longer than that. He advised the husband not to show 'weak submission' or 'sentimentality' but 'consideration and technical proficiency' because 'the course of a marriage is determined by the wedding night.'[41]

Another reason suggested for women's reluctance to engage in sexual intercourse or their inability to relax and enjoy it, was anxiety over unwanted childbearing. Hannah Stone advanced this argument in her paper for the Sex Reform Congress entitled 'Birth Control as a Factor in the Sex Life of Women'. The case studies that she describes show that one woman at least was 'obtaining sexual gratification at times through mere external contact or auto-erotic practice'.[42] Such practices are described by Stone as 'unnatural sex habits'. The husbands in the case studies are those revealed as suffering trauma through lack of sexual intercourse. Her evidence suggests that birth control was more necessary to men's sexual pleasure than to women's. Another birth controller contributing to the Sex Reform Congress offers birth control as a solution to a woman who describes brutal battering and rape by her husband.[43] The birth controllers' belief in the necessity of sexual intercourse seems to have made them blind to women's right to abstain, to engage in alternative erotic practices and to control access to their bodies. These were demands which feminists up to the 1920s had been making as central to the struggle for women's emancipation. In the 1880s there was a demand for rape in marriage to be made a crime.[44]

Some historians have praised the birth controllers for separating sex and reproduction. The opposite seems more likely to have been the case. Sexual intercourse is only one of many possible sexual practices within heterosexuality, and the only one which is specifically reproductive. Whilst joining in the conscription of women into sexual intercourse in the 1920s the birth controllers helped to link sex and reproduction inextricably together.

Solutions

To solve the problem of the non-participating woman the sex reformers had to deal with the large number of women who would not or could not marry, and with the frigid wife. The solution which was favoured for the problem of the spinster was concubinage. Concubinage was aired as a solution before the First World War in the *Freewoman* magazine which carried articles about the satisfaction and happiness that accrued to women in societies in which polygamy was practised. In *Women under Polygamy* (1914) Walter Gallichan shows clear approval of the Indian system where he imagines that women are more compliant, and conform closely to his image of the ideal woman.

> Spinsterhood, and the 'right to live one's own life', – the
> supreme consummation of a large number of revolutionary
> British women – make no appeal to an Indian woman. Her

strongest impulses are to fulfil her womanhood, to experience love, and to bear children. That is her vocation, her
ambition, and her joy.[45]

Gallichan's impulse to write the book came from his alarm at
the numbers of unmarried women in Britain and their feminist
ideas. He sees polygamy as applicable to the problem of these
intransigent women.

Another cause of (reason for ?) polygyny especially in
Great Britain, is to be sought in the preponderance of women
in the population. The surplus of marriageable women who
remain single is often overstated. Nevertheless there is an
immense army of compulsorily celibate women. Certain city
areas are inhabited chiefly by unmarried women.[46]

Walter Heape, in his pre-war anti-feminist work *Sex Antagonism*, stated a preference for polygamy because, 'it may
perhaps be claimed that polygamy amongst savage people is
associated with a minimum of sex antagonism.'[47] Ludovici in
Lysistrata suggests the legal recognition of concubinage as the
solution to the central problem of the book, that of 'surplus
women'. Norman Haire, in the foreword, enthusiastically
seconds Ludovici's proposition about concubinage and states
that he agrees that 'Sound and desirable women cannot be
happy unmated.'[48] Charlotte Haldane, in her book *Motherhood
and its Enemies*, was deeply worried about that particular
category of 'enemies', the spinster. She devotes a chapter of the
book to 'An Experiment in Polygamy' in which she eulogizes
the Oneida community in the US because of the holding of
women in common which took place there.[49]

Behind the interest in polygamy lay, for all these authors
whose political views ranged from high Tory or fascist to liberal,
a concern at the existence of 'surplus women'. The concern was
not primarily for the sexual or emotional satisfaction of these
women, many of whom, anyway, were engaged in passionate
relationships with each other.[50] The concern was for the management of a group of women who were seen to be the mainstay
of the feminist movement and deeply critical of men, marriage
and the form taken by male sexuality. They were also seen to be

alarmingly independent of men and to threatened the maintenance of male domination. The institution of polygamy was
seen to be desirable because it would attach these women to
men in a form of marriage and as we can see from much of the
sex reformers' work, marriage was understood to be an institution which maintained the submission of women.

There was no simple solution to the problem of ensuring that
married women would participate actively in sexual intercourse. One panacea that was recommended was sex education
since ignorance was held to be a prime cause of women's shock
and trauma at the outset of marriage. In the 1920s there was an
avalanche of sex advice literature. Many of the homilies upon
marriage seem to be designed not so much to explain to women
how to achieve sexual satisfaction as to enjoin upon them the
necessity of entering marriage prepared to engage in sexual
intercourse and not object to it. Dire warnings are issued to
women as to what will happen if they refuse to co-operate,
usually posed as the loss of their husbands permanently or
temporarily to affairs, or to prostitutes. Isabel Hutton writes a
'special word' to 'women who feel disinclined to begin the
sexual life, and who feel that the idea is distasteful to them'.[51]
The recalcitrant woman is assured by Hutton that only by
enthusiastic participation in sexual intercourse can she prove
that she is 'normal', ensure her own health and ensure that her
husband will not abandon her.

Van de Velde had a similarly stern approach to sex education
for women. He writes that, 'The wife must be taught, not only
how to behave in coitus, but, above all, how and what to feel in
this unique act.'[52] No wonder the period of training was
expected to last so long. In cases where simple education was
not enough the manuals advised husbands to call in gynaecolog-
ists or psychoanalysts to deal with their wives. Van de Velde
describes here the treatment of a woman who was, according to
his analysis, creating hostility in marriage.

The patient is shown the necessity of changing her manner of
thinking after she has been brought to see the whole situation
clearly. She must then be freed from egocentricity, and attain
to a high degree of adaptability to any given circumstance.[53]

Another way in which the conscription of reluctant women into active participation in sexual intercourse was carried out was through marriage advice centres. One of these was opened in 1929 by Mrs Janet Chance in the East End of London. From a report on this centre in the papers of the Sex Reform Congress comes a picture of the way in which sex reforming ideas were filtered through such centres to those women who might not be reading sex advice literature. Chance writes that the centre was opened to deal with the following: first, the sex education of children; second, abdominal hygiene for women; and, third, sex-satisfaction for women. One aim of the centre was to give advice in the technique of orgasm. Chance was totally confident of the rightness and necessity of sexual intercourse for women despite the lack of enthusiasm of some of her clients. The following shows the kind of attitude she sought to change:

> By many [women] it is not to be expected that the marriage relationship should be enjoyed by the wife. As one woman, Mrs Eyles tells us, put it in 1914 to a young wife who was grieving over the departure of her husband: 'No, my dear, you don't know what you're up agen yet. But you wait till you've been to bed over 3,000 nights with the same man like me, and had to put up with everthing, then you'd be blooming glad the old Kayser went potty.'[54]

Her comments on the 'spinster' and those women who had different views on the significance of male sexuality and sexual intercourse for women come close to the most extreme pronouncements of the anti-feminist sex reformers. She was convinced that 'non-orgasmic' women should be kept out of politics, and wrote,

> The effect of your spinster politicians, whether married or single, has yet to be analysed and made plain to the women they represent. I consider the lack of orgasm by women a fundamental question which deserves serious consideration.[55]

The Sex Reform Congress

At the congress of the World League for Sex Reform in 1929

the viewpoint of those feminists who had been launching a critique of male sexual behaviour and its effects on women, was represented by only a single voice, that of Joanna Elberskirchen. The congress in London brought together many of the sex reformers mentioned in this chapter. It was organized by the British branch of the World League which was set up in 1928. The main organizing work was done by Dora Russell and Norman Haire. The contributors included Dora Russell, Marie Stopes, Stella Browne, Norman Haire, and the supporters and members of the congress included Havelock Ellis and August Forel (who shared with Magnus Hirschfeld the presidency of the World League), Walter Gallichan and Wilhelm Stekel. The contributors and supporters also included an impressive cross-section of the best-known names in the arts, the academic world (particularly anthropology), the biological sciences, medicine and psychoanalysis, and in politics. Literary figures included Vera Brittain, Naomi Mitchison, Ethel Mannin, G.B.Shaw, Arnold Bennett, E.M.Forster, D.H.Lawrence and Somerset Maugham. Such a distinguished list of personnel indicates the strength, influence and respectability which the sex reform movement had gained. The congress brought together many whom one might otherwise have thought to have little in common. Politically, sex reform seems to have created some very strange bedfellows, including Alexandra Kollontai and Sylvia Pankhurst along with the high Tories.

Joanna Elberskirchen's paper was the only one at the congress which represented the pre-war feminist understanding of the link between male sexual behaviour and women's oppression, She had been a militant suffragist in Germany before the war. She argues that the matriarchate was suppressed by the patriarchal state when sexual periodicity gave way to men's preoccupation with woman as an object of pleasure. 'Sex, the desire for pleasure, became the great power in the life of man. Man became the slave of pleasure. Woman became the victim, the slave to man's pleasure.'[56] The result of this according to Elberskirchen, was the 'sexual dictatorship of men over women' which led to the general dictatorship of men over women. Rather than seeing frequent sexual intercourse as vitally necessary for health and happiness as do the other contributors, she argues that 'too frequent' sexual intercourse 'does terrible harm' to women's interests. The whole tone of her contribution is at total variance with others at the congress. Though the equality of women was one of the planks of the World League platform of reform, the form of feminism espoused by the league was carefully circumscribed, Only that propounded by 'modernists' like Dora Russell was acceptable. Elberskirchen was the lone representative of a defeated tradition.

Feminists such as Stella Browne and Dora Russell who were committed to fighting the idea that sex was unclean or shameful found themselves in the position of having to deny or reject the ideas on sexuality which the militant feminists had proclaimed.[57] They did not wish to reject the idea of sexual relations with men but to assert that they could be pleasurable for women and demanded more consideration for women within these relationships. In the pursuit of their aim they echoed the anti-feminist sex reformers in portraying the 'spinster' feminists as old-fashioned prudes and glossed over or ignored the critical analyses that these women were making of the connection between male sexual behaviour and the oppression of women. The sex reforming feminists set out to create a new form of feminism to reflect their new concern with the joy of sexual intercourse. Russell's ideal form fits closely with that held by the male sex reformers from Havelock Ellis onwards. She writes of the importance of motherhood and says that the most important task of 'modern feminism' is to 'accept and proclaim sex; to bury the lie that has too long corrupted our society – the lie that the body is a hindrance to the mind, and sex a necessary evil to be endured for the perpetuation of the race.'[58]

The routing of the feminist critique was accomplished through the assertion by the sex reformers that there were only two sides to the debate on sexuality. The two sides were the 'prudes' and the 'progressives'. The feminists were characterized as 'prudes' who were defined as anti-sex, thwarted, repressed and dangerous. There was no space left in the discussion for those who wished to criticize male sexual behaviour and its effects on

women. Women's campaign to transform male sexual behaviour and protect women provided a strong motivating force
to the women's movement for 50 years. By its defeat militant
feminism was seriously undermined. The decline of militant
feminism was facilitated by the sex reformers through the
creation of an alternative, non-challenging form of feminism, a
concerted attack on the ideas of the militant feminists and their
most vociferous proponents, the spinsters.

As the sex reformers gained ground in the battle of ideas
around sexuality the foundations of male domination were
structurally reinforced through the conscription of women into
the heterosexual couple and into active participation in sexual
intercourse. The construction of the category of the 'frigide'
was of vital importance in reinforcing the heterosexual unit.
The spinster, and resisting women in general, were classified as
deviant and dangerous. Those sex reformers who made plain
their belief that submission to the man was an intrinsic part of
female sexual pleasure were unambiguous in promoting sexual
intercourse as the antidote to feminism and to women's independence.

Sexuality remains a central concern of the women's liberation
movement today. The orchestration of women's sexual response through the science of sexology, through sex therapy
and sex advice manuals from the 1920s to the present can be
seen as a means of maintaining men's domination over women.
It cannot be assumed that the pursuit of sexual pleasure for
women in relationships with men is automatically in women's
interests. The construction, not merely of sexual practice, but
of sexual pleasure itself needs to be analysed and it is necessary
to question whether sexual response within the power relationship that is the heterosexual unit, can be positive and
liberating for women.

Postscript: The London Feminist History Group

In the summer of 1981 some of the women who had given papers to the London Feminist History Group in the course of that year met together to plan this book. Many of us felt that the theories which feminist historians in Britain had been using up until then were inadequate to deal with the problems we had been grappling with, particularly in the areas of sexuality and sexual violence. What we wanted to talk about was patriarchy and male power.

We want to stress that we only represent the views of the women involved in producing this book and not the London Feminist History Group as a whole.

The London Feminist History Group 1973–1983*

The group started in 1973 as an informal discussion group meeting in the houses of members, and was the first Feminist History Group in Britain. For many years it had strong links with the Women's Research and Resources Centre (WRRC) but this connection is less strong now, and over the last few years it has met at different women's centres in London: at the Women's Aid building and at 'A Woman's Place'. At present it is meeting at the New Mary Ward Centre, Queen's Square, WC1.

The London Feminist History Group is open to all women, meets fortnightly on Friday evenings, and draws its participants from advertisements in the WRRC newsletter, *Spare Rib*, the

---

* With grateful thanks to Anna Davin and her article on the FHG in *History Workshop Journal*, 9, spring 1980.

London Women's Liberation newsletter, *WIRES* and *City Limits*.

A major function of the group has always been to provide a supportive and stimulating environment for women writing feminist history, and supports the increasing number of women involved in women's studies courses and WEA classes. The group also provides a forum for women without an academic base, who work at their history full- or part-time, often in virtual isolation, who need to talk about their findings. We try to break down the isolation and individualism which can make research work so alienating, by sharing sources and information, and by establishing contacts between women, very often women from other countries who are staying in London or visiting the Feminist History Group.

The London Feminist History Group is certainly not confined to those actually working on historical projects – up to 40 or 50 women will turn up for popular subjects. By talking about our work with other feminists we are able to make links between the struggles which many of us are involved in today, and the women's history we're exploring. It is clear that present and past members of the group feel that the existence of the London Feminist History Group has been important for maintaining a space for feminist history within the British Women's Liberation Movement. Many currents of feminist thought have been debated within the Feminist History Group; such theoretical discussions have been very popular.

The London Feminist History Group consists solely of the women who come to the weekly meetings. One or two women act as convenors and do the administrative work, for about a year, and then the job is passed on to others. Speakers include regular members of the group, irregular members and visitors. We also hold frequent work-in-progress sessions, where everyone talks about their work for five minutes. The presentation may be as loose or as formal as the speaker wants, but on the whole people are encouraged to be relaxed about it, so that discussion can be as free as possible.

The subjects discussed in the group have always varied widely. From time to time we have attempted to group papers in subjects; during the last few years – family history, women's work, education, medical and nursing history, and sexuality. However, we have found that some areas haven't been adequately covered and we would welcome papers on black women's history, lesbian history and papers which address the problem of heterosexuality.

The Feminist History Group is also involved in activities such as putting on films and plays, and organizing feminist history walks.

How to start a Feminist History Group

There are already Feminist History Groups in Birmingham, Manchester, Sheffield and Liverpool and probably in other towns as well. Women often write to us asking if there is a local group or how to set one up. We felt that our experience in London may be very different from that of other groups and so we asked the Manchester Women's History Group if we could reprint their suggestions from the 1983 Spare Rib diary:

> Think about what kind of group you want. In our experience the initial impetus may come from a number of different sources, but these are not mutually exclusive and the group will no doubt change over time.
> — a support group for women actively engaged in historical research and others interested in history, to share their work and the common problems of isolation, working in an unsympathetic environment and struggling with the new questions which women's history necessarily raises, for us, one of the recurring questions has been the relationship between marxism and feminism. We also continue to discuss what constitutes feminist history and how it differs from women's history. Needless to say, we have not resolved either of these questions yet!
> — a group to study local women's history as a collective enterprise, arising out of a common interest in your community. For example, were local women involved in the struggle for the vote? Have there been local campaigns for birth control and for abortion, such as the Manchester and Salford Mothers' Clinic set up in 1926 for local

working women and which provoked considerable hostility in some sections of the community?

— a group which draws on the shared experience of its members to explore our recent history. This is more than a consciousness-raising group in that it is part of remaking our history as women. The Birmingham Feminist History Group have been working on feminism and femininity in the 1950s (see bibliography) building on their own experience of that period.

— a group which springs from a shared commitment to a particular campaign such as the peace movement, or Right to Work campaign, or an abortion campaign, and looks for its historical roots and the ways in which women in particular have taken up these issues in the past. This work can serve both as an inspiration and can help us to learn from earlier successes and failures.

Advertise your interest, using the local press, local radio, local women's networks, local bookshops and national publications like *Spare Rib* and *WIRES*. Advertisements do not need to be limited to the classified columns of the local paper: why not provide material for an article or use an old photograph – for example, of a local suffrage campaign – to draw attention to your group and to invite participation? Just asking for similar photos and other documents or memories can produce a good response and attract members. Another way to meet interested women and to begin to work on women's history is to start a class with the co-operation of the Workers Educational Association, the extra-mural department of your local university, or the County/City education department. You could run a class yourselves or suggest to one of these bodies that there is sufficient interest for them to arrange a course. A single lecture or public meeting with a speaker from a women's history group in another area or from a local history group could fulfil the same function.

Once a group is formed it is obviously a good idea to continue to advertise your meetings, and to stick to a regular date and place for meetings if possible so that it is easy for other women to join you.

Notes

1. Rape or seduction? A controversy over sexual violence in the nineteenth century

The best source for the Thornton trial is John Hall, ed., *The Trial of Abraham Thornton* (Notable British Trial Series), London and Edinburgh: Hodge 1926. For background on the early nineteenth century, Barbara Taylor's *Eve and the New Jerusalem*, London: Virago 1983, is very useful. Susan Edward's *Female Sexuality and the Law* (London: Martin Robertson 1981) provides some information on the legal treatment of sexual violence, mostly in the late nineteenth century. Aside from the Thornton trial, many of the conclusions in this article are based on a sampling of newspaper reports of incidents of sexual violence, taking three months out of every year between 1815 and 1845 of *The Times* and out of every other year between 1815 and 1845 of the *Weekly Dispatch* (also a London publication).

1. T.C.Smout, 'Aspects of Sexual Behaviour in 19th century Scotland', in *Social Class in Scotland,* ed. A.A.Maclaren, Edinburgh: John MacDonald 1976, pp. 77–9; David Levine, *Family Formation in an Age of Nascent Capitalism,* New York: Academic Press 1972, p. 137.
2. Hall, *op. cit.* p. 72
3. *The Times*, 19 August 1824.
4. (G. Ludlam), *The Mysterious Murder* (2nd edn), Birmingham: ca. 1818. Ballads found in Madden Collection, Cambridge University Library; *Gentleman's Magazine* (1817) II, p. 464.
5. Hall, *op. cit.* p. 110.
6. *Ibid* pp. 98, 78–9.
7. S. Farr, *Elements of Medical Jurisprudence*, London: 1815, p. 45: T.R.Beck, *Elements of Medical Jurisprudence,* London: 1825, pp. 55–7; Michael Ryan, *A Manual of Medical Jurisprudence,* London: 1831, pp. 182–3.

8. *The Times*, 29 October 1829; *The Times*, 2 March 1838; *Independent Whig*, 17 August 1817; *The Times*, 31 March 1838.

9. Madden Collection, Cambridge University Library.

10. *Hints to the Public and the Legislature, on the Prevalence of Vice and the Dangerous Effects of Seduction*, London: 1811, p. 6.

11. *Weekly Dispatch*, 15 February 1835.

12. 'Report from the Select Committee on Criminal Law' Parliamentary Papers 1819 (585) VIII.1.

13. Edward Holroyd, *Observations on a Case of Abraham Thornton*, London: 1819, pp. 24–87.

14. *Wager of Battle: Thornton and Mary Ashford, or an Antidote to Prejudice*, London: 1818, p. 16.

15. Edward Hyde East, *A Treatise on the Pleas of the Crown*, vol. 1, London: 1803, p. 444.

16. *The Times*, 30 August 1824.

17. Quoted in H.A.Snelling, 'What is Rape?' in L.Schultz, ed., *Rape Victimology*, Springfield, Illinois: Charles C. Thomas 1975, p. 153.

18. The Rev. Luke Booker, *A Moral Review of the Conduct and Case of Mary Ashford*, Dudley: 1818, p. 54.

19. *Ibid.* p. 10.

20. Broadsheet, 'Confession, though not the Dying Speech of Ab. Thornton', from Nottingham City Library Broadsheet Collection.

21. 'Friend to Justice' *Reply to the Remarks of the Rev. Luke Booker*, Birmingham: 1818, p. 34.

22. *The Times*, 16 September 1824.

23. Madden Collection, Cambridge University Library.

24. *The Murdered Maid*, Warwick: 1818, p. 43.

25. Madden Collection, Cambridge University Library.

26. John Gillis, 'Servants, Sexual Relations, and the Risks of Illegitimacy in London 1801–1900', *Feminist Studies*, spring 1979, p. 146.

27. *Horrible Rape and Murder! The Affecting Case of Mary Ashford*, London: 1817, p. 51.

28. *The Murdered Maid*, p. 12

29. *The Mysterious Murder*, p. 58.

30. *The Terrific Register*, vol. 2, London: 1825, pp. 401–3.

31. *The Murdered Maid*, p. 22.

32. J.Chitty, *A Practical Treatise on Medical Jurisprudence*, London: 1834, p. 378.

33. *Ladies Monthly Museum*, March 1818, pp. 121–6.

34. *The Times,* 1 December 1836.
35. *The Times,* 5 April 1830; *Weekly Dispatch,* 1 June 1845.
36. *Weekly Dispatch,* 17 May 1829; *The Times,* 5 July 1844.
37. *The Times*, 13 October 1837; *Weekly Dispatch*, 3 December 1843.
38. M. Ignatieff, *A Just Measure of Pain,* New York: Columbia Univerity Press 1978, p. 133.
39. *The Times,* 12 December 1843; *The Times,* 20 September 1819; *Weekly Dispatch,* 1 March 1829.
40. *The Times,* 8 August 1834; *Weekly Dispatch,* 26 July 1840; *The Times*, 18 December 1829 *The Times*, 11 December 1827.
41. The Associate Institute for Improving and Enforcing the Laws for the Protection of Women, *First Report,* London: 1846, p. 14.
42. Sheila Jeffreys, 'Free from All Uninvited Touch of Man: Women's Campaigns around Sexuality, 1880–1914', forthcoming, *Women's Studies International Quarterly.*

2. Rape in England between 1550 and 1700

1. J.S Cockburn, 'The Nature and Incidence of Crime in England 1550–1625: A Preliminary Survey', in J.S.Cockburn, ed, *Crime in England 1550 – 1800,* London: Methuen 1977, p. 58.
2. Geoffrey Quaife, *Wanton Wenches and Wayward Wives*, London: Croom Helm 1979.
3. J.B.Post, 'Ravishment of Women and the Statutes of Westminster', in J.H.Baker, ed., *Legal Records and the Historian,* Cambridge University Press 1978; J.B.Post, 'Sir Thomas West and the Statutes of Rapes, 1382', in *Bulletin of the Institute of Historical Research,* vol. 53 no. 127, May 1980.
4. E.W.Ives 'Agaynst taking awaye of Women: The Inception and Operation of the Abduction Act of 1487', in E.W.Ives, R.J. Knecht and J.J. Scarisbrick, eds., *Wealth and Power in Tudor England,* London: Athlone 1978.
5. J.S.Cockburn, *Calendar of Assize Records, Essex, Hertfordshire, Kent, Surrey, Sussex: Elizabeth I and James I*, London: HMSO 1976.
6. F.Pollock and F.W.Maitland, *The History of English Law Before the Time of Edward I,* Book II, Cambridge University Press 1952, p. 490.
7. J.B.Post 'Ravishment of Women'.
8. J.B.Post, 'Sir Thomas West'.

9. E.W.Ives, 'Agaynst taking awaye of Women'.

10. Michael Dalton, *The Country Justice: Containing the Practice, Duty and Power of the Justices of the Peace*, London: Professional Books 1973, p. 483.

11. Anthony Fitzherbert, *The New Boke of the Justices of the Peas*, London: Professional Books 1972, p. 19.

12. Conyers Read, ed., *William Lambarde and Local Government: His 'Ephemeris' and Twenty-nine Charges to the Juries and Commissions,* New York: Cornell University Press 1962, p. 81.

13. Nicholas Brady, *The Lawes Resolution of Women's Rights or The Lawes Provision for Woemen*, 1632.

14. F.Pollock and F.W.Maitland,*op. cit.*

15. In an unusual case at the 1655 Kent Assizes, Henry Grundee was indicted for the rape of Mary Fynn. Susan Austen and Annke Baker were indicted as accessories. In the home counties over the whole period 1558–1700 this was the only case where women were indicted in a rape prosecution. These women were given a particularly hard time, especially considering the proportion of men acquitted of rape and released unconditionally. Austen and Baker were bound in August 1655 to 'to remayne in gaole until delivered by due course of law'. Three years later in March 1658 they were still in gaol and no notice is given of their release. Grundee went uncaptured, untried, unpunished and finally was outlawed.

16. Brady, *The Lawes Resolution of Women's Rights,* book 5, section 29, p. 392.

17. *An Account of the Proceedings at the Sessions of Oyer and Terminer and Gaol Delivery of Newgate*, 1683.

18. Sir Henry Finch, *Law, or a Discourse Thereof*, 1627; Brady, *op. cit.* p. 396; William Lambarde, *Eirenarcha, or Of the Office of the Justices of the Peace*, 1611.

19. Sussex Record Office, Chichester, *QR*.W83/72, W138/90, W137/90.

20. *Brockman Papers,* vol. 12 ADD.MSS 42598, 18 October 1697. British Museum.

21. William Lambarde, *Eirenarcha, or Of the Office of the Justices of the Peace.*

22. PRO *Ass.*44/4.

23. Surrey Record Office, *Sessions Rolls XXV*, 16 April 1667, m.24.

24. Sussex Record Office, *QR*.W201/10.

25. *Lancashire Quarter Sessions Records,* vol. 1. Quarter Sessions

Rolls 1590 – 1606, James Tait (ed.), Chetham Society, Manchester, 1917, p. 170.

26. PRO *Ass.*45/1/5/29.
27. PRO *Ass.*45/2/1/13.
27. PRO *Court of Requests,* bundle 5, no. 35, Item 1.

Fitted for her place: introduction

1. Patricia Brancia, *Silent Sisterhood*, London: Croom Helm 1975. See particularily Catherine Hall's 'Early Formation of Victorian Domestic Ideology', in Sandra Burman, ed., *Fit Work for Women*, Croom Helm 1979; and Leonore Davidoff's 'Landscape with Figures: Home and Community in English Society' in Juliet Mitchell and Ann Oakley, eds., *The Rights and Wrongs of Women*, London: Pelican 1976. Catherine Hall and Leonore Davidoff will be publishing shortly the results of their joint project on family lives, housing and domestic activity in an urban and a rural area (Birmingham and East Anglia).
2. Ellen Malos, ed., *The Politics of Housework,* London: Allison & Busby 1980, p. 36. See also other articles in this collection, which has an extensive bibliography of the major historical and sociological works on domesticity.

3. Thomas Tryon's regimen for women: sectarian health in the seventeenth century

1. Most vividly shown in Michel Foucault's historical works. For an introduction to Foucaultian structuralism, see Alan Sheridan, *Michel Foucault: The Will to Truth*, London: Tavistock Publications 1980.
2. See Neil McKendrick, 'Home Demand and Economic Growth: A New View of Women and Children in the Industrial Revolution', in N.McKendrick, ed., *Historical Perspectives: Studies of English Thought and Society,*London: Europa Publications 1974. Also: N.McKendrick, J. Brewer, J.H. Plumb, *The Birth of a Consumer Society,* London: Europa Publications 1982.
3. Catherine Hall, 'The Early Formation of Victorian Domestic Ideology', in Sandra Burman, ed., *Fit Work for Women,* London: Croom Helm 1979.

4. See Christopher Hill, *The World Turned Upside Down: Radical Ideas during the English Revolution*, Harmondsworth: Penguin Books 1980.

5. *Ibid*. chapter 15; see also E.S.Morgan, *The Puritan Family* (first edn. 1944), New York: Harper & Row 1965.

6. Christopher Hill, *op. cit.* p. 376.

7. A.D.Gilbert, *Religion and Society in Industrial England*, London: Longman 1976, p. 40; see also chapter 2. 'Patterns of Religious Practice 1740–1914'.

8. The results of a long study on gender and the English middle class in the late eighteenth and early nineteenth centuries are due to be published by Leonore Davidoff and Catherine Hall during 1985–6. See also Davidoff and Hall, '*The Architecture of Public and Private Space; English Middle-Class Life in a Provincial Town 1780–1850*', in A. Sutcliffe and others, eds., *The Pursuit of Urban History*, London: Edward Arnold 1983.

9. For revolutionary Puritan medical ideas see Charles Webster, *The Great Instauration*, London: Duckworth 1975.

10. These are listed in Sir J.Sinclair, *Code of Health and Longevity*, vol. 2, Edinburgh: 1807, p. 297. They can be found in the British Library and Wellcome Institute collections.

11. Alexander Gordon, *A Pythagorean of the 17th century*, Liverpool Literary and Philosophical Society 1871, p. 5.

12. Thomas Tryon, *Memoirs*, London: 1705, pp. 26–7.

13. Thomas Tryon, *Health's Grand Preservative*, London: 1682, p. 7.

14. Thomas Tryon, *Memoirs*, pp. 29–30.

15. *Ibid*. p. 37.

16. *Ibid*. pp. 1–3 (35–7).

17. Thomas Tryon, *Health's Grand Preservative*, titlepiece.

18. Thomas Tryon *A Treatise of Cleanness*, London: 1682, p. 4.

19. Thomas Tryon, *Memoirs*, pp. 4, 14.

20. *Ibid*. pp. 13–14.

21. See on male professional rivalry, Jean Donnison, *Midwives and Medical Men*, New York: Schocken Books 1977.

22. Thomas Tryon, *The Knowledge of a Man's Self*, London: 1704, p. 131.

23. See Mary Douglas's works *Purity and Danger*, London: Routledge & Kegan Paul 1966, and *Natural Symbols*, London: Barrie & Jenkins 1973.

24. G.E.R.Lloyd, *Polarity and Analogy*, Cambridge University Press 1966, gives an analysis of symbolism in Greek science and other early cultures.

25. Maryanne Cline Horowitz, 'Aristotle and Women', *Journal of the History of Biology*, vol. 9, no. 2, 1976, pp. 183–213.

26. Thomas Tryon, *Pythagoras His Mystic Philosophy Reviv'd: The Mystery of Dreams Unfolded*, London: 1691, p. 43.

27. Thomas Tryon, *Health's Grand Preservative*, pp. 11–12.

28. Prefixed to the Wellcome edition of *The Way to Health*, London: 1683

29. Thomas Tryon, *Memoirs*, p. 32.

30. *Ibid.* pp. 92–198.

31. C.Hall, *'The Early Formation of Victorian Domestic Ideology'*, p. 26.Quoted from W.Wilberforce, *A Practical View of the Prevailing Religious System of Professed Christians in the Higher and Middle Classes of this Country*, 1797, p. 453.

4. Ellen Silk and her sisters: female emigration to the New World

1. Ellen Silk was born in Ballindooly, a tiny hamlet in Co.Galway about 1846. She emigrated to New Zealand at the age of 20 aboard the *Bombay* with two other women from Ballindooly, Mary Broderick and Catherine Francis. She married John Crow in 1868 and had four children, three sons and a daughter. Her grand-daughter Winnie Davin, remembers Ellen dictating letters to friends and relatives back in Ireland when she was a young girl. Ellen's great-grand-daughter, Anna Davin, was a founding member of the London Feminist History Group in the early 1970s.

2. 'Assisted Emigration to Otago', application form in OP 8/1 – Encl. to 75 (1863) Otago Provincial Archives, National Archives, Wellington, N.Z.

3. A.James Hammerton, *Emigrant Gentlewoman: Genteel Poverty and Female Emigration, 1830–1914*, London: Croom Helm 1979. See also his 'Feminism and Female Emigration, 1861–1886', in M.Vicinus, ed., *A Widening Sphere,* Bloomington and London: Indiana University Press 1977, pp. 52–71; and ' "Without Natural Protectors": Female Immigration to Australia, 1832–36', *Historical Studies*, vol. 16, (1975), pp. 539–566.

4. Barbara Roberts, ' "A Work of Empire": Canadian Reformers and British Female Immigration', in Linda Kealey, ed., *A Not Unreasonable Claim*, Toronto: Women's Educational Press 1979.

5. Marilyn Barber, 'The Women Ontario Welcomed: Immigrant Domestics for Ontario Homes, 1870–1930', *Ontario History*, no. 3, September 1980, pp. 148–172.

6. Joy Parr, *Labouring Children: British Immigrant Apprentices to Canada, 1869–1924*, London and Montreal: Croom Helm and McGill-Queen's University Press 1980.

7. Margaret Kiddle, *Caroline Chisholm*, Victoria: Melbourne University Press 1969; Mary Hoban, *Fifty-One Pieces of Wedding Cake – A Biography of Caroline Chisholm,* Kilmore, Victoria: Lowden Publishing 1973.

8. Anne Summers, *Damned Whores and God's Police – The Colonization of Women in Australia*, Ringwood, Victoria: Penguin Books Australia 1975.

9. Mary Taylor was born in Gomersal in the West Riding of Yorkshire, where she was a close friend to Ellen Nussey and Charlotte Brontë. In 1845 she sailed to Wellington, New Zealand, and ran a successful retail business until, at the age of 42 she returned to England in 1859. She was a political and social radical and a feminist whose firm belief it was that women had a duty and a right to earn an independent income to secure their economic independence.

10. Wakefield proposed a plan of systematic colonization whereby land, labour and capital would be held in such a balance as to create a concentrated and hierarchical settlement. Land was to be sold at a 'sufficient price' so as to restrict the dispersal of the founding population. He hoped to combat the indiscriminate and disorderly settlement which resulted from 'shovelling out paupers', and create a 'New Old England'.

11. The rates of assistance offered by New Zealand's provincial governments varied over the period 1853–71. Single women never had to pay more than half the cost of a steerage berth (approximately £8), and for several years entirely free passages were granted.

12. Approximately 600 people – about one third of the 2,200 individual women whose names were transcribed from passenger lists and were found in tracings through marriage registers. What happened to the remaining 1800 or so is impossible to tell – some will have never married, some died soon after arrival, many went to Australia or California, some went back to England. But in what proportions it is impossible to know.

13. *Lyttelton Times,* 14 September 1865, p. 4.

14. Loose letters, 15 May 1884, Hawkes Bay Museum (NZ).

15. Tom Arnold to Mrs Arnold, 11 March 1849, in James Bertram, ed., *New Zealand Letters of Thomas Arnold The Younger,* London and Wellington : OUP and Wellington 1966, p. 108.

16. Rollo Arnold, *The Farthest Promised Land.* Wellington: Victoria University Press with Price Milburn 1981, p. 12.

17. James Adam, *Twenty-Five Years of Emigrant Life in New Zealand* (2nd edn.), Edinburgh: 1876, p. 58.

18. Quoted by Jeanine Graham in W.H.Oliver and B.R.Williams, eds., *The Oxford History of New Zealand*, Oxford and Wellington: Clarendon Press and Oxford University Press 1981, p. 124.

19. Arthur Clayden *The England of the Pacific or New Zealand as an English Middle-Class Emigration Field,* London: 1879, p. 9.

20. Quoted in *The Times,* 29 August 1862.

21. *Manchester Examiner and Times*, 16 May 1863, p. 6.

22. In New Zealand 'the bush' is a general term describing the natural countryside, especially where it is uncultivated, but not necessarily referring to vegetation or aforestation of any particular variety.

23. Bessie R. Parkes, 'A Year's Experience in Woman's Work', *Transactions of the National Association for the promotion of Social Science*, London: 1860, pp. 817–18.

24. 'A Letter From Sydney', in M.F.Lloyd-Pritchard, ed., *The Collected Works of Edward Gibbon Wakefield,* Auckland: Collins 1969, p. 138.

25. Report of Select Committee on Immigration, Nelson Provincial Council, *Votes and Proceedings,* Session 6 (1859).

26. *The Saturday Review* (Dunedin), 7 January 1865, p. 314.

27. R.S.Neale, '"Middle-Class" Morality and the Systematic Colonizers', in *Class and Ideology in the Nineteenth Century,* London and Boston: Routledge & Kegan Paul 1972.

28. *Statistics of New Zealand*, Auckland, NZ: Blue Book 1864.

29. Summers, *op. cit.* pp. 268–269.

30. Erik Olssen, 'Social Class in Nineteenth-Century New Zealand', in David Pitt, ed., *Social Class in New Zealand,* Auckland: Longman Paul 1977, p. 36.

31. Roger Thompson, *Women in Stuart England and America,* London and Boston: Routledge & Kegan Paul 1974.

32. *Ibid*. p. 22.

33. *Ibid*. p. 23.

34. *Ibid*. pp. 23–4.

35. Jock Phillips, 'Mummy's Boys: Pakeha Men and Male Culture in New Zealand', in Phillida Bunkle and Beryl Hughes, eds., *Women in New Zealand Society*, Auckland: George Allen & Unwin 1980, pp. 217–43.

36. The current feminist movement has mounted an extensive critique of marriage, identifying it as an institution of oppression. Feminist historians have begun to scrutinize the family and marriage in past times – see, for example Rayna Rapp, Ellen Ross and Renate Budenthal, 'Examining Family History', *Feminist Studies*, vol. 5 no.1, spring 1979.

37. Summers,*op. cit.* p. 305.

38. Arnold, *op. cit.*p. 247.

39. Theresa McBride, *The Domestic Revolution – The Modernisation of Household Service in England and France 1820–1920*, London: Croom Helm 1976.

40. *Ibid.* p. 34.

41. Tamara K.Hareven, 'The Family as Process: The Historical Study of the Family Circle', *Journal of Social History*, no. 7, spring 1974, pp. 322–9.

42. City of London Board of Guardians, Minutes. CBG 45 (1864), p. 602, and CBG 44 (1863–64), p. 611. Julia Burns emigrated to Otago, New Zealand aboard the *Silesia*, 1863.

43. Emily (aged 26) and Mary Tregarnowarn (aged 25) both sailed to New Zealand aboard the *David Fleming*, arriving at Lyttelton on 9 December 1863. They both gave their occupations as 'domestic servants'.

44. Private communications R. Gerson, Palmerston North (NZ), August 1979, September 1982.

5. 'Our women are expected to become . . .': women and girls in further education in England at the turn of the century

1. An early draft of this paper was given to the Standing Conference on the Sociology of Further Education, Garnett College, London on 7 – 8 July 1981. Substantially revised, it was presented to the London Feminist History Group on 18 September 1981. I should also like to acknowledge the help that the following women have given me in the writing of this paper: Sandra Acker, Enid L. Blunden, Miriam E. David and Noelle Whiteside. I am also grateful to the county archivists and the county education officers and their staffs of Gloucestershire and Wiltshire and to the principals and staffs of the Mid Gloucestershire Technical College, Stroud; the West-Gloucestershire College of Further Education, Cinderford; and the College, Swindon, for their support and interest.

2. Cd 2175 1904, para 230.
3. *Ibid*, para. 259.
4. *Ibid*, para. 232.
5. *Ibid*.
6. Gloucestershire Education Committee: report of the minor committee 1905.
7. Swindon and North Wilts Technical Education Committee: annual report 1898–9.
8. Swindon Education Committee: annual report 1906–7, p. 8.
9. *Ibid*.
10. Swindon Education Committee: school managers' subcommittee minutes, 18 May 1908.
11. Gloucestershire County Council, Technical Education Committee: annual report 1897.
12. Gloucestershire Education Committee: annual report 1907–8, p. 45.

6. Women and psychiatric professionalization, 1780–1914

1. See e.g. Phyllis Chesler, *Women and Madness,* New York: Avon 1972; Dorothy E. Smith and Sara J.David, *Women Look at Psychiatry*, Vancouver University Press 1975; Luise Eichenbaum and Susie Orbach, *Outside in . . . Inside Out,* Harmondsworth: Penguin 1982.
2. For an account of the Women's Therapy Centre in London, see Eichenbaum and Orbach, *op. cit.*
3. See e.g. Barbara Ehrenreich and Deirdre English, *Witches, Midwives and Nurses,* London: Writers & Readers 1973; Jean Donnison, *Midwives and Medical Men*, New York: Shocken 1977.
4. The *Town and Country Registers* were lists of lunatics and where they were confined kept by central government. A copy of the *Country Register* is available in the Public Record Office, MH 51 735.
5. W.L.Parry-Jones,*The Trade in Lunacy: A study of private madhouses in England in the Eighteenth and Nineteenth Centuries,* London: Routledge & Kegan Paul 1972, p. 132.
6. Thomas Bakewell, *Domestic Guide in Cases of Insanity,*London: 1805, p. x.
7. *Ibid.* p. xi.
8. Leonore Davidoff, 'The Separation of Home and Work? Landladies and Lodgers in Nineteenth- and Twentieth-Century Eng-

land', in Sandra Burman, ed., *Fit Work for Women*, London: Croom Helm 1979, p. 64.

9. Catherine Hall, 'The Early Formation of Victorian Domestic Ideology' in *ibid*. p. 15.

10. Michael Ignatieff, *A Just Measure of Pain: The Penitentiary in the Industrial Revolution, 1750–1850*, London:1978, p. 38.

11. *Select Committee Report* (1807); *Parliamentary Returns* (1819, 1830).

12. Parry-Jones, *op. cit.* p. 81.

13. *Ibid.* pp. 134–5.

14. *A prospectus of Earl's Court House, Mrs. Bradbury's Establishment at Old Brompton, for the recovery of ladies labouring under affections of the mind. With plans and illustrations*, London: 1836.

15. *Ibid.* p. 8.

16. *Parliamentary Returns* (1830).

17. *Hanwell Reports*, 31st Report, Easter QS (1835) p. 109.

18. *Ibid.* 34th Report, Epiphany QS (1836) p. 124.

19. Sally Alexander, 'Women's Work in Nineteenth-Century London: A Study of the Years 1820–50', in Juliet Mitchell and Ann Oakley, eds., *The Rights and Wrongs of Women*, London: Penguin 1976, p. 6.

20. W.C.Ellis, *A Treatise on the Nature, Symptoms, Causes and Treatment of Insanity*, London: 1838, p. 221.

21. *Ibid.* p. 259.

22. John Conolly, *The Construction and Government of Lunatic Asylums*, London: 1847, p. 137.

23. *Seventh Annual Report of the Commissioners in Lunacy* (1852), p. 115; PP (1852–3), xlix.1.

24. *Ibid.* p. 114.

25. *Ibid.* pp. 44–112.

26. J.C.Bucknill, 'Tenth Report of the Commissioners in Lunacy to the Lord Chancellor', *Asylum Journal of Mental Science*, 3 (1857), pp. 19–20.

27. Leonore Davidoff, *op. cit.* p. 65.

28. J.C. Bucknill and D.H. Tuke, *Journal of Mental Science*, 1885, p. 140.

29. *Fourteenth Annual Report of the Commissioners in Lunacy* (1860) pp. 41–2. PP (1860), xxxiv, 231.

30. John Arlidge, *On the State of Lunacy and the Legal Provision for the Insane with Observations on the Construction and Organization of Asylums*, London: 1859, p. 147.

31. Sally Alexander, *op. cit.* p. 74.

32. *Annual Reports of the Commissioners in Lunacy* PP (1860) xxxiv.231–; (1870) xxxiv.1–; (1880) xxix.1–; (1890) xxxv.1–; (1900) xxxvii.1–; (1910) xli.1–.
33. *Journal of Mental Science,* 1894, p. 158.
34. *Ibid,*,1909, pp. 270–80.

7. 'So extremely like parliament': the work of the women members of the London School Board, 1870–1904

1. *The Times*, 29 November 1870.
2. Elizabeth Garrett to Emily Davies, 24 October 1870, quoted in Barbara Stephen, *Emily Davies and Girton College,* Cambridge University Press 1927, p. 120.
3. Emily Davies to Mr H.R. Tomkinson, 7 November 1870, quoted in *ibid*. p. 121.
4. J.S.Hurt, *Elementary Schooling and the Working Classes 1860–1918,* London: Routledge & Kegan Paul 1979, pp. 85–6.
5. *Women's Penny Paper,* 17 November 1888, p. 4.
6. *The Times,* 7 January 1871, quoted in Jo Manton, *Elizabeth Garrett Anderson,* London: Methuen 1965, p. 214.
7. Edith Simcox, *'Autobiography of a Shirt-maker',* manuscript journal held in the Bodleian Library, Oxford.
8. Emily Davies to Barbara Bodichon, 6 January 1874, quoted in Stephen, *op. cit.* p. 285.
9. Peter Gordon, *The Victorian School Manager*, p. 182.
10. Simcox,*op. cit.*
11. *Ibid.*
12. Elizabeth Garrett to J.G.S.Anderson, 15 December 1870, Fawcett Collection, London.
13. Thomas Gautry, *Lux Mihi Laus: School Board Memories*, London: Link House 1936, p. 78.
14. *South London Chronicle,* 28 October 1882.
15. *School Board Chronicle* 21 October 1882, p. 411.
16. *Ibid.* 28 October 1882, p. 436.
17. *Women's Penny Paper,* 23 August 1890, p. 518.
18. Ethel E.Metcalfe, *Memoir of Rosamond Davenport-Hill,* London: Longmans Green & Co. 1904, p. 115.
19. *The Telegraphist,* 2 February 1885, p. 30. (I am grateful to Anna Davin for this reference).
20. Elizabeth Garrett to J.G.S.Anderson, 16 December 1870, Fawcett Collection,London.

21. *'The Other Side of the Question'* (1885), Manuscript of paper presented to the Men and Women's Club, Karl Pearson Papers.
22. Quoted in Margaret Stacey and Marion Price,*Women, Politics and Power* London: Tavistock 1981, p. 154.
23. *Spare Rib,* November 1981.

8. Serving two masters? The introduction of a marriage bar in teaching in the 1920s

1. Department of Employment Gazette, August 1978.
2. For discussion of this idea see Irene Bruegel, 'Women as a Reserve Army of Labour', *Feminist Review* no. 3, 1979; and V.Beechy, 'Women and Production', in Annette Kuhn and AnnMarie Wolpe, eds., *Feminism and Materialism*, London and Boston: Routledge & Kegan Paul 1978.
3. See Annmarie Turnbull's chapter in this volume.
4. PRO Board of Education papers Ed 24/1744. Minute to President from Selby-Bigge, 31 January 1923.
5. *Price v. Rhondda UDC* 1923, see *Daily Telegraph*, 4 May 1923.
6. *Short v. Borough of Poole* 1925, *The Times*, Law Report, 1 August 1925, also *Fennel and others v. East Ham* 1925.
7. *Daily Mail,* 2 October 1922.
8. LCC Record Office, EO/STA/2. 13; letter to LCC 28 October 1922.
9. LCC *ibid.* printed report to TSSC, 4 November 1920.
10. LCC *ibid.*see reports and papers, 29 July 1922, and 15 November 1922.
11. LCC *ibid.* letters sent by Education Officer 6 and 13 November 1922 and replies from inspectors.
12. LCC *ibid.* letter to LCC 28 October 1922.
13. LCC *ibid.* letter to LCC from E. West, 4 October 1922.
14. LCC *ibid.* letter to LCC, 27 September 1922.
15. LCC *ibid.* letter to LCC from Mr Pearson, 8 November 1922.
16. Letter to *Daily Mail,* 2 October 1922.
17. Letter to *New Statesman*, 3 March 1923, p. 628–9.
18. *Ibid.*
19. Annual Reports of the NUT, 1921, 1922 and 1923.
20. NUT Law Committee Minutes, 1 December 1922, letter from the Rhondda women.
21. NUT Parliamentary and Superannuation Committee Minutes, 16 July 1926, 21 May 1927, 22 October 1927.

22. NUT Annual Reports for these years.
23. Letter to *Times Educational Supplement*, 12 August 1922, p. 378.
24. See NUWT, *A Short History of the Union to 1956*.
25. PRO Board of Education papers, Ed 24/1744.
26. Board of Education papers, Circular 1404, 1929.
27. *The Times*, 5 November 1929.

Sexuality: introduction

1. Lilian Faderman, *Surpassing the Love of Men*, London: Junction Books 1981.
2. W. Chapkis, ed, *Loaded Questions: Women in the Military*, Amsterdam: Transnational Institute 1981.
3. Adrienne Rich, *Compulsory Heterosexuality and Lesbian Existence*, London: Onlywomen Press 1981. Also appears in *Signs: Journal of Women in Culture and Society*, vol. 5 no. 4, 1980; *Love your Enemy?*, London: Onlywomen Press 1981.
4. Judith R. Walkowitz, 'Male Vice and Feminist Virtue: Feminism and the Politics of Prostitution in 19th Century Britain', *History Workshop Journal*, no. 13, spring 1982, pp. 79–93. See also the introduction to this article by Jane Caplan, 'The Politics of Prostitution', in *ibid*. pp. 77–8.
5. Judith R. Walkowitz, *Prostitution and Victorian Society: Women, Class and the State*, Cambridge University Press 1980.
6. Sheila Rowbotham, *A New World for Women: Stella Browne: Socialist Feminist*, London: Pluto Press 1977.

9. Distasteful and derogatory? Examining Victorian soldiers for venereal disease

1. Some of the issues covered here are discussed in greater detail in my thesis, 'Marriage and the Victorian Army at Home: The Regulation of Soldiers' Relationships with Women and the Treatment of Soldiers Wives', PhD thesis, University of Bristol, 1981.
2. See Alan Ramsay Skelley, *The Victorian Army at Home*, London: Croom Helm 1977; Olive Anderson, 'The Growth of Christian Militarism in Mid-Victorian Britain', *English Historical Review*, no. 86, 1971, pp. 46–72.
3. Farnham Union: Report of Enquiry into the Charges Contained in *The Lancet* with respect to the State and Management of the

Workhouse of the Farnham Union, Parliamentary Paper (PP), 1867–8 (134), LX, p. 5.

4. Report on the Soldiers' Institutes at Aldershot and at Portsmouth, PP, 1862 (126), XXXII, p. 11.

5. Army Medical Department, Report for 1859, PP, 1861 (C.2853), XXXVII, p. 15.

6. See Judith R. Walkowitz, *Prostitution and Victorian Society,* Cambridge University Press 1980.

7. Report from the Select Committee on the Contagious Diseases Act (1866), PP, 1868–9 (306), VII, Q.1139.

8. Report of the Committee Appointed to Enquire into the Pathology and Treatment of the Veneral Disease, with the View to Diminish its Injurious Effects on the Men of the Army and Navy (Hereafter the Skey Committee), PP, 1867–8 (C.4031), XXXVII, Q.2062.

9. *Ibid.* QQ.5652–5674.

10. See the Skey Committee.

11. *Ibid.* p. xxxi.

12. *Ibid.* Q. 480.

13. *Ibid.* p. xxxii.

14. William Acton, *Prostitution,* London: Frank Cass 1972 (reprint of 1870 edition).

15. *Ibid.* p. 194.

16. 'Prostitution: How to Deal with it', *Westminster Review,* no. 37, 1870, p. 508.

17. Royal Commission upon the Administration and Operation of the Contagious Diseases Acts, PP, 1871 (C.408, 408–1), XIX.

18. *Ibid.* (C.408) p. 17.

19. Paul McHugh asks this question in his *Prostitution and Victorian Social Reform,* London: Croom Helm 1980, p. 27.

20. Frances Finnegan's *Poverty and Prostitution: A Study of Victorian Prostitutes in York,* Cambridge University Press 1979, raises this issue.

21. See Sheila Jeffreys, 'Prostitution', *Revolutionary and Radical Feminist Newsletter*, no. 6, spring 1981, pp. 13–18 (women only).

10. The illegal operation: abortion, 1919–39

1. *The Times,* 7 February 1920, p. 4; 13 February 1920, p. 9.

2. The various changes in the abortion law were made in 48

Geo.III, c31 (1803), 9 Geo.IV, c31 (1837) 1 Vic. c85 (1837), 24 and 25 Vic. c100 (1861).

3. *The Medical Press and Circular,* 28 July 1931, p. 74
4. *British Medical Journal* (hereafter *BMJ*), 2 February 1929, p. 203; Marie C. Stopes, *Mother England: A Contemporary History,* London: John Bale, Sons & Danielsson 1929, p. 178.
5. *The Times,* 22 January 1920, p. 7.
6. Letters to Marie C.Stopes, in files MCS/A3, MCS/A5, and her reply ACS/A9. Contemporary Medical Archives Centre, Wellcome Institute, Euston Road, London (hereafter CMAC).
7. *Select Committee on Patent Medicines*, London: HMSO 1914, p. 237.
8. MCS/A1 CMAC.
9. *The Times,* 13 February 1920, p. 9; 6 March 1925, p. 11; 3 December 1925, p. 11.
10. *The Times,* 21 January 1920, p. 7.
11. MCS/A3, MCS/A5, CMAC.
12. *Birth Control News,* 30 June 1930, p. 30.
13. *BMJ,* 4 October 1930, p. 566.
14. H.R. Andrews, C. Berkeley, and J.S. Fairburn, eds., *Midwifery by Ten Teachers,* 3rd edn, London: Edward Arnold 1925, p. 726.
15. *BMJ,* 13 July 1929, p. 59: 14 December 1929, p. 1095.
16. *BMJ,* 25 September 1937, p. 636; *The Times,* 1 July 1936, p. 18.
17. *Lancet,* 31 January 1920, p. 268.
18. *BMJ,* 12 January 1935, p. 84.
19. House of Commons Debates, vol. 304, c.1163; vol. 300, c.1634.
20. 'The Mothers' Clinic', included in M.C. Stopes, *Wise Parenthood,* London: G.Putnam & Sons 1921.
21. M.C.Stopes, *Mother England,* p. 183.
22. F.W.Stella Browne, 'The Sexual Variety and Variability among Women and their bearing upon Social Reconstruction', in Sheila Rowbotham, *A New World For Women: Stella Browne: Socialist Feminist,* London: Pluto Press 1977, pp. 104–5.
23. Dora Russell, *Hypatia, or Woman and Knowledge,* New York: E.P.Dutton & Co. 1925, p. 24.
24. Dora Russell, *The Tamarisk Tree: My Quest for Liberty and Love,* London: G.P. Putnam & Sons 1975, p. 169.
25. J.Chance in N.Haire, ed., *Sexual Reform Congress, World League for Sexual Reform,* London: Kegan Paul, Trench, Trubner & Co. 1930, p. 37.
26. A.Jenkins, 'Abortion and Maternal Mortality', Abortion Law Reform Association Archives, file 2/1/25, Aberdeen.

27. This discussion of the Abortion Law Reform Association is based on the ALRA Newsletters and Archives in the Medical Sociology Unit, Aberdeen.

28. Stella Browne, 'Women and Birth Control', in Eden and Cedar Paul, eds., *Population and Birth Control*, New York: The Critis & Guide Co. 1917 p. 249.

29. Rowbotham, *A New World for Women*, p. 75.

11. Sex reform and anti-feminism in the 1920s

1. Wilhelm Stekel, *Frigidity in Woman in Relation to her Love Life,* 1st edn. 1926. vol. 2, New York: Livewright Publishing Corporation 5th edn., 1936.

2. Sheila Jeffreys, '"Free from all Uninvited Touch of Man": Women's Campaigns around Sexuality, 1880–1914', *Women's Studies International Forum,* 5 June 1982.

3. *Ibid.*

4. Margaret Jackson, 'Sexual Liberation or Social Control? Some Aspects of the Relationship between Feminism and the Social Construction of Sexual Knowledge in the Early Twentieth Century', *Women's Studies International Forum,* 6 January 1983.

5. Havelock Ellis, *The Task of Social Hygiene,* London: Constable 1913.

6. Lillian Faderman, *Surpassing the Love of Men,* London: Junction Books 1981, pp. 241–8.

7. Havelock Ellis, *The Erotic Rights of Women,* London: British Society for the Study of Sex Psychology 1917.

8. Stella Browne, *Sexual Variety and Variability among Women,* London: British Society for the Study of Sex Psychology 1915.

9. Marie Stopes, *Married Love,* 1st edn. 1918, London: G.P.Putnam & Sons 16th edn. 1924.

10. A.M.Ludovici, *Lysistrata or Woman's Future and Future Women,* London: Kegan Paul, Trubner, Trench & Co. 1924.

11. *Ibid.* p. 37.

12. *Ibid.* p. 89.

13. K.A.Weith Knudsen, *Feminism – The Woman Question from Ancient Times to the Present Day,* London: Constable 1928, p. 119.

14. *Ibid.* p. 121.

15. Walter Gallichan, *The Poison of Prudery,* London: T.Werner Laurie 1929, p. 184.

16. *Ibid.* p. 11.
17. *Ibid.* p. 12.
18. Wilhelm Stekel, 'Frigidity in Mothers' in V.F. Calverton and Samuel D. Schmalhausen, eds., *The New Generation*, London George Allen & Unwin 1930, p. 249.
19. *Ibid.* p. 259.
20. Walter Gallichan, *Sexual Antipathy and Coldness in Women,* London: T.Werner Laurie 1927, p. 13.
21. Thomas Van de Velde, *Sex Hostility in Marriage,* London: Heinemann 1931, p. 16.
22. Isabel Hutton, *The Hygiene of Marriage,* London: Heinemann 1923, p. vii.
23. Walter Gallichan, *Sexual Antipathy and Coldness in Women,* p. 20.
24. A.M.Ludovici, *op. cit.* p. 80.
25. Sigmund Freud, 'The Taboo on Virginity', in *On Sexuality,* Pelican Freud Library, vol. 7, London: Penguin 1977, p. 266.
26. *Ibid.* p. 266.
27. Wilhelm Stekel, *Frigidity in Woman in Relation to her Love Life,* vol. 2, p. 1.
28. *Ibid.* p. 3.
29. Thomas Van De Velde, *op. cit.* p. 64–5.
30. K.A.Weith Knudsen, *op. cit.*p. 116.
31. Wilhelm Stekel, *Frigidity in Woman in Relation to her Love Life,* p. 3.
32. K.A.Weith Knudsen, *op. cit.* p. 97
33. Thomas Van de Velde, *Ideal Marriage,* 1st edn. 1928, London: Heinemann 37th impn. 1961, p. 227.
34. Charlotte Haldane, *Motherhood and its Enemies,* London: Chatto & Windus 1927, p. 154.
35. Walter Gallichan, *The Poison of Prudery.*
36. Thomas Van de Velde, *Ideal Marriage,* p. 227.
37. Isabel Hutton, *op. cit.* p. 51.
38. Thomas Van de Velde, *Ideal Marriage,* p. 89.
39. Sheila Jeffreys, *op. cit.*
40. Isabel Hutton, *op. cit.* p. 51.
41. Thomas Van de Velde, *Ideal Marriage*, p. 228.
42. Hannah Stone, 'Birth Control as a Factor in the Sex Life of Women', in Norman Haire, ed., *Sex Reform Congress*, London Kegan Paul, Trench, Trubner & Co. 1930, p. 158.
43. Elise Ottesen-Jensen, 'Birth Control Work among the Poor in Sweden', in *ibid.* p. 175.

44. Ignota, 'Judicial Sex Bias', *Westminster Review,* vol. 149, 1898, pp. 279–88.
45. Walter Gallichan, *Woman under Polygamy,* London: Holden & Hardingham 1914, p. 73.
46. *Ibid.* p. 295.
47. Walter Heape, *Sex Antagonism,* London: Constable 1913, p. 14.
48. A.M.Ludovici, *op. cit.* p. 7.
49. Charlotte Haldane, *op. cit.*
50. Lillian Faderman, *op. cit.*
51. Isabel Hutton, *op. cit.* p. 54.
52. Thomas Van de Velde,*Ideal Marriage,* p. 232.
53. *Ibid.* p. 283.
54. Janet Chance, 'A Marriage Education Centre in London', in Norman Haire, ed., *op. cit.* p. 38.
55. *Ibid.* p. 38.
56. Joanna Elberskirchen, 'The Altero-Centric Dynamics of the Female and the Ego-Centric Dynamics of the Male: Their Part in the Development of Life and Civilisation, and the Transformation of the Relations between Man and Woman', in Norman Haire, ed., *op. cit.* p. 651.
57. Stella Browne, *op. cit.*; Dora Russell, *Hypatia,* London: Kegan Paul 1925.
58. *Ibid.* pp. 24–5.

Cynthia Enloe

Does Khaki Become You?
The militarisation of women's lives

More and more women are being drawn into an invisible khaki net; not just as soldiers, but as a support system for the military, who are dependent on women but do not like to admit it.

Cynthia Enloe looks at the many roles played by women in relation to the military: as mothers and wives, as nurses, prostitutes and social workers, as workers in munitions and other industries dependent on military contracts.

She gives a feminist analysis of the army's use and abuse of women, in Vietnam and in the Falklands, in the USA and in Britain. She argues for urgent resistance to such military manoeuvres.

'*Does Khaki Become You?* draws into a clear framework many moving and enraging examples of exactly how far the military and men in general can go in exploiting women . . . it makes inspiring reading.' Connie Mansueto, Greenham Common activist.

'*Does Khaki Become You?* traces the military's ambivalence and awkwardness in dealing with its dependence on women. Cynthia Enloe's book is both informative and most absorbing.'
Nick Bloomfield, co-producer and co-director of the film *Soldier Girls*.

272 pages   ISBN 0 86104 704 4   paperback   £4.95

Margaret Ward
Unmanageable Revolutionaries
Women and Irish Nationalism

How women have fought for Irish independence — whilst being
consistently excluded from positions of influence in the Republican
movement.

'invaluable for the wealth of historical detail it gives... this book has
done a great deal towards rectifying (a)serious omission' *Troops Out*

0 86104 700 1   paperback   £5.95